The Chameleon Poet
Bob Dylan's Search For Self

John Bauldie

Introduction by Bill Allison

route

First published by Route in 2021
Pontefract, UK
info@route-online.com
www.route-online.com

ISBN: 978-1901927-83-2

First Edition

John Bauldie asserts his moral
right to be identified as the author of this book

Bob Dylan lyrics reproduced with permission.

Cover Photos:
Björn Larsson

Cover Design:
John Sellards

Typeset in Bembo by Route

Printed & bound in Great Britain by TJ Books

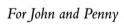

For John and Penny

Introduction
Portrait of the Artist as a Bob Cat: Bill Allison

Portrait of the Artist as a Bob Cat: Bill Allison   7

1. Stranded   49
2. In Another Lifetime   58
3. To Live Outside the Law You Must Be Honest   66
4. Gazing in the River's Mirror   74
5. The Titanic Sails at Dawn   88
6. Desolation Row   100
7. Blonde On Blonde: Bob Dylan's Nigredo   121
8. Songs of Love and Hate   128
9. She's Your Lover Now   145
10. A Painted Face on a Trip Down Suicide Road   162
11. Drifter's Escape: A New Kind of Innocence   184
12. I'll Be Your Baby Tonight   198
13. Back to the Starting Point   209
14. Tangled Up in Blue   223
15. Still on the Road   240
16. Changing of the Guards   259
17. Lost or Found?   278

Acknowledgements   280
John Bauldie Appendix   281

Portrait of the Artist as a Bob Cat
Bill Allison

On his untimely death at 47 years old in October 1996, not only did John Bauldie sit at what could be called the high table of Dylan Studies, but from the early nineties, when he was invited by Dylan's management to write the booklet of liner notes that accompanied *Bootleg Series Volumes 1-3*, many would attest that he was chairman of the board.

Ever since he had been moved by the power of Dylan's lyrics in early songs like 'A Hard Rain's A-Gonna Fall', he had somehow sensed the need to try and understand what he felt by writing about it. In later years not only did he develop this skill, he also had a growing interest in bringing this writing to others, for them to be excited by new insights and arrive at a deeper understanding just as he had. John knew that this was the challenge and he wrote about it in an early issue of *The Telegraph*:

> I'll tell you something that bothers me. If you write seriously about Bob Dylan, chances are people will look at you as if you're some kind of curiosity. Scorn isn't generally heaped upon groups who get together to discuss or write about D. H. Lawrence and yet enthusiasts for Dylan's work are still regarded as oddball freaks or a lunatic fringe. I ask what is the difference between a writer about Dylan and a writer about Robert Lowell? And if that age-old 'real writer' argument raises its ugly head again, I swear I'll scream. Dylan's songs depend upon nuance, mood and intonation, and the words are inseparable from the song blah blah blah blah. Don't we all know that, admit it and accept it? But aren't Shakespeare's words, for example, also dependent upon nuance, mood and intonation, and aren't his words inseparable from their dramatic context? People do write about Shakespeare's work and the process isn't questioned. Shakespeare wrote plays. Dylan writes songs. What's the difference?

John knew that the power of Dylan's work was not just contained in his official albums but also in tapes of live concerts and outtakes that weren't in wide circulation. During the late sixties and throughout the seventies he built up a worldwide network of people who collected these recordings and exchanged them with each other, but he was also looking for critical writing about Dylan's lyrics, which seemed to be very thin on the ground at that time.

Dylan's concerts in London in the summer of 1978 brought together many of these collectors and created a bigger audience for Dylan's work than had perhaps been envisaged. There seemed to be an insatiable appetite for information about Dylan which was not forthcoming, particularly in the UK. This need was becoming so strong that John, with a little help from a small circle of friends, started Wanted Man, The Bob Dylan Information Office and *The Telegraph*, which he wanted to become a quarterly critical journal to examine and explore Dylan's work.

During 1978, 1979 and 1980 he worked on the manuscript of *The Chameleon Poet*, his critical study of Dylan's art, as till now unpublished in full. I will come back to that in good time, but first it seems appropriate to take a brief look at John's life and how he came to have such a high standing in the world of what he called Dylan Studies.

***

It was always a joke amongst friends: John Bauldie professed total dedication to Bolton Wanderers and Bob Dylan, in that order. His family had originally come from Fife in Scotland, so, amusingly, it was said that he should have supported Cowdenbeath, a football club that plays in the lower leagues of Scottish football, but anyone that knows anything about football will tell you that it is not as simple as that. Nothing ever is. The team you choose to support runs through you like the word Blackpool runs through Blackpool rock. In John's case, Bolton Wanderers ran through him.

John's great-grandfather, David Bauldie, moved from Fife to Manchester with his wife, Maggie, looking for work in the coal-mining industry. Their son, James, married a Manchester girl in 1919 at St Wilfrid's Church in Newton Heath. John's father, Robert Stewart Bauldie, was born in 1925. Clearly the middle name, Stewart, was there in order to preserve the Scottish heritage. John's mother, Betty, came from Farnworth, then a small outlying district of Bolton. She married Robert in early 1949 and gave birth to their first and only son, John Stewart Bauldie, on 24th August 1949 at the family home in Newton Heath. John's birth certificate shows his father listed as a 'Journeyman Electrician', his mother is listed as a civil servant, a job she kept all her working life. The young couple soon moved with their baby boy to a two-up two-down terraced house in Farnworth, near to Betty's family. John's parents would live there for the rest of their lives.

Together as a family, mum, dad and young John had season tickets in the grandstand for Bolton Wanderers. The Wanderers' ground, Burnden Park, was a twenty-minute walk down Manchester Road from Farnworth. L. S. Lowry, the Salford artist, painted several pictures that had links with Burnden Park, the most famous of these being *Going to the Match*. The Bauldies would have traversed the painting from right to left so to speak as they came to the ground every other Saturday. John loved this painting and always kept a print of it on his desk wherever he lived in later years.

John was one of the thousands of 'baby boomers' born in Britain after the Second World War. Forces had returned from Europe and Japan knowing that they had defeated alien political regimes in other countries and now they perhaps felt that it was time to change their own country. The Labour Party, who described themselves as the party of working people, won a landslide victory in the 1945 general election. Their manifesto 'Let Us Face The Future' included promises of nationalisation, economic planning, full employment, a National Health Service, a revised education programme and a system of social security. The National Health Service came into effect on 5th July 1948 and gave everyone medical care free at the point of entry. Unknowingly, 'free' could well have become a theme for the baby boomers' lives – free health care, free school milk and, in later years, free university courses and ultimately free love.

At the age of six, John went to his local primary school in Farnworth and at the end of his time there, as with the rest of his generation, he took what was the standard examination for entry to secondary school, the Eleven-plus. The results of this examination would stream pupils into a tripartite system of presumed different intellectual ability. John's result meant he was offered a place at a prestigious direct grant grammar school which had previously been fee paying but now, because of the 1944 Education Act, had to make twenty-five percent of its places free to pupils who had demonstrated intellectual prowess in the Eleven-plus examination. Devastatingly, John's parents would not let him take up the place. Instead they made him go to the local authority Farnworth Grammar School just a short walk from where he lived.

★★★

I thought I heard it on a jukebox
All the things I couldn't say.

Iain Matthews, 'Stealin' Home'

If T. S. Eliot's J. Alfred Prufrock felt he'd measured his life out in coffee spoons, it may not be a stretch to say that John's life was measured out in his record collection. In his essay 'Simple Twist of Fate', published in a collection called *Love is the Drug* edited by John Aizlewood and published in 1994, John chronicles some of his adventures in music during his early years. In 1962, transistor radios were the vogue and the 'must have' Christmas present for teenagers. John was given one by his parents. Suddenly for the young Bauldie (whose mind may well have been full of Latin, mathematics, the novels of Charles Dickens – all good grammar school fare – and, of course, Bolton Wanderers) this opened up a new world of blue bayous, two girls for every boy and good rocking tonight. He was smitten and there would be no turning back. There were so many who had come to music this way, so many writers whose work he would explore and come to respect later, even Dylan himself, who wrote about the holy spirit of rock'n'roll and how they all had come to it through the radio. When John's parents bought the family's first record player, he was allowed to pick one LP. He chose *Kent Walton Presents Honey Hit Parade*, a Radio Luxemburg compilation album full of the hit songs he had heard on the only station playing pop music at that time.

By late 1962, John's musical tastes had matured with astonishing rapidity. The Beatles were please pleasing what seemed like the whole world. They created a new universe of their own for the baby boomers and led them into it like Pied Pipers. They turned everything upside down. In later life, John kept his records in a filing cabinet. In the top drawer before the albums, two Beatles EPs were stacked one in front of the other – *The Beatles' Hits* and *Twist and Shout*. These must be good contenders for his first Beatles purchases. By mid-1963 he had bought the first Beatles album and put his name on the back with a John Bull printing kit to show the world that it was his.

Among his first few LPs was the debut album by The Animals, who were said to have spearheaded the arrival of American Rhythm and Blues in England. On the album were the customary twelve tracks with two Chuck Berry songs, but it also had two by a grizzly old blues singer called John Lee Hooker: 'Dimples' and 'Boom Boom'. John went on to listen to Hooker, Howlin' Wolf and Sonny Boy Williamson. This led him back to the sources, picking up singles on the Pye International label which revealed a world of untold wonder. He said later that their grizzly voices helped him understand where Dylan was coming from when he sang.

In March 1964, Pete Bryan, his cool school friend who had told him about The Beatles, The Rolling Stones and the blues singers, told him about Bob Dylan. Pete had always been right before, so John, with due accord, checked him out. He returned home the following day with *The Freewheelin' Bob Dylan* and *The Times They Are A-Changin'*. The latter had just been imported from America, so he was showing early signs that there were no lengths he would not be prepared to go to get otherwise unavailable Dylan material.

John discovered that there were songs that Dylan had written but not released himself that others had recorded. Being a quiet little boy from the suburbs, John was never really a risk taker, certainly at this time in his life, but he skipped school once in a while to go to Ralph's Records in Manchester, next to Victoria Station. This was a paradise all of its own. He soon developed the skill of flicking through two browsers at the same time to soak up as many album covers as he could, looking for... he wasn't quite sure what. In later life he was to say that if you looked through album covers in record shops long enough you would find the album you never knew you had made. You wish.

At Ralph's Records he found a 1964 album called *Paths of Victory* by Hamilton Camp that contained seven Dylan songs, six of which he didn't know and were not on any of his albums. There were other songs too. The beautiful 'Farewell Angelina' and 'Daddy, You Been On My Mind' were on Joan Baez's *Farewell Angelina* album.

If The Beatles and early Bob Dylan albums had opened the gate for John, what happened next kicked down the front door. We don't know what John felt when he first heard the holy ghost of the airwaves play 'Like A Rolling Stone', but we do have a piece by the late Bob Carroll (who would go on to be one of the original Wanted Men) written several years later, where he tried to sum up what happened to him when hearing that song for the first time. John told Carroll how much he admired this piece and he wished he had written it for he'd felt just the same. Carroll, like John, was sixteen in 1965 and recalls wallowing in teenage angst:

> That single bang, shotgun like, on the radio caught my attention. Then the pounding swirling organ and then what seemed like a recognisable fairy tale beginning – once upon a time – but I had ever come across a fairy tale like this. There could be no happy never after ... and suddenly while I was trying to make sense of it all – the chorus...

How does it feel
To be on your own
With no direction home
Like a rolling stone?

Somehow in a bizarre way I thought it was talking to me. It was calling out to me. I had never known imagery like this before … This wasn't pop music. It wasn't folk music … The singer was taunting me. Go on do something about it. If you can. If you dare. It made me feel that I wanted to dare. Don't let other people get your kicks for you. I had to respond but I felt pathetic. I didn't know how to.

Dylan's imagery had not been like this before nor had the music been so heavily aggressive. It seemed to be laughing at you and wanted to kick you in the face for as long as it went on, and it went on for a while. Even that was groundbreaking. John and Carroll and thousands of others wanted it to go on forever. John didn't know it at this point but he had heard something he would spend the rest of his life trying to find the meaning of; for himself and to share with others. As he said years later, if he didn't do it, who would?

John had heard about a Dylan concert in Manchester in 1965, but he didn't go. When Dylan returned with an electric band in 1966, John's mother didn't think it was a good idea that he went the eleven miles to Manchester when he had to be at school the next day. John wrote this later about the show:

The furore over Dylan 'going electric' had been raging for a good year. He'd put out *Bringing It All Back Home* and *Highway 61 Revisited* and I loved them both. My faith was total, absolute, unswerving. But I didn't go to the concert. If I had I would be able to tell you about the guy who shouted 'Judas!' Where he was sitting, perhaps, maybe even what he looked like. But I can't because I wasn't there.

Whilst being seduced by the lyrics on Dylan albums, John was also beginning to develop a love of literature, devouring plays and poems and novels with a ravenous hunger. All for the love of words.

In September 1967 he started his degree in English Literature at the University of Leeds. One of the prize possessions he took with him was the 'I Want You' single because on its B-side was a live cut from the Liverpool 1966 concert. Five minutes of that 'thin, wild mercury sound' as Dylan would describe it.

In the second-anniversary issue of *Rolling Stone* magazine in November 1969, there was an article by Greil Marcus that catalogued, in serious detail, Dylan's recordings, both official and, more importantly for fans, unofficial. Marcus spilled the real beans and got worldwide coverage. The list took up a whole six pages of an eleven-page article alongside five full-page monochrome photos of Dylan, though Marcus exhorts readers to believe that the list was by no means complete. John said that that article literally changed his life. He wrote to Marcus asking him to send some of those tapes. At the same time he stuck a notice on a board in Leeds University Student Union asking if anyone had any unreleased Dylan tapes. A student turned up with what would become known as *The Acetate,* containing fourteen songs put out by Big Ben Music of demos from *The Basement Tapes* for other artists to record themselves.

> I loved it. I wanted it. I bought it. And consequently went without food and drink for a month or two – okay, maybe it just seemed that way. Then Marcus sent me a little reel of tape with the Liverpool 66 tracks on and told me he'd got the stuff by 'scrambling and hustling' and suggested that I do the same and that for starters I should write to a guy called A.J. Weberman. I did. A.J. told me that he didn't have any money but if I sent him $5 he'd send me hours of stuff. I did. He did. Suddenly I had got what was the best unreleased Dylan tape collection in England, maybe in Europe.

John may have missed Dylan in 1965 and 1966, but he didn't repeat the mistake in 1969 when Dylan next came to these shores; he made the 250-mile trip to the Isle of Wight to see him. Even though the backing band was the same, the 'thin, wild mercury sound' was no more.

I was at the Isle of Wight ... What do I remember of the Isle of Wight? By the time Dylan came on at eleven o'clock at night I was just about asleep on my feet, knocked out by the physical exhaustion of getting there in the first place. Ragged, jingle-jangle, laughing sleep, sleep, wanna sleep – such is my report from the Isle of Wight.

John graduated from Leeds in 1970 with a BA in English. However, as with so many of the baby boomers who were first-generation graduates in the family, he was unsure as to what kind of career he could follow. Unsure of many things, he registered for a one year Postgraduate Certificate in Education course (PGCE).

John was by now slowly making contact through small ads and word of mouth with other people in Britain and America who wanted to feed the same habit, wanted to know more and more about Dylan and, most importantly, to track down unreleased material. An Englishman, the late Geoff Styche, who has never really been given the credit he deserves amongst Dylan collectors, began research that was to produce the first ever attempted comprehensive listing of 'otherwise unavailable' Dylan material in the form of a discography booklet. Styche wrote:

I felt that there had to have been more going on than we were getting to hear about. Through my then wife, a San Francisco girl, I had built up a few musical contacts in both California and New York City and it was around the first half of 1969 that I came to hear about (and maybe even got to listen to – I can't remember) these things called *The Basement Tapes*. Clearly this material was nothing like the official Columbia output of the day and I became intrigued. In August 1969 I arranged to meet up with a few Dylan contacts from the UK and overseas whilst attending Dylan's concert at the Isle of Wight Festival, his first real public outing for years. We all kept in touch off and on throughout the next few years, continuously exchanging and updating our collective Dylan knowledge.

By late 1970/early 1971 I had built up quite a catalogue of confirmed and suspected Dylan recordings, knowledge of which was not necessarily generally in the public domain. I began to advertise my little catalogue in the small ads of the more popular music papers of the day (the likes of *Melody Maker* and *New Musical Express*). Using a simple manually-operated, single-sheet, foolscap screen print device which produced its printed pages using stencils cut by typewriter, I sent them out as the postal orders came in.

The Dylan bootlegs started to become available for everybody if you looked hard enough. In a *Melody Maker* article of June 1971, Richard Williams announced the release of a new bootleg of Dylan in 'London' in 1966. John read the article and bought his copy on Leeds Market for 10 shillings (50p!). Over a short period of time he bought every bootleg he could find.

In September 1971 John gained his PGCE and started teaching English at Bury Technical College, a further education college that provided qualifications for school leavers pursuing A-levels, vocational qualifications or apprenticeships. It might be rather peevish to say that he drifted into this, but he needed a job if only to pay for his bootleg addiction. However, he realised quite quickly that he didn't enjoy teaching.

★★★

[Collecting is] dudes hanging out together relating to each other's objects … It's such a manifestation of dude culture, where guys tend to gather and not talk about their actual lives if they can avoid it, but instead refer to the engine of their car or whatever third thing they can talk about. And then through the aesthetics of that, they'll relate to one another and get a sense of whether somebody is trustworthy or not and if they can actually open up to them … It's a compensation for all kinds of male skills that are supposed to be present in adolescence that may not be present so you compensate with other things – the superiority of specialisation in some arcane field.

Amanda Petrusich, *Do Not Sell At Any Price: The Wild, Obsessive Hunt for the World's Rarest 78rpm Records*, 2014

This is where I come into the story. In spring 1972, I was living at home and in the early stages of my own teaching career. I replied to a small ad in *Melody Maker* placed by someone who wanted to exchange Bob Dylan tapes. The bloke got back to me pretty quickly and it turned out that he lived three streets away from my mum's house; I had delivered evening papers there when I was a kid. He was called Bob Richardson and his claim to fame, amongst other things, was that he had been on the television pop show *Thank Your Lucky Stars* on a panel with other fans who passed judgement on whether new releases would be hits or misses. He also ran the Gary US Bonds fan club, and because of that, a certain Bruce Springsteen would get in touch with him at some point in the future.

Bob, like me, was a Bolton Wanderers fan and suggested that before we went to the match one Saturday we should make a trip to the Virgin record store in Liverpool. Virgin at that time was predominantly a mail order organisation that sold cut-price records. They also sold Bob Dylan bootlegs, even over the counter in the shops. When he picked me up, he introduced me to John Bauldie who was already in the car. On our return we travelled back down the M61 to go to the Wanderers match at Burnden Park. Just past the Bolton West motorway services, Wanderers' manager Jimmy Armfield drove past us. We all broke into a chant of 'Ji-mm-y Armfield' as he sped by on his way to the game.

John and I were rooted in so much from that very beginning. We were born within a few weeks of each other and had grown up the same way. We were both northern working-class kids who had made it to grammar school on our own merit. We grew up with the all-embracing influences of football and music. We were both just starting out in teaching careers, and we were both still living at home.

I didn't have much of a Dylan collection, not in comparison to him anyway, but he was always generous to a fault. There were a few things I was able to do to help the collection along. The school I was working in had a rather large language laboratory with a bank of high quality open reel recorders where I was able to copy tapes for both of us. One I particularly remember copying was the hilarious so-called CBS Message Tape from 1965. He never said where he got the tapes from but it was obvious his connections were fairly good.

Quite soon after we met I moved to a flat above a chemist's shop in Horwich and John bought a house in a row of cotton weavers' cottages in Padiham, a small town with a population of less than 10,000 that was once a thriving part of the Lancashire textile industry. The house had all its primitive early nineteenth-century features including a picture rail three quarters of the way up the wall in what was described as the best room. The most striking feature of this room hit you as soon as you went in; all along the picture rail John had put empty cans of McEwan's Tartan Bitter, a beer popular at the time that was sold in tartanised pop-art style cans. The picture rail brought Andy Warhole style to this tiny house on the edge of the Pennines and a smell of stale beer too.

As for Bolton Wanderers, this was one of the darkest periods in their history. In 1971 they were relegated to Division Three of the English Football League. To bring together his two passions, John rewrote the words to Dylan's 'Ballad in Plain D' and was known to perform it to other Bolton Wanderers fans. With a can of beer in his hand he would sing:

> Now is the time for all good loyal Bolton men
> To get down to Burnden Park again.

In the middle of the song, he would pause and say that the audience had to imagine there was a harmonica break going on whilst he had a drink as if the can was a harmonica cradled around his neck. The song ended by comparing the desolate Bolton ground to a graveyard.

John would buy books in WH Smith's on Victoria Square in Bolton. Their new books section was down a set of stairs. It would have been one day in 1972 when John walked in there and found on display *Bob Dylan: An Intimate Biography* by Anthony Scaduto. If publishers were picking up on the fact the people wanted books about him, Dylan seemed to have hit mainstream. For John, this seemed too good to be true. In a further visit to WH Smith's that year he found *Song & Dance Man: The Art of Bob Dylan* by Michael Gray. This turned out to be a critical study of Dylan's lyrics. Indeed it was the first and in truth became a seminal work. As a student of literature, John realised for the first time this was really where his interest in Dylan's work lay.

During that time John and I saw each other pretty often, going to matches and gigs including Jackson Browne, Loudon Wainwright and Ralph McTell. I had a particular penchant for The Incredible String Band – a sign of a wasted childhood perhaps – and we went to see founder member Robin Williamson who was well into that period of his where he was regaling the audience with long, long, long tales of Celtic heroes. I don't recall John being too impressed, he was almost on the edge of being into glam rock of a mild kind; Thin Lizzy, Cockney Rebel. He also saw David Bowie on the Ziggy Stardust tour.

After a relatively long period without any official output from Dylan, he burst back onto the scene in 1974 with the release of *Planet Waves*, followed by a twenty-one city comeback tour with The Band. Shows were taped, copies made and instantly posted off all over the world. Suddenly tapes were everywhere, dropping through letter boxes on a daily basis. This is where the network of Dylan contacts came of age. Open reel tapes came by post from America – this was the time just before everyone had access to a cassette player. Every show seemed to spawn tapes and single, double and triple bootleg records too.

The American collectors thought that bootleg records were for part-time fans. They were interested in what they thought was the real deal: tapes. These tapes were a veritable Dylan cornucopia of studio outtakes, concert recordings, media appearances and private recordings Dylan had made way back in 1962 at the houses of friends. Often with scribbled notes stuck in the boxes to offer some kind of detail, the tapes found their way to John, including the *Blood on the Tracks* outtakes which arrived almost before he had turned the officially released album over on his turntable to play side two. This was Dylan heaven.

Then, lo and behold, the 1975 Rolling Thunder tour. More

gigs, more tapes, more delight. Not only were these shows documented by live audience tapes, but sometimes unofficial soundboard tapes too, and countless TV and radio spots. Novelist and playwright Wes Stace, aka recording artist John Wesley Harding, wrote in his liner notes to *The Rolling Thunder Revue: The 1975 Live Recordings* box set, 'Dylan scholar John Bauldie said he'd give up all the rest if he could just keep 1975.' Stace acknowledged that when he was a young student at Cambridge, John had taken him under his wing and nurtured his interest in listening to and writing about Dylan.

In late August 1975, John helped me move from Bolton to Runcorn in Cheshire to take up a new teaching post. We drove along with the bootleg version of *Blood on the Tracks* playing loudly and proudly through the open windows – everything we did was set against the background or indeed the foreground of new Dylan albums and tapes as they appeared. As we drove into the town on this warm, August morning, John turned and said in a very matter of fact, much unembellished manner, 'I've met this girl. She's called Penny.' John had first seen Penny in July 1975 when she had got a job at Bury College. Penny Garner was a science graduate from an affluent family in London. She'd had many of the opportunities in life that John had been denied and in many ways had lived a life up to this point as different to John's as mushy peas to guacamole.

Our lives continued to be intermingled. John and Penny and me, amongst other company, visited eateries, drank wine and generally tried to be grown-ups. We went to Greece, taking in the Acropolis and the Parthenon, but also looking for obscure Dylan Greek picture sleeves in record shops. John and Penny fell in love with Greece and spent every summer there from that time on.

Like many intelligent and creative people, John didn't often give much of his deepest self away, but his personal papers reveal he did express his inner feelings in writing. Not many people know that John was also a competent guitarist. He had a friend who was a merchant seaman who, when on leave, would turn up at John's and play very tasteful Bruce Langhorne-style guitar to John's renditions of Dylan songs. We used to play a game together too. He would send me songs he had written and recorded on cassette tape and I would send him mine. His were good. Mine were awful. He would send my tape back and say 'I can't sing this so I've rewritten it in the style of Tom Rush' and proceed to play a more than competent Tom Rush-style guitar. He often made my terrible songs sound less terrible.

Amongst his personal papers there is a hand-bound book of 11 songs he'd written for Penny called *Songs that Begin and End with You – 1976-1977.* If there's a general theme to the songs, it would be of John's insecurity, manifested here in expressing his fears that Penny would leave him.

These songs were written at the time when young men and women in their mid-twenties were searching for a new identity. The sixties were long gone; peace and love had run its course. Anguish and identity in the music were seemingly the new norm. Lyrics of songs by James Taylor and Joni Mitchell perhaps attest to this and Neil Young, always one to say it like it is, was 'Helpless'. So it is not surprising then that John, now in his mid-twenties too, was searching for identity, searching to find ways of dealing with new emotions that Penny had brought into his life and searching to quell his own insecurity – not a sensation that anyone who knew the John Bauldie that he gave to the world would associate with him.

There were signs too, to me at least, of his growing dissatisfaction with teaching. After a trip with his students to the Royal Shakespeare Theatre at Stratford-on-Avon he told me that while the trip had been successful, the performance probably did more to educate his students than a hundred of his lessons. He also felt the time he spent working on lessons took him away from the things which he wanted to do – like his own reading, which he never felt was as extensive as it should be.

★★★

Friendship arises out of mere companionship when two or more of the companions discover that they have in common some insight or interest or even taste which the others do not share and which, till that moment, each believed to be his own unique treasure (or burden). The typical expression of opening friendship would be something like, 'What? You too? I thought I was the only one.'

C.S. Lewis, *The Four Loves*, 1960

It was announced that Dylan would tour the world in 1978, including six nights at Earls Court in London. These shows, and the long-queues for the tickets outside the designated shops that sold them, would be a real catalyst for the progression of what John would describe as Dylan Studies. John Lindley from Stockport, who in a matter of months would go on to become one of the five Wanted Men, recalled the scramble to get tickets.

People at work told me that Dylan would be coming to Britain for six shows at Earls Court London in June. I made some hurried and illicit phone calls from my desk and discovered that the tickets would go on sale at 9am Sunday morning, May 7th. From these enquiries I learned the location of the nearest ticket office outlet would be the Hime & Addison store in Manchester. On the morning of Saturday 6th May, a friend drove me into Manchester to pick up some things. Around 11am we passed by Hime & Addison to check out where it was. I saw a queue of what looked to be about 80 people beginning at the shop's doorway, continuing down the block and snaking around the corner for what I fully expected to be a twenty-two hour wait until nine the following morning. The queue seemed to be growing all the time.

Without thinking, I jumped out and joined the queue ignited by goodness knows what. I asked my friend to make contact with people to tell them where I was and told him to ring another friend who was as crazy about Dylan as I was and get down here to get some tickets for himself. Chatting to others around me, sharing thoughts about albums, if we had seen him before and what Dylan meant to us, relationships were formed in the queue that became long lasting. I recall John Cooper Clarke, the punk poet, strutting up and down without his Bob Dylan mask but with his best Dylan hairstyle.

Around 2am on Sunday morning, a member of staff was instructed to open the shop, presumably above and beyond the call of duty, and start selling tickets to a queue of people that were now in their hundreds. My friend had joined me. We went to where he had parked his motorbike. I climbed on the back and off we went after I had stuffed the haul of tickets into my pockets thinking we might be mugged.

John and I slept on people's floors in London for the Earls Court shows and met people whose names we had only ever seen at the bottom of notes stuffed into tape boxes or whose voices we only ever had heard on the telephone telling us about new Dylan tapes in circulation. In meeting them face to face we did indeed remove our hats.

On 27th July 1979, the first Bob Dylan convention – 'Zimmerman Blues' – organised by Richard Goodall, cemented the loose associations built up around the Earls Court shows and brought fans together from all over the world. The convention also brought together what we might call some of the big league Dylan tape collectors, John being one of them, plus luminaries in the form of Robert Shelton and Professor Christopher Ricks, who championed Dylan in the academic world. Goodall had set the high standard for everything that followed his convention. John knew this and was always grateful for what he had done in putting it on and getting things moving. Goodall says, rather embarrassingly for him, that John, ever gracious, never let him forget.

After the convention, even larger networks began to spring up that circulated tapes and information by post, nationally and internationally, to increasingly larger circles of interested people. For everyone concerned this was taking up an enormous amount of time, especially when much of the same information was repeated over and over again.

The following year, 'Dylan Revisited' took place at Owen's

Park Conference Centre Manchester over the weekend of 29th–31st August 1980. John was invited to speak and answer questions on the Saturday afternoon of the convention. He called his talk 'A Look at Some of the More Rare Dylan Songs'. John offered responses to a variety of questions about these songs. When asked what Dylan was all about, he replied that there is more than one Dylan: 'I think that Dylan has gone through a series of explorations of self which relate to one huge SELF written in capital letters.' In answer to a question about the possibility that Dylan is vague and often writes about things that few can understand, John replied:

> It is surely up to the listener to investigate the song. Dylan, in writing songs, an art form that needs to be listened to, is offering the listener the opportunity to do this for themself. This is what art is about: an invitation to deduce something from it for yourself. What you find in it is up to you. Dylan puts it in the song for you to find. If you listen to 'Isis' for example you might want to investigate vegetation rituals, an understanding of which is perhaps crucial to the understanding of the song itself. You have to investigate the song yourself. What you find out is up to you but Dylan puts it in the song for you to find.

John first got the idea for The Bob Dylan Information Office at this convention. He wrote a letter afterwards to Ian Woodward, another major international player:

> I have been working on a critical survey … spending most of my spare time on that for the last year. It may be another year before it's finished. However I don't see any publication possibilities. What I'm really interested in are articles from literary publications or articles which deal with Dylan's words from a literary or otherwise analytical perspective. Do you know anyone who has done a literature search on Dylan for an academic thesis?

Ian Woodward, like Bauldie, was a dignified, well-read, well-spoken, well-mannered and well-dressed English gentleman; one of the last people on Earth you might expect to have a fascination with Dylan. In fact, if you put both of them together it would take you a long, long time to work out their common, abiding fascination. Woodward was the major influence on what would happen next. One of the first things that The Bob Dylan Information Office set out to do was distribute Ian Woodward's fact sheet *The Wicked Messenger*.

The Wicked Messenger started in December 1980, initially for private circulation only. Later published by *The Telegraph* and then, for many years, by *ISIS* magazine, it ran for 2271 issues, ceasing publication in January 2009. During those 28 years, it carried 6648 entries, each entry being numbered sequentially to allow for cross-referencing. There was no set schedule but, on average, it was produced once or twice a week. Each issue was a single-sided A4 sheet, gathering current news and historical information, often based on contributions by many Dylan collectors and fans from around the world, as well as contacts in the music business. In terms of content, its accuracy and thoroughness were rarely surpassed at the time.

Now we need to consider the formation of Wanted Man, The Bob Dylan Information Office and *The Telegraph*. The place, the hour and the men. It was perhaps one of those quirks of history that all the Wanted Men lived in Manchester or its environs. So for them to meet up in pubs on a regular basis after the 1980 convention to trade tapes and keep up to date with what they thought Dylan was up to seemed a natural thing to do. These Wanted Men came together with all the wide-eyed excitement of little bright boys sharing their stamp collections with each other.

John Lindley again tells a little of the story:

> I had just heard about this guy who supposedly had all these Dylan tapes. We were having a bit of what I suppose you might call a meeting in a pub. John turned up. I got the impression he was a bullshitter and con artist but I liked him. We met several times like this. There were other people there too, like the late Dave Dingle. Dave

took a big part in what happened in starting Wanted Man. I met Dave in a record store. We were both buying the same Dylan album. There was no plan to all this stuff. It happened by what seemed a kind of an accident. We started to go to John's house in Radcliffe. The idea came from John. It started as a jokey idea really. Somehow something a bit like a rag mag.

Dave Heath came from Leeds and would later go on to form *My Back Pages* with Dave Dingle to track down hard to find Dylan books. He remembers John's house with some affection:

> We were just in the middle of trying to set something going and there was a scratching at the window. John got up and said 'Scuse me for a sec, I've got to let Neil in' and left the room almost like Charlie Chaplin. He came back in with his cat. 'Neil? What kind of name for a cat is that?'

The cat was named after Neil Whatmore, something of a Bolton Wanderers hero at the time. Like I said, Wanderers first, Dylan second. (He didn't have a cat called 'Bob' did he?) Dave Heath also says that he got a shock when he went into John's bathroom and spotted a very tacky picture-mirror of Rod Stewart hanging there. John admitted it was a guilty pleasure.

The meetings carried on and ideas were kicked around. Pretty soon Wanted Man was advertised in the British pop music papers for anyone who was interested. These adverts initially turned up 146 respondents. The first edition of *The Telegraph* went out to these initial subscribers in November 1981.

The Wanted Men were introduced:

> There is John Bauldie, secretary and editor who opens all your letters and then passes them on to other people to do the mugging and unrewarding jobs. Dave Dingle is chief book pusher and does a hell of a lot of chasing around and generally being a Johannes factotum or something like that. John Lindley is book distributor. All your book orders are handled by John. It must be a God awful chore for him at the post office with all those packets. A most important guy is Bob Carroll the treasurer. Then there's

> Clinton Heylin, who, well Clinton serves an important
> function in that he's the one who gets all the flak from
> everyone else. He's a kind of tension reliever. Clinton's
> mind retains a lot of sources for the answers to questions
> that are passed on to me.

Of course, Clinton Heylin would eventually be considered as the world's foremost writer about Bob Dylan. However, at this point in time on the formation of The Bob Dylan Information Office, Clinton, who came up with the name Wanted Man for the group, was so much younger then, just out of short pants and punk rock. On close examination of the first issue of *The Telegraph*, it is John's voice that we hear and we can perhaps sense that the majority of what has been written is already coming from his pen. One of the real problems of running a newsletter of any kind is getting material from people to put in it. Ask anyone who has run one of these things and they'll tell you. John wasn't averse to making things up to fill odd spaces. Look for letters by Alex from Crewe. Football fans should be able to work that one out.

In the sixteen-page newsletter there were eight pages of questions and answers, one page for collectors' corner, two pages of letters and two pages of tapes and records for sale. On the inside front cover are the lyrics to 'Caribbean Wind', an unreleased song, and on the back cover is a black and white poorly reproduced photo of a young Dylan. Hey Presto, the first issue of *The Telegraph*, the Wanted Man newsletter.

The first six issues followed using this same format. Issue 7 would establish what would become an annual tradition. While John had his teacher's endless summer break, Dave Dingle took over editing *The Telegraph*. John spent that summer in Greece with Penny, ruminating on the direction of Wanted Man. He felt that *The Telegraph* was spending too much time in dealing with the trivia of Dylan's life. He wanted to make it into the critical quarterly that he had always envisaged. He and I, with others like Nigel Hinton, discussed this at some length. Nigel was a contributor to *The Telegraph* and over time became a close friend of John's. He was himself a renowned British writer of teenage fiction.

At the 1979 'Zimmerman Blues' conference, Richard Goodall had introduced John to Robert Shelton, the journalist whose *New York Times* review of Dylan's 1961 show at Gerde's Folk City had been reprinted on the back of Dylan's first album. Shelton and John became firm friends. He wrote a letter to John asking him about the direction of Wanted Man:

> I'm wondering what the 'Information Office' could possibly be. Is it going to avoid gossip and tales and concentrate on scholarship and discographical information? I think that it ought to be rigorously defined, or first thing you know, you'll have your hands full of nutters.

John was back in the driving seat for Issue 8 of *The Telegraph* in October 1982. His column is a long statement, covering many pages, with John maybe seeing himself as Martin Luther nailing his thesis for change to the church door in Wittenberg.

> We're a year old now. We look like becoming the longest running Dylan magazine. We have to get things organised and visualised if we are not to limp and splutter to a whimpering conclusion. I know from feedback most are happy with what we have done so far. I think we've done okay too. But I am anxious about Wanted Man policy and direction. What are we to do with gossipy items that cannot in any way act as information and yet which nevertheless are very much part of the Dylan story? I've been guilty in the past of seizing the opportunity to add smart alec comments to communications included on letter box pages. Mea culpa. But I do take Dylan seriously as a writer. Unfortunately *The Telegraph* does not give me the opportunity to make this clear. I have been writing about Dylan for three years, but I have a great deal to do before I am finished.
>
> Just as with Shakespeare it isn't the mystic that makes him great as with Dylan – it's the work. Most of the time Wanted Man particularly, but *The Telegraph* seems to have nothing to do with Dylan's work. People ask what is the point of it all? If I try to answer that question – I would have to answer that we're writing history. We're trying to get it right before the chance disappears. Write in if you

can help get some dialogue going here – I need your help.
I want *The Telegraph* to develop.

He ends by saying that he felt that it was 'grand to be back at the helm and this ship will go exactly where I want it to go'. You can hear the nails being banged in the church door.

Issue 9 did publish one or two articles along the lines that John had suggested, but it also revealed that there was resistance to what he wanted to do, which provoked a vibrant interchange of views on the letters page of the next few issues. From the very beginning John could sense a tension between those who wanted tape lists and those who wanted critical writing and understanding. In light of this, after he thought *The Telegraph* had taken a misguided direction, he took over completely and to go alongside contributions from the Wanten Men he invited critical work from acclaimed writers such as Professor Christopher Ricks, Aidan Day, Patrick J. Webster, David Pichaske, John Hinchey, Roy Kelly, Nigel Hinton and Michael Gray. In a relatively short period, John turned *The Telegraph* into the foremost critical work of Dylan Studies in the world. *The Telegraph* was published every three months or so for the next fourteen years, and distributed to a subscription base that reached 3500 people around the world. During that time John wrote more than fifty critical articles about Dylan's work.

In 1983, John launched The Wanted Man Study Series. In the preface to the first publication, *Bob Dylan's Slow Train* by John Hinchey, he laid out his raison d'être for the series. This could well be his manifesto for everything that he was trying to achieve.

> The object of this series is to provide studies of individual LP records by Bob Dylan, or of particular themes in Bob Dylan's written and recorded work. The emphasis is placed firmly upon critical discussion and critical assessment. It is assumed that the reader has a good knowledge of the work under discussion. Furthermore it is important that Bob Dylan's songs should be heard, so that the reader may be aware of the component parts of Dylan's art, even as he reads an assessment of perhaps only one of

these components, the lyrics to the songs. It is hoped that the critical judgements offered in this series will help to develop a more thorough understanding and appreciation of the work of this important modern writer and also help to bring about further recognition of his achievement as a poet of the first order.

★★★

John used his summer break in 1986 to follow the Dylan tour of the Northeastern states, travelling with his close friend Christian Behrens, a lawyer from Germany and fellow Dylan collector. John sent me a postcard from the tour, it read: 'Dear Bill, Been to three shows. Hartford was great not only the concert but because I talked with Dylan for ten to fifteen minutes. Radios are full of our music. You must come next time. John.' After the concert in Hartford, Connecticut, they were walking back to their car. Suddenly in front of them they saw a white Volkswagen they had seen on the tour and recognised it as the vehicle that Dylan used to travel from gig to gig. I'll let John tell the story. This is what he wrote:

> Unbelievably at the very moment we reached the van, the sliding door opened and out popped Bob Dylan, right next to us, still in his stage clothes. He must have known that if he got out he would bump into people who had been to the gig. What perhaps he wouldn't know is that he would bump into a guy from Germany who was following the tour and a guy from England who for the last five years had edited a fan magazine about him with an enthusiasm that occasionally had veered towards the fanatical. So what's the first thing you say when you meet Bob Dylan? Hi Bob I'm a great admirer of your work. One thing I've always wanted to know... and other bubble gum stuff like that?
>
> So what was I to say that would immediately capture his imagination and let him know that this guy ambling along with him wasn't just some lame-brain bozo? He was a real fan, a knowledgeable, intelligent, understanding kind of fan who meant no harm, who didn't want a piece of him, who himself was worth talking to.

'Hey Bob. "Lay Lady Lay". Last time I heard you sing that was in Barcelona.'

'You were at that show?'

'Yes,' I replied. It was one of my favourite shows. 'Do you remember it?'

'Yeah I do remember.'

I couldn't live a lie, I had to tell him something about myself so he'd know just who he was dealing with here. I knew that he knew about *The Telegraph*.

'Err, Bob I should tell you I'm the guy who does the fan magazine *The Telegraph* about you.'

Suddenly Dylan stopped dead in his tracks, turned his face for the first time towards me and slowly lifted his shades.

'Is that you? You do that?'

'Yes,' I said half proud, ready to duck. 'Is it okay?'

'Yeah I've seen it a few times. It's pretty interesting ... So what are you guys doing here?'

'We're here for the shows.'

'Make sure you tell the truth about me. A lot of people tell lies. Make sure you tell the truth.'

And as if he couldn't reinforce the point enough he added just for good measure, 'Don't forget now – check your sources.'

We must have been walking for twenty-five minutes or so dribbling on about this and that. Then Bob's big tour bus drove into view and a minder skipped out and hustled Bob brusquely towards it. He was about to say 'Goodbye' but all he could do was manage a half turn and a wave. And then he was gone.

***

When will the bell ring, and end this weariness?
How long have they tugged the leash, and strained apart,
My pack of unruly hounds...
I shall keep my strength for myself;
they can keep theirs as well.
For if I should sell it all for them
I should hate them
I will sit and wait for the bell.

D. H. Lawrence, 'Last Lesson of the Afternoon'

It is perhaps a myth that most English teachers really want to be writers, but it certainly crossed John's mind. Towards the end of his teaching career he told a story about a time he was patrolling the classroom, walking round and round between the rows of desks, when he found a student writing on a desk in big letters. The boy had written 'Weed, Whites and Wine' from Little Feat's song 'Willin''. He said that instead of admonishing the boy, he felt that although he wasn't into weed or whites himself, but maybe into a little wine, that there was some hope left and the promise of rock'n'roll hadn't died.

Things came to a head for John and Penny when, due to a combination of ill-health, problems at the school she worked at and a sense of isolation, Penny took up a teaching job nearer to her family. Faced with this, John decided to quit his job, up sticks and move south to be with Penny. In one of those wonderful twists of fate, something miraculous happened during his train journey to London. A fellow passenger was Mark Ellen, one of the co-founders of *Q*, a new British music magazine. *Q* was a grown-up magazine for people who had grown up with what they thought was the music that mattered. At that time, Ellen along with *Q* co-founder David Hepworth, was also presenting BBC's music TV show *The Old Grey Whistle Test*. It transpired that Ellen was aware of John and the quality of his writing in *The Telegraph* since he subscribed under his wife's maiden name. He asked John to make an appointment to meet him, which he did. He offered John the post of sub-editor. Within a couple of days, he started at their Great Portland Street office. The unemployed English teacher had become a full-time journalist within seven days of his arrival in London.

From Romford, where he was now living, he carried on with *The Telegraph*. By now he was recognised as an expert in Dylan's work. John was a brilliant raconteur and now he was in and around London he was often invited to speak at conventions and on radio about his work and *The Telegraph*. In 1987 he co-edited with Michael Gray a collection of 50 or so critical articles from contributors to *The Telegraph* published by Sidgwick & Jackson. As well as critical articles, another of the impressive features of *The Telegraph* was that John was able to conduct interviews with musicians who had worked with Dylan and who trusted him enough to offer insights into various aspects of Dylan's work, knowing that he would ensure that what they said would be faithfully reproduced. In 1990 many of these interviews were collected together in the book *Wanted Man: In Search of Bob Dylan*.

At Q magazine, John usually submitted five or six short reviews for each issue, considering latest releases from artists as diverse as The Clancy Brothers and Tom Paxton to Carly Simon, James Taylor and Neil Young. Sometimes he commanded half a page to review albums from the big stars, albums such as Van Morrison's *Enlightenment* and a Cat Stevens box set reissue amongst others. Q knew that he always wrote well in his vibrant, meaningful, bouncy style. He was charged with writing a six-page article every month called 'Systems' where he reviewed the latest hi tech audio-visual gear. Hi-fi wasn't particularly where his interest lay, but he dutifully went off to all kinds of sales conventions to gather details. In one 'Systems' feature he was looking ahead to the sound system of the future. He wrote, 'No matter how loyally you may want to cling to your dear old, much-loved records, it's only a matter time before vinyl is a black plastic thing of the past.' He didn't always get it right.

John had a skill for reviewing hi-fi gear that was recognised by others. He wrote a column called 'Behind the Lines' for *High Fidelity* magazine with a big photo of him and his name above the title. Real recognition. Made it at last. He also managed to sneak into the same issue a two-page review of Dylan's album *Oh Mercy*, and a full overview of Dylan's career with a plug for Wanted Man to boot.

For Q he also wrote a column called 'Where Are They Now?' looking up 'stars' like Mike Heron of The Incredible String Band and Jesse Winchester, and asking them over the phone what they were up to. His greatest thrill at Q was to be sent to Los Angeles to interview Jackson Browne. John did have other singer-songwriters that he listened too as well as Dylan. Jackson Browne had been one of these since his first album in the early 1970s. John got a personal preview of the new album *I'm Alive* with a dozen or so others where Browne and his band played the songs from the album in full. Then he got to interview him. Such was his overwhelming little-boy-meets-a-hero delight that he rang me in the middle of the night and said, 'I bet you can't guess where I am or what I am doing?'

John had followed Dylan on tour around Europe and the United States in 1984, 1986 and 1987, and always kept a diary, although he called it an 'on the road record of gossip and recollection'. It didn't occur to him to print it in *The Telegraph* at first. The idea was a simple one, it was merely a matter of writing down the kind of thoughts and conversations that occurred each day in between shows, in hotel rooms, in bars and mostly in cars on highways and interstates, autostradas and autobahns with his travelling companion Christian Behrens. Journeys like this in literature have often been used as a device, a foundation on which to build something else. There are only characters and the road. Interaction between the characters often provides situations where these characters take us down roads of their own. John's diary had nothing to do with Bob Dylan, just as Chaucer's Pilgrims had nothing to do with Thomas à Becket.

In 1995 he published *Diary of a Bobcat* in an edition of 300 through the good auspices of Wanted Man. The book brought together the four instalments of his diary that had first been published in various issues of *The Telegraph*. It is wonderful. The first thing he does in the foreword is, in fact, debunk the term Bobcat which he says he hated, although Bobcat was coined by him and some friends journeying by car from one gig to another:

> The idea of Bobcats was meant to be a joke and yet somehow it has become a generic term for Dylan's keenest followers. Many *Telegraph* readers hate the word. I pretty much hate it myself. But alas it's too late to do anything about it now. We're all of us Bobcats, whether we want to be or not.

> do Not create anything. it will be
> misinterpreted. it will not change.
> it will follow you the
> rest of your life.

Those lines are a quote from a Dylan poem called 'Advice for Geraldine on Her Miscellaneous Birthday'. Despite mock hatred he seems to feel for the term, John, in fact, defines it in the book maybe just for the hell of it. You can judge for yourself if you qualify.

> As so many 'would-be Bobcats' seem to be claiming full membership just because they collect tapes and go to a few shows I think that I should remind everybody that you must have either:
>
> > a) Been mentioned in *The Telegraph* by name more than once.
> > b) Been the first person to put into collecting circulation a previously unheard tape.
> > c) Have seen at least 58 Dylan concerts.
>
> There are no other qualifications and no 'honoraries'. This is definitely an exclusive cliquery. Let's keep it that way, eh?*

So there! And here we have a wonderful example of John at his best. A tongue-in-cheek passage, pared right down to its basic gentle irony, comic but barbed, making the reader delight in its style but at the same time getting the point. In the body of the book we meet obsessive fans who are following the tours, members of the bands who back Dylan, security guards, sometimes fellow rock stars. We travel though small town America and hit the big cities too.

In March 1988, John privately published *The Ghost of Electricity* in a print run of 500 copies. In the introduction he says:

> The intention of this book is to document Bob Dylan's 1966 world tour. I have no wish to provide a wiser-with-hindsight account of events but have tried to offer a summary of the way in which the concerts were reported at the time. A large part of what follows is therefore, verbatim reportage. It is hoped that the reader will come out of the experience of the book as Dylan came out of the tour; bewildered, bleary-eyed and completely exhausted.

---

* Just in case you ask, I am a fully qualified Bobcat having entered this esteemed body by virtue of a and b. Thank you.

John's adventures in the Dylan trade got bigger and better and more exciting as the years went on. He was approached by Jeff Rosen, Dylan's business manager, to write the liner notes for *Bootleg Series Volumes 1-3*. We cannot begin to understand how he must have felt. From nothing to everything in a roller-coaster ride of twenty years or so. In 1987, in the space of a week he went from being a teacher of English to being a full-time journalist on an international pop magazine. Only four years later he would be nominated for a Grammy for his notes in the box set. All this not only based on his passion about Dylan's work but through his ability to express this passion in writing.

At a convention in October 1992, John gave a talk about his involvement in the project. In a witty ninety minutes he entertained the audience with his description of how it happened. The first fifteen minutes of the talk were taken up by, believe it or not, Bolton Wanderers Football Club. As he moved the subject on to the liner notes, John recalled how from the very beginning of *The Telegraph*, complimentary copies had gone to Jeff Rosen, who was aware of the high standard that John set for the journal. In the summer of 1990, Rosen had suggested that John had about six months to write the notes. With other commitments in mind, John decided he would start the project at the beginning of the New Year 1991. However, he got a phone call from Rosen on Boxing Day; unforeseen circumstances meant that the release of the box set had been moved forward and that they needed the notes in six days. Not even seven days, six! John managed to talk ten days out of him. With seventy songs on the list that Rosen had sent him, he worked out he had about an hour of available time to write about each song. No pressure.

The booklet itself is seventy-two pages long. Each of the songs is described in depth and in detail. For example, of 'Every Grain of Sand' he says:

> The great song which concluded *Shot of Love* here as Dylan demoed it. It's one of the most moving lyrics Dylan has ever written – a self-portrait of isolation, even desolation, an admission of failure in a lifelong attempt

at coming to terms with what he calls 'The Reality of Man' and, perhaps, a confession of spiritual doubt in what is described in the opening line as 'the hour of my deepest need'. The consolation that he offers to himself in the song – the Biblical reassurance that 'every hair is numbered', that there's providence in the fall of a sparrow, that the world is governed by, as he wrote in the song's alterative penultimate line, 'a perfect finished plan' – seems convincing enough compensation for the pains of the journey through the veil of tears.

'I can see the master's hand/ In every leaf that trembles, in every grain of sand' he sings at the end of the second verse, echoing William Blake's 'Auguries of Innocence'. Dylan had addressed the concept before – 'I can see God in a daisy' he said in 1976. But, it seems, there are debilitating moments of doubt, when he's not always conscious of the creator's presence within the world. In the very last verse of 'Every Grain of Sand' he turns, hearing those 'ancient footsteps' which betray the presence of God (again the image is borrowed from Blake), but it's only 'sometimes' that he feels as if he's not alone – 'other times it's only me'. It's a chilling moment, and anything but a statement of assured faith.

He provided details about each song, how it came to be written, where it was recorded and, more often than not, which album it had been left off in favour of something else, reigniting the game Dylan fans like to play and which he, naturally, loved.

The Bootlegs Series Volumes 1-3 set up what would become a paradigm for much of the record industry from there on in. Every recording artist and band worth, or not worth, their salt, was able to scrape up dubious recordings from the bottom of the barrel of their back catalogue and market them as box sets. More often than not these were actually scrapings from underneath the barrel. Some were even given the title of *Bootleg Boxes*, imitating the manner in which Rosen had established the Dylan box sets. While they were able to copy the marketing, none of this material had anything like the quality that the Dylan recordings had. But what these sets did have in common is that they all continued detailed notes in the style that John had established for the Dylan box.

In the early nineties my life was turned upside down more than a little. I was going through a divorce and, without wanting to be too melodramatic, I was involved in a very nasty traffic accident. By then I was living outside Blackpool and John wrote to me:

> I'm not going to wither on too much, not going to offer any meaningless advice or consolation because I know that during the course of our lives, we've read the same books, listened to the same songs and each of us has used them to give shape and meaning to our lives.
>
> Just as I've always sorted things out for myself so I know that you have the strength and resources to come to terms with whatever this crazy, ridiculous and unfortunately outrageous existence has to throw at you.
>
> Like Bob, I think that life is sad, life is a bust – but it's also true that all you can do is do what you must do and do it well.
>
> The clock ticks on – and you can't turn it backwards.
> John

Clearly his writing skills weren't reserved for words about Dylan.

In 1993 Q was joined by a new sister publication, *Mojo*, and John moved across the room so to speak, to write for *Mojo*. In truth, he wasn't very happy and quickly grew frustrated. As chief sub editor at Q and *Mojo*, he worked with some of the best music writers in the world – the likes of Mat Snow, Barney Hoskyns and Paul Du Noyer – but like so many successful, creative and seemingly gregarious people, he was troubled by self-doubt. Periodically he even doubted his own writing ability.

In March 1996 he left *Mojo* and joined the staff of *House and Garden*, a high-end monthly magazine that focuses on interior design, entertaining and gardening. He applied for the job at *House and Garden* simply to prove to himself that he was where he was not just by writing about Bob Dylan, but that editors wanted him for his ability as a true journalist who could write about anything. Given what we know about his Rod Stewart mirror and picture rail decorated with Tartan Bitter cans, we know his experience of interior design was minimal.

Ever since he'd moved to Romford, John travelled to Bolton every other weekend to watch Wanderers' home games. He did this with an old friend from secondary school, Barry 'Swifty' Swift. John and Swifty had been going to matches together since they were little boys. So when Bob Dylan was scuffling in New York in the early sixties to get gigs, these little boys were travelling to watch their team. In the late 1980s, Swifty lived in Northampton and worked in the City of London for an international oil company. On Saturdays, John drove to Northampton, picked up Swifty on the way to Bolton, watched the match and then generally drove straight back. For nearly ten years they would share the intimacy of that 500-mile round trip. Their conversations would have been predominately about football, goals, players, wins, losses and Neil the cat, but Swifty does remember John playing him stuff by Crash Test Dummies on one occasion and how John got really excited.

On the evening of Monday 21st October 1996, John rang me at home. The following night Bolton were playing Chelsea at Burnden Park.

'How do you fancy coming down to the match tomorrow? I'm coming up with Matthew in his helicopter. We can meet up. You can meet him and we can go in the directors' box. Pretty good eh?'

The Matthew he referred to was Matthew Harding, Chairman of Chelsea Football Club. They had common interests, football and Bob Dylan.

'John, I can't I've got a parents' night at school,' I told him.

'Okay, maybe next time? Keep your eye on the score if you can.'

I was listening to the news early on Wednesday morning when a voice said that they were getting reports of a helicopter crash over Cheshire with high ranking Chelsea Football Club officials on board.

I rang Penny straight away. 'We're just waiting for confirmation,' she said. Confirmation came far too soon. Everyone on board the helicopter had died.

For most people, words aren't much use for making sense of the things that really matter. That's why we need poets who forge their own meanings from language to make sense of their experiences to help us in the process too. John and I dropped lines from Dylan into our conversations, so perhaps it is inevitable that I turn to Dylan's work at this point:

> And there's no use in tryin'
> To deal with the dyin'
> Though I cannot explain that in lines.

In my copy of his book about Dylan's 1966 World Tour, *The Ghost of Electricity*, John wrote:

> Many a day has passed and gone
> Many a gamble has been lost and won
> And many a road taken by many a friend
> Happy Trails Bill
> John

John's partner Penny also died far too young, succumbing to cancer in 2004. They'd been together for over 20 years. One of the songs that he wrote for her contained the line, 'I remember the first time I saw you, you were dressed in black and talking on the telephone'. Presumably she was on the phone to tell her family that she had got the job at Bury College where they first met. Like the best of relationships, John and Penny were very much their own people. Even though they didn't share the same interests – Penny wasn't seen at Dylan shows or Bolton Wanderers football matches – they had each other in common. Penny was always there behind John; she helped him, cajoled him, drove him on, supported him, loved him and encouraged his indulgences. Penny never got involved in the business of Wanted Man, except once when John was working on a book with journalist Patrick Humphries. Penny came into the room, saw what they were doing and said, 'Oh no! Not another Bob Dylan book,' which duly became the title of the book. John only ever mentioned Penny once in *The Telegraph*. It was issue number 55 and it went like this:

> So there we were in Ferrara, Italy. A lovely town, about half an hour's drive north of Bologna with my long suffering girlfriend Penny looking for a place to eat a couple of hours before the show that Dylan was to play in the castle square. It was a terrific setting with the great Castello Estense built by the d'Este family in the late fourteenth century.

In *The Telegraph* issue number 50, John invited Mike Wyvill and John Wraith to write a regular column called 'Jotting Down Notes'. For several years they had produced a booklet documenting all the gigs that Dylan had played in that particular year, including set lists where possible. After John's death, Wyvill and Wraith carried on the work of *The Telegraph* by editing and publishing *The Bridge*.

★★★

Even though John's life was cut short and his papers and projects would be largely unfinished, did John meet the challenge he'd set himself? In his mid-twenties he said that if he didn't do it who would? Twenty years later what had he achieved?

In the sixties and seventies he had been a major international player in a network of people interested in Dylan's work. In the eighties he had brought this network together to create The Bob Dylan Information Office and, more importantly for him, *The Telegraph*, which he steered to be the quarterly journal of Dylan Studies he had originally envisaged. It is clear that Dylan himself read *The Telegraph*. John wrote about how on one occasion a new *Telegraph* was due, Dylan phoned filmmaker D. A. Pennebaker to ask if his copy had come. Pennebaker said that it had and Dylan asked if he could borrow it because his hadn't arrived. John attracted serious articles from writers who were able to explore Dylan's work in depth, and he also encouraged young writers to take up the mantle and write for *The Telegraph* too. Throughout this time, magazines, booklets and books seem to have been never ending about Dylan. It would be very rare indeed to find one without a credit to John Bauldie for his influence, help, advice or support.

John was not an elitist. He was a supreme communicator and teacher with an engaging, vibrant style in both speaking and writing. His aim had been for everyone to understand what he and others saw and heard in Dylan's work. By the early nineties there were a multitude of writers about Dylan. Some good, some bad and some ugly. John stood head and shoulders above them all.

In what almost might seem to be a valedictory statement, John wrote in his essay 'Simple Twist of Fate' published in the book *Love is the Drug* in 1994:

> Because of *The Telegraph* I've met people and been places and done things that I could never have dreamed of doing. I've rattled through Manhattan in the back of a van with Allen Ginsberg gleefully spouting William Blake lyrics at me. I've stared not a little apprehensively down both barrels of a loaded shotgun waved towards me by A. J. Weberman, fabled raider of Dylan dustbins. I've sat in an ancient amphitheatre in Jerusalem listening to Bob and I've seen him play on top of a mountain in Greece, the air heavy with heat and perfume. I've seen him awesome and amazing. I've seen him delighted and dancing. I've seen films and heard tapes that even the hardest of hard-core Dylan fans couldn't begin to dream of.

Nevertheless there is a seemingly apparent irony. Despite writing more than fifty articles for *The Telegraph*, creating The Wanted Man Study Series, publishing two volumes of articles and interviews from his journal by other writers, working in conjunction with others to co-author books about Dylan and petitioning the Nobel Academy to honour Bob Dylan with the Nobel Prize for Literature in the early nineties much earlier than anyone else even considered the idea, John never published his own book about Dylan's work. People, agencies and publications seemed to be queuing up for his energy and it would seem that these things diverted his attention away from publishing *The Chameleon Poet*.

John had written *The Chameleon Poet* by 1980 but never came back to it fully. He had doubts about its worth, but I and others tried to convince him that it was far better than he himself thought. During his lifetime only small extracts from it saw the light of day. One of the many magazines that appeared about Dylan after the conventions in 1979 and 1980 was *Endless Road*. It first appeared in September 1981, two months before the first issue of *The Telegraph*, and ran for seven issues. The most important thing about it was that it was the first time that John had appeared in print. He allowed them to print an extract from his 'as yet unpublished work on Dylan's writings entitled *The Chameleon Poet*'. They printed the passage on 'Isis'.

Perhaps this was John testing the waters. John said to Ian Woodward about the extract: 'I was disappointed with how it came out. It seemed pretentious and because it was ripped out of context it lost far more than I thought it would.' However, he did go on and use further pieces from the book in *The Telegraph*. This made perfect sense in a great many ways; he already had this material written and they were the kind of pieces he wanted to publish. He could see how they sat in print to allay his anxieties about the 'Isis' passage in *Endless Road*. He could further test the waters.

In *The Telegraph* issue number 14 of November 1983 he published an extract on 'Tangled Up in Blue'. In the footnotes to the article he wrote 'these ideas are explained and explored at length elsewhere in my book *The Chameleon Poet*'. What is of interest now is that he calls it 'my book'. He must have felt that whatever he had written several years before was more than worthwhile and had stood the test of time to make it worth publishing in *The Telegraph*.

In 'Tonal Breath Control', *The Telegraph* issue number 19, spring 1985, he makes another reference to the book. Writing about 'I'm Not There' on the second page of the article he asks himself – tongue in cheek – 'I suddenly wondered if I'd said anything at all in *The Chameleon Poet* about "I'm Not There". Long-time readers of *The Telegraph* and *Endless Road* will know well enough that *The Chameleon Poet* is my own heftily unpublishable critical book about Bob Dylan.' He looks for *The Chameleon Poet* on his book shelf and sure enough in Chapter Ten he finds a paragraph about the song and quotes from it. The last extract to appear, 'Tarantula', was in Issue number 41, winter 1991. This was a revised extract from Chapter Five.

The Chameleon Poet: Bob Dylan's Search For Self, to give it its full title, is like an American quilt. Popular in the nineteenth century, American quilts were assembled in blocks, often fifty or more, in vibrant colours, each telling a tale that, when put together, formed a vast and rich story, often of family history or particular achievements. The tales are cross-referenced and a motif in one block could well allude to motifs in another. The main quilter would be responsible for ensuring that the quilt hung together well and the vision of more than just one individual tale was achieved.

John approaches Dylan's work chronologically, dealing with each album as it appears, each collection of songs or groups of songs. To expand the metaphor, each block on the quilt represents an individual album which John has laid out and stitched together to make up something that had never been done before up to that point: a synthesis of Dylan's work into one canon to ensure, like a faithful Boswell to his own Johnson, that Dylan is given his rightful worth in the literary world.

As the book moves through each of Dylan's albums, from the beginning there is a sense of what has often been called the long march of everyman. John leads us on this journey and shows how each stage of Dylan's own development is revealed in his lyrics. This long march also reveals how the lyrics themselves grow in richness and maturity in both style and content. This is often done by not just considering individual songs but also writing about groups of songs that deal with a similar theme.

I am not going to offer a running commentary on the text of *The Chameleon Poet*, but will try to indicate some broad brush sweeps. The book was a child of its time and we are reading it now, on its first full publication, some forty years after it was written. There is naturally some residual juvenilia, though it doesn't detract from the insight, power and quality of the text. John was thirty and still very much in the process of understanding, and coming to terms with his own self. He found a clear path through Dylan's work, finding interrelating themes, by drawing on his own experience. But the book isn't limited to his own experiences; the scholarship that he brings to his text is remarkable. Dylan's work is cross-referenced with major literary figures such as Shakespeare, Eliot, Blake, Keats and Hesse, with prima facie psychologists such as Jung and Joseph Campbell. It goes without saying that the Bible is a major influence, but also Gnostic gospels, Greek legends, alchemy and the Egyptian *Book of the Dead*. And he does it all succinctly. The gypsy girl in 'Spanish Harlem Incident' is suddenly Cleopatra at Cydnus. The pretty dancing girl in 'Went to See the Gypsy' could well be Hermine in Hesse's *Steppenwolf*.

John considers Dylan's prose work as an integral part of his oeuvre. Up to the point that he wrote *The Chameleon Poet* no one else had done this. He writes at length about *Tarantula* and Dylan's sleeve notes and other writing, highlighting the fact that not only do these texts offer insight to songs from that period, Dylan's prose often gives a greater idea of what is going on than the songs themselves. Characters from this writing are, sometimes, much larger than the characters in the songs. He also writes about Dylan's adventures in film, demonstrating that *Renaldo and Clara* is not a tributary of Dylan's work but mainstream and reflects his artistic vision just as much as the songs and prose.

The 'camelion poet' is a phrase associated with Keats, even though he only used it once in a letter written to Richard Woodhouse in 1818. The chameleon is used to illustrate the notion of 'self' endowed with the ability to change. Academics have suggested that by exploring ideas about transformation and disguise, sympathetic responsiveness, hypocrisy and the stability of 'selfhood', Keats's works reveal him engaging in a self-reflective manner with implications directly relevant to a chameleon-like model of poetic self. With this concept in mind, John uses his analysis of songs, prose and film to argue that, from the very beginning, Dylan's work demonstrates an exploration of his own ever changing 'self'. Everything in the book is about this search. You'll emerge from it knowing each piece better than before and return to the work more informed and more excited by its breadth and depth than before you went in.

As a baby boomer, John grew up with so many others listening to Dylan's music as it was happening. His book documents that development – both Dylan's and his own. However, *The Chameleon Poet* is far more than just a testament of baby boomers who were blowing in the wind or changing with the times, shouting 'Judas' or retiring to Woodstock et al. For baby boomers, this is a documentation of something contemporaneous with their own lives. But, as a major writer, Dylan's work is timeless, and younger generations have come to it by virtue of its continuing relevance. For them, reading John's book could be compared to reading James Joyce's *A Portrait of the Artist as a Young Man* or listening to *The Young Person's Guide to the Orchestra*. As John said at the conference in 1980, 'This is what art is about: an invitation to deduce something from it for yourself. What you find in it is up to you. Dylan puts it in the song for you to find.'

What you have in your hand is John Bauldie's *The Chameleon Poet: Bob Dylan's Search For Self*, finally published in full for the first time forty years after it was written. In the sleeve notes to *John Wesley Harding* Frank asks:

> 'And just how far would you like to go in?'
> 'Not too far but just far enough so's we can say that we've
> been there.'

Bauldie takes us in, just far enough, leaving the rest to us. Enjoy the ride.

The Chameleon Poet

Bob Dylan's Search For Self

1. *Stranded*

Well, now time passed and now it seems
Everybody's having them dreams
Everybody sees themselves
Walkin' around with no one else.

— 'Talkin' World War III Blues'

Like all of Bob Dylan's talking blues songs, 'Talkin' World War III Blues' is anything but a joke. Even though it's sung and played for a lot of laughs, it contains subtle and grimly ironic glimpses of the dilemma of the individual and some of the problems inherent in their relationship to the world in which they find themselves. The speaker in the song discovers, on an otherwise 'normal day', that he is one of the apparently few survivors of a fifteen-minute-long world war. He has been preserved, it would seem, by being 'down in the sewer' at the time of the big bang. His emergence into the now 'lonesome town' is expressed in terms of a metaphorical birth, from darkness, warmth and security into glaring light. He immediately has to face up to problems. There is an initial bewilderment, expressed in terms of aimlessness: 'I stood a-wondering which way to go'.

Having chosen a direction, he makes various attempts to communicate with other survivors he encounters, but each attempt meets with its own kind of failure. The narrator briefly occupies his time by fulfilling an ambition of driving a stolen Cadillac. Though this provides a temporary purpose, it has its own dissatisfactions – the radio doesn't work so well and the record player offers only 'Rock-a-day Johnny' and his formulaic pop lyrics. Eventually, the speaker is driven to near despair:

I was feelin' kinda lonesome and blue
I needed somebody to talk to

49

So I called up the operator of time
Just to hear a voice of some kind.

The true indication of the speaker's feelings is not that he has to resort to this pathetic phone call, nor is the point in the irony that the recording is jammed at the time of the explosion and the 'operator of time' repeats infinitely 'when you hear the beep it will be three o'clock'. It rests in the fact that the speaker actually *listens* to the recording for 'over an hour' before finally hanging up – such is the extent of his need to communicate.[1]

The point is made by a doctor's interruption to speak of his own dream about his own post-nuclear isolation, and the last stanza's observation that 'everybody sees themselves walking around with no one else' – the experience of such loneliness, isolation, purposelessness, non-communication and ultimately spiritual despair, is not that of one man but of everyman. What Bob Dylan is writing about here is the twentieth-century human condition. It may be his own experience of – and response to – the world in which he exists, but as he recounts his feelings to others, he finds that these feelings are not, or would seem not to be, his alone.

A long list of such feelings is offered in the somewhat immature poem 'Last Thoughts On Woody Guthrie', which is directly addressed to the universal 'you', who are offered various aspects of their own intimations of isolation, helplessness and of the apparent purposelessness of their existence:

And to yourself you sometimes say
'I never knew it was gonna be this way
Why didn't they tell me the day I was born'.

The poem is relentless in its crescendo. Lines are piled upon lines, most beginning with an almost inevitable 'And' as Dylan points out to his reader (or more properly to his audience, for the poem was spoken at a 1963 concert) just the kind of desperate feelings and thoughts to which he himself is subject and which he knows are shared to some degree by each of his hearers:

[1] It could be argued that the true 'operator of time' with whom the speaker attempts to communicate here is, in fact, God, who fails to respond to the speaker's call.

And you say to yourself just what am I doin'...
Am I mixed up too much...
Why am I walking, where am I running
What am I saying, what am I knowing.

Having listed many aspects of modern man's world in which solutions or satisfactions will not be found, Dylan asserts that the only two places to look for 'this hope that you know is there, and out there somewhere' are in the 'church of your choice' or in the 'Brooklyn State Hospital' with the dying Woody Guthrie.

The poem is verbose and sentimental, often weakly constructed or expressed. Dylan is much more terse and direct in expressing this kind of dilemma in such a song as 'Talkin' World War III Blues' or as in 'Mixed Up Confusion', a clipped and pared down statement of a state of mind:

I got a mixed-up confusion
Man it's a-killin me...
My head's full of questions
My temp'rature's risin' fast
Well, I'm lookin' for some answers
But I don't know who to ask.

The song ends without a realisation of any solution, simply an exasperation of ultimate desperation: 'Seein' my reflection, I'm hung over, hung down, hung up!' The 'reflection' which Dylan is to encounter many times in later songs ('Tomorrow Is a Long Time' or 'I Shall Be Released' are notable examples) may be his own real image, or very likely that image of himself which he sees reflected in other people whose heads are similarly 'mixed up'.

Without wishing to labour the point, I would offer just a couple more of Dylan's expressions of his own and of modern man's feelings of ignorance, helplessness, aimlessness or despair, and his own relation to the world in which he finds himself sometimes pointlessly existing. The *11 Outlined Epitaphs*, printed as sleeve notes on Dylan's 1964 album *The Times They Are A-Changin'*, are among the most overtly personal and truthful of Dylan's early writings. The first begins with a cameo of his own situation:

I end up then
in the early evenin
blindly punchin at the blind
breathin heavy
stutterin
an blowin up
where t go?
what is it that's exactly wrong?

It's very much Dylan's own version of T. S. Eliot's 'Preludes', but with significant allusion not simply to style but more importantly to content – the expression of urban disillusion and personal frustration. In the sleeve notes to his 1965 album *Bringing It All Back Home*, Dylan announces to the prospective listener:

I am about t sketch You a picture of what goes around here sometimes. tho I don't understand too well myself what's really happening.

Some of Dylan's most fully realised lyrics on that album present a picture of 1960s America in songs such as 'Maggie's Farm', 'Gates of Eden' and 'It's Alright, Ma (I'm Only Bleeding)'. But it's his subsequent album *Highway 61 Revisited* which really hits home the hardest. 'Like A Rolling Stone' may on one level be a vicious personal attack, but its chorus addresses a question to everyone:

How does it feel
To be on your own
With no direction home
Like a complete unknown
Like a rolling stone?

Although Mr Jones in 'Ballad of a Thin Man' has been identified as an uniformed reporter or any unhip person who does not acknowledge what is currently happening, Michael Gray quite rightly pointed out: 'The song implicates its narrator quite consciously and so makes clear that we are each of us the Mr Jones whose confusion we witness.'[2]

[2] Michael Gray, *Song & Dance Man, The Art of Bob Dylan*, Hart-Davis, MacGibbon, 1972.

You raise up your head
And you ask, 'Is this where it is?'
And somebody points to you and says
'It's his'
And you say 'What's mine?'
And somebody else says 'Where what is?'
And you say 'Oh my God
Am I here all alone?'

So each of us is Mr Jones, an occupant of Desolation Row, 'lost in the rain in Juarez' or ends up with 'the Tombstone Blues' – the 'tombstone' at the end of each stanza never allowing us to forget our own mortality, to forget that we're bound to end up on 'Rue Morgue Avenue' eventually. In the meantime, the truth is: 'We sit here stranded though we're all doing our best to deny it'.

In many of his songs and poems from the early 1960s right through until perhaps 1967, Dylan confronts the problem of the lack of meaning and significance of life for modern man.

> The story of Dylan's art and poetry ... is the story of a
> personal quest ... a search for personal identity carried out
> as an ever-expanding dialogue between the many facets
> of his own personality.[3]

The Swiss psychologist Carl Jung propounded the idea that modern man found life to lack meaning and significance because he had become alienated from a part of his being. That part of modern man which Jung suggested was lacking was a substratum of existence which was common to all men and which was the source of mythological, cosmogonic notions. Jung conceived that this mythological material had a positive function in giving meaning and significance to man's existence, perhaps as compensation for his actual insignificance.

This myth-creating level of mind was, Jung argued, common to people of different times and different cultures. He named it the 'collective unconscious' – collective as opposed to personal, for this level of mind was in no way dependent upon any direct influence

---

[3] Gregg Campbell in *Bob Dylan And The Pastoral Apocalypse*, Journal Of Popular Culture, Spring 1975.

of experience, either in maturity or in forgotten childhood. Jung regarded creative people as being in touch with this collective unconscious to such a degree that they were granted superior or new insights. Furthermore, artists acknowledged that their creations are shaped by, and take origin from, a source beyond conscious control.[4]

As it is only through the mythic level of existence that man can overcome the sense of his own futility, the individual needs to journey towards this centre within his psyche. This journey is termed the process of individuation and the ultimate goal is for man to relinquish the power of his ego and acknowledge its dependence upon that part of the mind greater than itself. This consciousness would be 'detached from the world' and was named by Jung as the 'self'. This concept of self is, I believe, what Bob Dylan as artist concerns himself with, and it is possible to trace a cohesive, coherent movement – which might be termed the process of individuation – in Dylan's work.

Any art which impresses, also intrigues. And though we may be superficially satisfied by the art itself, the temptation to know more than meets the eye, to understand the art more fully, often drives us to look beyond the art to its creator. An understanding or a knowledge of the artist is often believed to enhance the truth of the art and to make it more accessible and rewarding.

But does knowledge of an artist really help us understand their work? The problem is that it's too easy to confuse someone's life with their work. The resolution may depend upon how the writer presents themself. Some writers may be primarily concerned with using their work to make their personal experiences accessible to their readers, but because these aims are clearly autobiographical, it is quite easy to recognise them in their work. Still, we are inclined to forget that what we are reading is not literal autobiography but a reflection, and thus a transformation of it. If art is produced by a person, it presents not the person, but a persona – a reflection seen through the artist's eye – not themself but another, perceived, self.

Both artist and persona have consciousness, but they do not

[4] *Collected Works of C. G. Jung Vol. 13.*

always operate on the same level. Arthur Rimbaud's observation 'Je est un autre' ['I is someone else'] is clearly relevant here. In the 'Lettres du voyant' to Georges Izambard, Rimbaud wrote:

> One has to be born a poet, and I know I am a poet. This is not at all my fault. It is wrong to say; I think. One ought to say people think me... I is someone else. It is too bad for the wood which finds itself a violin and a scorn for the heedless who argue over what they are totally ignorant of!

'Je est un autre' expresses the idea that in the poet there are two selves: the deeply hidden, mysterious self who, in his creation of poetry, destroys the 'familiar self of the controlled and predictable responses'.[5]

In relation to Bob Dylan, the problem is compounded. We do not simply have two selves to consider – that is 'Bob Dylan the man' and 'Bob Dylan the artist' – because there is also a third, that of 'Bob Dylan the performer'. Because Dylan's art is expressed in a new medium – a synthesis of not merely articulate, but artistically conceived and organised lyrics, the musical setting and the vocal delivery of lyrics that were primarily meant to be heard rather than read – our response is to the art and to the performer simultaneously, while our intrigue is directed towards the 'self' beneath both artist and performer. But while this self is one and the same, the *selves* of artist and performer are not so.

Furthermore, because Dylan's medium of expression is within an aspect of popular culture, which for the sake of simplicity I'll call *rock music*, Bob Dylan the performer inevitably becomes subject to the pressures of that culture. Although it could be argued that initially at least Bob Dylan the artist and Bob Dylan the performer are one and the same self, even if Bob Dylan the man – Robert Zimmerman – was separated when he became Bob Dylan, gradually these two selves are divorced, and Bob Dylan the performer begins to move beyond the control of either the artist or the man, as his identity is imposed and defined from without – by the public – rather than from within. The

---

[5] Wallace Fowlie, *Rimbaud; A Critical Study*, University of Chicago, 1965.

more success Bob Dylan the performer achieves – success which is reflected upon Bob Dylan the artist, and which provokes persistent and curious attempts to probe beneath the mask in the hope of bringing to light Bob Dylan the man (or Bob Dylan the artist!) – the more the performing self becomes autonomous. Indeed, the performing self is subject to such development that it can be argued to be, in fact, not one self at all, but a multiplicity of selves. Thus Bob Dylan the performer of 1962, for example, is a different self from Bob Dylan the performer of 1966 or 1969 and so on. This public self is a masked man – a fictive persona created by Robert Zimmerman, a sensitive Jewish kid with an artist's soul who found his imagination suffocated in the petite bourgeoisie milieu of his home town. Bob Dylan was a figure who could conceal and perhaps protect what was most essential in Zimmerman's artistic soul, from the stares, threats and scorn of an uncomprehending, unsympathetic and even hostile society as Gregg Campbell considered in *Bob Dylan and the Pastoral Apocalypse*:

> More than a mask, Bob Dylan was an extension of Robert Allen Zimmerman – a fantasy, a mythic persona that could be altered, expanded upon and perhaps abandoned as his vision of himself grew richer, fuller and more complete.

The artist in Bob Dylan, meanwhile, attempts to direct his art towards the realisation of the self lying at the centre of his psyche, as Campbell suggests:

> Dylan took the road in the early sixties seeking to resolve the riddle of his own identity and to affirm his destiny.

I'm going to begin to trace the process of this search in Bob Dylan's work by looking at some of his early songs and simultaneously offer observations on the affinity of the processes presented in other literary works, particularly within Shakespeare's *King Lear*, which has many significant parallels to Dylan's work and search for self-realisation. In subsequent chapters, I will regularly return to this play, hoping that by presenting Dylan's artistic progress and Shakespeare's archetypal hero's dramatic progress in parallel, the significance of the stages of Dylan's artistic development may be illuminated.

2. In Another Lifetime

Cornwall: Whither is he going?
Gloucester: He calls to horse; but will I know not whither.
Cornwall: 'Tis best to give him way; he leads himself.

— *King Lear* 2.4

One of the greatest difficulties posed by Shakespeare's *King Lear* is that of the appropriateness of the reader's or audience's response to the experience of tragedy. We witness, or endure, the spectacle of an old man who was and is a mighty king – an archetype of human potential in a society which depends upon an ordered structure for its unity and strength – deliberately and foolishly removing that strength of society by his abdication. The folly is compounded by his senile belief in the flattery which has inflated his ego and by his willful pride in his casting off of his true, loving daughter, Cordelia, and his most faithful retainer, Kent. Consequently, having destroyed his own locus, he is himself to suffer the consequences of folly by being cast out of the society in which there is no longer a place for him, and by being exposed to the elemental forces of nature.

Through suffering comes remorse and progress. Self-centredness becomes self-awareness; there is a reduction of egocentricity and a growth of altruism. More properly, there is a development of the awareness of the power of love and a recognition of common humanity – in Bob Dylan's words, 'the oneness of us all'.[6] Lear realises he is a part of a universe which contains both good and evil, but which exercises its forces impersonally. He wakes up after a storm in the arms of his loving Cordelia, who in her very being 'redeems nature'. She is a symbol of goodness, of heavenly grace, of natural rebirth. She is daughter and mother, an aspect

[6] Bob Dylan, *Writings & Drawings*, Alfred A. Knopf, New York, 1973.

of the archetypal Eternal Feminine who succours and supports, nourishes and nurtures.

In a twist in the final act, Shakespeare has Cordelia – temporarily forgotten by those who love her – hung by men who behave as beasts. Lear carries his dear daughter in his arms and dies, apparently broken hearted, experiencing a superfluidity of grief, knowing her to be 'dead as earth', and of joy, believing distractedly that she lives. One of his final questions is:

> Why should a dog, a horse, a rat have life
> And thou no breath at all?

A possible answer to this question is a simple one – Cordelia dies because the universe is an imbecile. Some critics have tried to draw sense and order, comfort and consolation, faith and hope from the play's conclusion. But Cordelia dies, and the play seems to me unavoidably pessimistic. This is not to say that Shakespeare always looked at life so gloomily. There is tremendous assertion of faith, strength, belief and hope in later plays, and of course such feelings are not totally absent from *King Lear*, even though many of Edgar's and Albany's hopeful assertions are immediately contradicted and repudiated by events.

King Lear may be read as a statement of art which is the product of the artist's experience at the time of its composition. The function of this art is to mirror life. It is the obligation of the artist to embody for mankind the mystery of his existence in order to bring meaning to the world. Yet it is the experience of being that the artist must undergo before transmuting that base matter into the precious metal of his art. He must know and accept himself totally to attain his true self. Thus Lear's journey is like that of the artist. Bob Dylan is no different: he experiences his humanity, transforms it into poetry and song, and undergoes the same journey towards self-attainment as King Lear.

Shakespeare's journey towards that realisation involved attaining an understanding of himself by being both man and artist, human and magician, Hamlet and Prospero, joker and thief, fool and king – by accepting both the Caliban and the Ariel in his soul. It requires patience to see trial after trial become error after error. Every old man may be a King Lear, every intellectual a Hamlet, every middle-aged lover a Mark Antony, every businessman a Macbeth – so each character may be read as an exploration of the artist's own nature and thus a step towards the realisation of his ultimate self.

Bob Dylan grew up in the 1940s and 1950s, and emerged as an artist in the 1960s. He was born into a world of wars, with confrontations in Europe, Korea, Cuba and Vietnam. In his earliest songs he portrayed a world seeking its own destruction; later writings – notably the novel *Tarantula* – depict somewhat more objectively the chaos which he would come to accept. Edwin Casebeer describes the America of Dylan's formative years as:

> A society dominated by pessimism and hyperrationalism: the universe was absurd, man and society were fragmented, institutions were empty of relevant content. The only demonstrable facts were that each of us is isolated from the other and that all of us are subject to death, facts that rendered meaningless all that we did, individually or collectively. Although the resultant responses to these 'facts' ranged widely from suicidal nihilism to heroic efforts to erect foundations in the quicksand, few disagreed with the basic pessimistic propositions. Thus, by its elders, was the problem defined for the silent generation.[7]

Bob Dylan's early stance, present in many songs from 1960 to 1963, is undoubtedly one of the 'heroic efforts to erect foundations in the quicksand' of contemporary society. Dylan saw all around him an absurd and violent world and he pointed his accusing finger. He hit out wildly and bravely at playboys and playgirls, fall-out shelter sellers, politicians, fountain-pen bandits, get-rich-quick organisations and boxing promoters, John Birchers, Ku Klux Klanners and masters of war. The latter were there but unnamed in 'Let Me Die in My Footsteps'. They weren't accused, Dylan simply asserted 'the meaning of life has been lost

[7] Edwin Casebeer, *Hermann Hesse*, Warner, 1972.

in the wind' and that people were 'learnin' to die' instead of to live. But, like John Wesley Harding, he took a stand, appealing to the heavens for aid or approval: 'Lawd God let my poor voice be heard'. The naivety is unconscious:

> If I had rubies and riches and crowns
> I'd buy the whole world and change things around.

Other hits at warmongers can be heard in 'Cuban Missile Crisis' and 'Long Ago, Far Away', but war was just one aspect of an unjust society full of hate and fear, violence and terror; a society portrayed in the image of an 'iron train a-travellin'' down the line to destruction 'with a firebox of hatred and a furnace full of fears' and carrying 'crazy mixed-up souls' in a 'murder-minded world' of 'kill-crazy bandits and haters'.[8]

'Masters of War' was, in Dylan's own words, 'a sort of striking out, a reaction of the last straw, a feeling of what *can* you do?'[9] All Dylan could do in late 1962 was to 'hope' that such people would die, without any conviction that there was a universal provenance on hand to ensure that such an undoubtedly deserved end could be depended on. The feeling of futility was already there – 'what can you do?' – and 'Blowin' in the Wind' is a song which reflects exactly that exasperation:

> How many times must the cannonballs fly
> Before they're forever banned?

Dylan's hope that the perpetrators of the world's evils would either be struck down or pay a price worse than death – eternal damnation – is expressed over and over in his songs of desperate and frustrated youth. The threats are heard in 'Masters of War':

> Even Jesus would never
> Forgive what you do.

---

[8] From 'Train A-Travelin''.
[9] From sleeve notes to *The Freewheelin' Bob Dylan*, 1963.

And later:

> All the money you made
> Will never buy back your soul.

The whole of 'I'd Hate To Be You On That Dreadful Day' is centred upon the threat of ultimate retribution:

> Well, your clock is gonna stop
> At Saint Peter's gate
> Ya gonna ask him what time it is
> He's gonna say, 'It's too late.'

As is 'Whatcha Gonna Do?'

> Tell me what you're gonna do
> When the devil calls your cards.

In these songs, a self-righteous narrator is confidently assured that his own values are beyond reproach and that his purpose in life is to point the finger and put things right with a strum of his guitar strings:

> If I can't help somebody
> With a word or song
> If I can't show somebody
> They are travelin' wrong.[10]

Such words betray a writer trapped by his ego:

> Ain't there no one here that knows how I feel
> Good God Almighty.[11]

But the most important song of this early period sees Dylan begin to transcend himself a little. The need to point the accusing finger and the self-righteousness are markedly absent from 'A Hard Rain's A-Gonna Fall'; for the first time Dylan becomes artistically

---

[10] 'Long Time Gone'.
[11] 'Last Thoughts On Woody Guthrie'.

objective in his depiction of a chaotic negative world, an absurd world, an imbecilic world of no contact and no compassion, of little light and less love.

The narrator is a child, a 'blue-eyed son' who, let loose in the world he is to inherit, finds himself stumbling and crawling over a landscape of death, facing 'a dozen dead oceans', struggling through ten thousand miles to find only the gaping jaws of a graveyard. All around is the fear and threat of death and destruction. A newborn baby is surrounded by 'wild wolves', young children have 'guns and sharp swords' in their hands, presumably in an effort to ensure their own survival in a world where, if you want to survive, you have to 'cut somethin''.[12] Chains of further flashing images present a 'young child beside a dead pony', the more immediate horror of 'a young woman whose body was burning' – piled up images of youth facing or experiencing premature destruction. There are two wounded men, one in love, the other with hatred. Most inhabitants of this world are isolated – a man walking a dog, others pounding their drums frenetically, trying to make themselves heard, others whispering but not listening, not heeding the starving, the wretched, disregarding the dying poet in the gutter.[13] Save for the outcasts, the only two figures that emerge from this worldview with credit are 'a young girl, she gave me a rainbow' – at least one gesture of charity in the face of catastrophe – and, removed from the earliest versions of the song, 'one man who cried he was human'. Such an attempt to assert basic humanity and have it recognised by others is doomed to go unheard, and Dylan disposed of his presence shortly after the song's composition.

What the narrator can't do in such a world is vainly try to put it to rights – such a hope is pointless in a world 'where souls are forgotten' and poets die in gutters. But he can 'reflect it from the mountain so all souls can see it'. Thus, by the end of 1962, Dylan comes to a realisation of new responsibilities. He is no longer setting himself up as a social reformer, or at least not primarily

---

[12] From 'Talkin' New York'.

[13] cf. Baudelaire's 'Spleen': 'l'âme d'un vieux poète erre dans la gouttière' ['the soul of an old poet wanders in the gutter'] with Dylan's: 'heard the song of a poet who died in the gutter'.

so. He does not have a 'duty to remake the world at large'[14] or to 'make this great land of ours a greater place to live'.[15] He is an artist; he lives on the edge of society, in it, yet not of it. It is his responsibility to create art from chaos by reflecting that chaos – by being a mirror. Dylan defined art as 'the perpetual motion of illusion'.[16] Through Hamlet, Shakespeare defined the purpose of his own art as 'to hold as 'twere, the mirror up to nature'.[17] Yet to be a 'mirror' the artist must experience what it is he is to reflect. Thus the blue-eyed boy must go back out into the world which is devoid of all values, where 'none is the number', and explore it to its very depths before he can reflect it or 'tell it and think it and speak it and breathe it'. The artistic act sustains the artist's life only as long as he creates. When it is done, he is totally emptied of experience. He must either gain more or die – both as man and artist, he must restore himself with experience:

> I'm a-goin' back out 'fore the rain starts a-fallin'
> I'll walk to the depths of the darkest black forest.

The experience of going back out into such a world, however, has its potential discomforts and extreme dangers. There are 'pellets of poison', a 'damp dirty prison', and an executioner waiting with a face 'well hidden', 'ugly' hunger, a swallowing ocean. Yet the artist has a responsibility to know what he's singing about before he starts singing at all. He is about to be flayed alive. Like Lear he must 'feel what wretches feel'. In *King Lear*, Edgar is forced to become Poor Tom, to:

> Take the basest and most poorest shape
> That ever penury in contempt of man
> Brought near to beast. My face I'll grime with filth.
> Blanket my loins, elf all my hairs in knots,
> And with presented nakedness outface
> The winds and persecutions of the sky.[18]

---

[14] From 'Wedding Song'.
[15] From 'The Death of Emmett Till'.
[16] In *Rolling Stone*, 26th January 1978.
[17] *Hamlet* 3.2.
[18] *King Lear*, 2.3.

Bob Dylan becomes the joker, the thief, the ragged clown. He leaves behind him the ego – the 'I' which Rimbaud divorced from the concept of self – and becomes 'the other', the outlaw on the edge of the chaos which he needs to experience before he can transmute it into his art.

3. To Live Outside the Law You Must Be Honest

> Poor naked wretches, wheresoe'er you are
> That bide the pelting of this pitiless storm
> How shall your houseless heads and unfed sides,
> Your looped and widowed raggedness, defend you
> From seasons such as these?
>
> — *King Lear* 3.4

In 1962, Bob Dylan walked out into the threatening storm just as King Lear had done before him. Lear, seeing and experiencing (and unconsciously perpetrating) injustice, violence, hatred and fear around him, becomes himself the victim of it – abused as he is by his cruelly self-centred daughters, Goneril and Regan. Just as Dylan 'saw through' the masters of war, Lear soon recognises who needs to be blamed – he points his accusing finger, threatening vengeance both in the world and beyond it. He invokes curses upon the wrongdoers, invokes the wrath of the gods, and takes up the stance of a god himself – only to have to face up to a frustrating impotence to change the horrors of reality. He is the victim of the ego which brought him to the edge of society and out on to the wind-blasted heath.

He rants and raves, crying out to the great gods for the bloody hand of justice to strike. It does not. Lear, like the other outcasts, feels wet and cold. The true innocents of society are cast adrift with him – Edgar, the Fool, Kent, Gloucester – the guilty are warm and safe in their castles. But of course the outcasts themselves form the nucleus of an alternative society, a society in which the individual members have nothing, not even ego. And it is in this society – the world of Poor Tom – that Lear comes to feel for others, and thus puts aside his own ego. No longer a king who can kill with a wave of his hand, he comes to recognise many truths. One is that of his oneness with all the other outcasts and victims of the storm. It is a sense of common identity, an intimation of the concept of universal self which lies beyond the ego:

> The Self is an ideal centre, equidistant between the Ego and the Unconscious, and it is probably equivalent to the maximum natural expression of individuality, in a state of fulfilment or totality. As Nature aspires to express itself, so does man, and the Self is that dream of totality.[19]

Another insight gained is that nature is impersonal. The thunder cracks and the lightning flashes, not symbolically as manifestation of Divine wrath at human vice, folly or injustice, but as forces which exist beyond the concepts of good and evil — concepts not of nature, but of man.

Bob Dylan's journey towards self took a major step forward with 'A Hard Rain's A-Gonna Fall'. In the years 1962, 1963 and 1964 he produced many songs in which having 'gone back out' into the storm, he began to identify with the outcasts and the victims of the world, the chaos of which he will gradually come to accept. Paul Simon cryptically portrayed the young Dylan in 'The Boxer':

> Layin' low, seeking out the poorer quarters
> Where the ragged people go
> Looking for the places only they would know.

Bob Dylan, of course, needed to look for such places because as the son of a moderately well off 'home and family', he would have a carefully defined social context — a locus which he abandoned fairly competently, shrouding his past in stories of travelling fairgrounds, pretending to be the new 'poor boy' whose true 'story is seldom told' and whose fake biography, which recurs in interviews and on record sleeves from 1960 onwards, is summarily dismissed in 'The Boxer's chorus — 'Lie-la-lie'.

This false biography is preserved in the songs too. Dylan's

---

[19] C.G. Jung quoted in *A Record Of Two Friendships*, Miguel Serrano, Routledge & Kegan Paul, 1966.

trip to New York is joyously celebrated in 'Talkin' New York' because he finally has 'hit the road' in his first idol's – Woody Guthrie's – footsteps. 'Poor Boy' Bob Dylan suffers 'Hard Times In New York Town', a city full of people who will 'kick you when you're up and knock you when you're down' and the daily grind is hard enough:

> Up in the mornin' tryin' to find a job of work
> Stand in one place till your feet begin to hurt.

But not *too* hard because this character is simply *playing* at suffering hard times and the lie is reflected in the jauntiness of the song's tune.

So he parodies the stances of the hobo in 'Standing on the Highway':

> Well, I'm standin' on the highway
> Tryin' to bum a ride.

And in 'Poor Boy Blues':

> Hey, stop you ol' train
> Let a poor boy ride
> Cain't ya hear me cryin'?

And in many others – 'Long Time Gone', 'Walkin' Down the Line', 'Down the Highway', 'Farewell' and perhaps most telling of all, the poem 'My Life In A Stolen Moment' – maybe 'stolen' for all the people whose lives the piece really did reflect.

Dylan's search for self progresses when he begins to identify with some of the:

> Rough riders, ghost poets
> low-down rounders, sweet lovers
> desperate characters
> sad-eyed drifters and rainbow angels.[20]

---

[20] In *Writings & Drawings*.

Sometimes they're anonymous – like the 'friend' in 'Ballad for a Friend', the 'Man on the Street',[21] or the hobo in 'Only a Hobo' – more often they're named. There are the drifters like 'Rambling, Gambling Willie' and 'Gypsy Lou', and the victims of society's perils and injustices: John Brown is the victim of war, Hollis Brown of poverty, Davey Moore of boxing superficially but basically of a mercenary and aggressive society. Emmett Till, we know from the lyrics, is black and Hattie Carroll may well be too but, as Christopher Ricks pointed out,[22] circumstantially so, and 'poor' anyway, like Hollis Brown whose very name may or may not be indicative of racial identity. They are victims because they are poor and black in a society in which to be either is unacceptable.

Emmett Till is brutally and pointlessly murdered by the 'race-haters' Dylan hit out at in the accusative songs. They are typical of those who go 'ghost-robed' in the Ku Klux Klan, and the murder is both violent and a 'dreadful tragedy', being committed 'just for fun'. Hattie Carroll is 'slain by a cane', wielded by a young wealthy white man 'who just happened to be feeling that way without warning' and of course the Klan and William Zanzinger deserve our condemnation and contempt.

But the finger of blame is not pointing specifically at the murderers in these two songs, but at the failure of justice – society's arbiter of right and wrong – to act appropriately. In Emmett Till's case 'this trial was a mockery, but nobody seemed to mind' and the scapegoat brothers, by complicity with the jury, are found innocent, provoking an exasperated outcry in the narrator which is both noble and futile. William Zanzinger doesn't quite get off scot-free, but his six-month sentence from the 'courtroom of honour' is something well worthy of society's tears.[23]

[21] cf. Dylan's lines: 'he jabbed him once with his billy club and the old man then rolled off the curb' with these lines from Bertolt Brecht's 'Litany of Breath': 'He had a rubber club loaded with lead. He smashed in the back of that man's head. And not another word was said.'

[22] In his radio broadcast Bob Dylan and the Language that he Used, BBC Radio 3, 22nd March 1976.

[23] cf. Dylan's chorus lines: 'Take the rag away from your face, now ain't the time for your tears' with Brecht's chorus line in 'Concerning the Infanticide, Marie Farrar': 'But you, I beg you, check your wrath and scorn'.

An evil judge is presented in 'Seven Curses', yet it is not absolute justice which is corrupted here. In terms of the law, Reilly is appropriately hung for his crime of horse-stealing. But the judge abuses his position and privilege by seducing Reilly's daughter, only to break his promise that her virginity should ransom her father's life.

In 'Ballad of Donald White' (again perhaps an indicative name) there is no doubt about Donald's crime. The poor orphan confesses quite freely:

> And so it was on Christmas Eve
> In the year of '59
> It was on that night I killed a man
> I did not try to hide
> The jury found me guilty
> And I won't disagree.

He has no doubt that many members of his audience (he is first person narrator of the song) will 'feel better' when he's hanged. But although justice may be done for murder, Donald White is portrayed, or portrays himself, as victim as much as enemy of society. The law is the means by which society maintains its own structure. Society imposes law upon itself, accepts all law's limitations and restrictions to preserve its own stability. The law is man's practical application of the abstract concept of justice. In Donald White, the young law-breaker is himself the victim of society – a society whose very fabric is woven with injustices: poverty, inequality of status, of opportunity, of education, a misdirected penal system. It is this paradox Dylan is hitting at here: the absurdity that a society riddled with inequality and injustice can presume to elect and maintain its own arbiters of absolute justice, which it cannot even serve upon itself.

It's a point Dylan will return to over and over again – and quite soon in 'It's Alright, Ma (I'm Only Bleeding)', where the 'rules of the road' may be well established but you must still dodge people's games and perhaps all you can do is resign yourself to laughing at justice as it attempts to administer itself:

> Old lady judges watch people in pairs
> Limited in sex, they dare
> To push fake morals, insult and stare
> While money doesn't talk, it swears
> Obscenity, who really cares...

If there is hypocrisy within the law, if morality is thus fake, what respect can it hope for? I think Dylan's exasperated anger has turned to an almost jovial incredulity by the time of this song's composition in 1964. He identifies it as 'a funny song' in 1965 concerts, announcing it on a tour of England in 1965 as 'It's Alright, Ma (I'm Only Bleeding) Ho Ho Ho!' and in this way he comes to an insight also gained by King Lear as a result of his exposure to the cruelty and injustice of his daughter's society from which he has been cast out.

In his madness, Lear comes to see the absurdity of a world in which the 'monsters' such as Goneril and Regan sit securely administering their own form of justice upon Gloucester, whose eyes are plucked out because he's both faithful to his king and 'honest', whilst out in the storm poor wretches have to suffer all the deprivation of society. Poor Tom is abject, a naked Bedlam beggar; Lear strips himself in sympathy. The Fool is bound to tell only the truth; he is whipped for it. Kent is honest, yet for telling his truth to Lear in the first scene, he is condemned to live outside the law.

In his deranged imagination, Lear finds himself 'playing' his former role and comes to see the preposterousness of that kind of social authority. The accused is Gloucester:

> What was thy cause? Adultery?
> Thou shalt not die. Die for adultery? No...
> Let copulation thrive![24]

Compare this with Dylan's, 'Obscenity, who really cares?'

The 'old lady judges' themselves are 'limited in sex' and reflected in Lear's 'rascal Beadle' who suffers sexual surfeits and lusts after the whore he is whipping for *her* lusts:

[24] *King Lear*, 4.6.

71

> The great image of authority
> A dog's obeyed in office...[25]

The inevitable conclusion is summary:

> None does offend, none, I say, none.[26]

So, Donald White the murderer is innocent; so is Reilly the horse-thief, Percy too, sentenced by the law (in 'Percy's Song') to a punitive 99-year sentence for the crime of 'manslaughter in the highest degree' having caused the deaths of four passengers in his (apparently) recklessly driven car's crash. 'Bad news' indeed, yet, sings Dylan:

> He ain't no criminal
> And his crime it is none.

The singer attempts to contribute personal knowledge of Percy as a friend:

> I knew him as good
> As I'm knowin' myself
> And he wouldn't harm a life
> That belongs to someone else.

As an audience, we contribute our own knowledge that 'what happened to him could happen to anyone'. But we must also acknowledge that personal feelings of right and wrong must be removed from absolute justice, which, after all, must concern itself with the facts of the case. As David Downing points out in *Future Rock*, 'The system can only operate in terms of a depersonalised consciousness.'[27]

When the judge feels threatened by the singer's personal pleas, he hardens himself, adopting the pose of the system that maintains him and that he in turn maintains; the judge's 'door', his ambiguous 'office', and the 'courthouse stairs' stand between

---

[25] idem.
[26] idem.
[27] David Downing, *Future Rock*, Panther, 1976.

the singer and total comprehension of what has just happened. The law remains immovable, the sentence 'cannot be repealed', the judge's face symbolically freezes hard as ice; the bewildered guitar-player, having confronted justice face to face has 'no other choice except for to go'.

Yet, in Dylan's terms, Percy will always remain innocent. 'He ain't no criminal' sings Dylan, 'None does offend' says Lear, and while both characters were once infuriated, exasperated, bewildered, they both journey to the point where they are able to see beyond the injustice to the absurdity. Such insights are hard won – the journey through the storm is a difficult one which has inevitable suffering. The young singer of 'Percy's Song' has to turn back towards the wind and the rain, though, before he can realise that 'it's life and life only'. Lear has to be wet and cold before he can see the joke and learn to laugh. Before either can reach shelter from the storm, each has to be 'burned out from exhaustion'.

4. Gazing in the River's Mirror

In times behind, I too
wished I'd lived
in the hungry thirties
an blew in like Woody
t New York City
an sang for dimes...
ah where are those forces of yesteryear?
why didn't they meet me here
an greet me here?

— Third *Outlined Epitaph*

Bob Dylan, of course, didn't live in the hungry thirties, but in the bewildered and bewildering sixties. If his initial attempts to define his own destiny began with his following in – or pretending to follow in – Woody Guthrie's footsteps, seeking out injustice with an accusative stance and attempting to put right the wrongs of society by exposing them, he soon found he had set himself an impossible task. Indeed, Dylan fell all too easily into the well-established type of the disenchanted adolescent: troubles with antagonistic authority figures, endless conflicts with cruel and impersonal systems – political, educational, legal and social – and vague wanderings into the bewildering realms of eros and sex.

The vestiges of his initial intentions remain in certain songs from 1963 and 1964 – in Dylan's identification with the persona of a juvenile criminal in 'Walls of Red Wing', with the daughter/sister/wife of North Country iron ore miners in 'North Country Blues', and perhaps his last-gasp expression of the belief that the world could be changed in 'When the Ship Comes In'. In this extended metaphor, Dylan sees himself on the bow of the ship of the future as it voyages with its cargo of hope, equality, justice, love, liberty and all those qualities that seemed in short supply in mid-sixties America. For the song's metaphor, Dylan is indebted to Bertolt Brecht. Compare this brief extract from 'Pirate Jenny', a song in *The Threepenny Opera*:

> And a ship with eight sails and
> With fifty great cannon
> Sails into the quay.
>
> When folk ask: now just who has to die?
> You will hear me say at that point: 'All of them!'
> And when their heads fall, I'll say: 'Whoopee!'
>
> And the ship with eight sails and
> With fifty great cannon
> Will sail off with me.

Dylan's ship, unlike Brecht's, brings with it not just destruction for the old bad world but change for the better. Nevertheless, the process of change it depicts is both sudden and violent – a 'hurricane' of pounding winds and sounding tides which will herald a new 'morning' for the world. The 'seas' of humanity will have to take a side; some, like 'the sands on the shoreline' will be 'shaking' in fear and apprehension for their own fate as a result of the new order of things; others will be 'smiling' and will 'laugh' or 'proudly stand' when the time comes, and no amount of the ship's crew who – somewhat like a Marxist revolutionary force – will break 'the chains of the sea'.[28]

The crew sing songs (of course) of coming equality for all, whatever the race, creed or social standing: 'The sun will respect every face on the deck'. The 'ship's wise men' – of whom the singer undoubtedly counts himself one – are the artists, intellectuals, philosophers of the new movement, a movement symbolised in 'The Times They Are A-Changin'' as a mighty flood or a raging battle 'outside', shaking the very fabric and structure of an outmoded,

---

[28] Dylan is alluding here to Marx's 'Workers of the world unite, you have nothing to lose but your chains', but there is a further allusion to Dylan Thomas's 'Fern Hill', the concluding line of which depicts the youthful poet: 'though I sang in my chains like the sea'. It is possible that Dylan has misinterpreted the line, in which 'in my chains' is, as it were, in parentheses.

'rapidly agin' … rapidly fadin'' society.[29] They set themselves against relatively foolish and hopeless foes (who have to 'pinch themselves' to determine even their own consciousness) before sweeping them aside, ironically with no mercy or gesture of conciliation to their abject surrender, drowning them or conquering them as David did Goliath, or as Moses did Pharaoh's tribe.

What Jon Landau names 'Dylan's apocalyptic vision'[30] is prominent on *The Times They Are A-Changin'* album. The prophesied change is righteously presented as being inevitable, unquestionable, inexorable. But with time and experience comes greater awareness and knowledge. The experience of 'Percy's Song' teaches that in reality when David takes on Goliath, the result is no contest. By 1964, Dylan realised that there didn't need to be a contest. Rather than attempt to change, he learned that he would have to accept and reflect. Indeed, if his art was to progress, 'reflection' would now need to become its primary purpose. By holding up his mirror to the society he had so fervently and enthusiastically wished to redirect, Dylan could determine the nature of that society, and define it with far more exactness and insight and thus gain for himself, and convey to his audience, images of truths which approached absolutes much more clearly than did the wishful-thinking dreams of his early twenties.

In 'My Back Pages', Bob Dylan announces the discovery of a new purpose for his art, renouncing stances which he now acknowledges to be either unreal or immature and most importantly, inappropriate to his development as a poet and an attainment of the self which he has yet to recognise within his psyche. When Dylan came to look into his own soul, he found as much conflict in himself as in the outside world, which meant he had no right to accuse and point fingers at the world for he shared a common guilt. Instead, his new attitude was one of acceptance in an effort to understand and learn.

---

[29] In his introduction to Hermann Hesse's *Demian*, Thomas Mann wrote, 'Towards the end of the novel, Demian says to his friend Sinclair "The new is a beginning and for those who cling to the old, the new will be horrible. What will you do?" The right answer would be: "Assist the new without sacrificing the old."' This may be compared to Dylan's 'your old road is rapidly agin', please get out of the new one if you can't lend your hand'.
[30] Jon Landau, 'John Wesley Harding', *Crawdaddy!*, 1968.

Initially, his 'high and mighty' stance had been to 'use' ideas. Dylan grants himself a picture of his own folly – 'proud 'neath heated brow' – a victim of that very sin that caused King Lear to embark on an ego trip to the brink of sanity and beyond. The vision of Dylan as society's emancipator may have been a 'romantic' dream, but he recognises the kind of 'half-wracked prejudice' which the conclusion of 'When the Ship Comes In' betrayed. An even greater insight comes with his acknowledgement that the view of life in terms of good and evil, 'black and white', is fallacious. In Thomas Pynchon's *The Crying of Lot 49*, Fallopian points out that if you think in terms of 'good guys and bad guys, you never get to any of the underlying truth ... Underneath, both are part of the same creeping horror'.

This particular step is one that Lear found difficult to take. If Dylan's 'monsters' of society were the masters of war, corrupt judges, politicians, the racialists and the moralisers, or the writers and critics who could rob or maim with their fountain pens, Lear's monsters were his own progeny – offspring of his own humanity. Lear could not initially acknowledge that Goneril and Regan could be his 'natural' daughters: 'Are you our daughter?' asked of Goneril, becomes 'Degenerate bastard!' a few lines later.[31] But with the experience of the storm, Lear can admit ''twas this flesh begot those pelican daughters'[32] though he still confesses difficulty in acknowledging that such evil could co-exist with good in a 'natural' fashion:

> Let them anatomise Regan: see what breeds about her heart.
> Is there any cause in nature that makes these hard hearts?

That good and evil, right and wrong, are values derived and determined by man's self-ordained morality and not by nature is a hard lesson. Life is not 'black and white'.

In *Some Other Kinds of Songs*, the poems that feature on the sleeve notes to *Another Side of Bob Dylan*, the album on which 'My Back Pages' appears, Dylan declares:

---

[31] *King Lear*, 1.4.
[32] *King Lear*, 3.4.

    nothin seems
    t be straight
    out there

And later:

    good an evil are but words
    invented by those
    that are trapped in scenes

Then:

    I know no answers an no truth
    for absolutely no soul alive
    I will listen t no one
    who tells me morals
    there are no morals

'My Back Pages' contains its own realisation in its own terms. Dylan looks back at himself speaking 'equality ... as if a wedding vow', 'memorising politics', aiming blows at his teachers, contemptuously labelled 'self-ordained' or even 'mongrel dogs', 'thinking I had something to protect'. Dylan said to Nat Hentoff in 1964:

> All I know is that so long as people stay so concerned about protecting their status and protecting what they have, ain't nothing going to be done ... nobody's going to learn anything.[33]

He may once have fooled himself into thinking he could define the terms 'good and bad', but the initial 'quite clear, no doubt' becomes 'somehow' and the terms are seen to be as deceptive as everything else Dylan once fooled himself into believing.

We've reached the point at which Dylan boldly states 'there are no morals' and later in the same set of *Some Other Kinds of Songs* 'I tell you there are no politics' repeated three times. Dylan speaks directly to a former fellow-worker for 'a world of peace'

[33] Quoted in 'The Crakin' Shakin' Breakin' Sounds', *New Yorker*, 24th October 1964.

who continues to offer the perspectives Dylan has transcended, only to have them rejected and denied as 'piles of paper slogans'. The friend is forced finally to tell Dylan how much he (Dylan) has changed. If we've reached this point, clearly there are new values, new insights, and new beliefs.

These same poems conclude with words which may well serve as pointers towards the determination of the content of Dylan's next three albums, and thus his writings from 1964 through to 1966:

> all is lost, Cinderella
> all is lost.

If Dylan has seen beyond good and evil, beyond morality, beyond politics, it is to a vision of chaos, of a world administered by forces of nature which are impersonal. I touched on this point in the last chapter, but I'll take it a little further by reference to two other compositions from this period – 'Chimes of Freedom' and 'Lay Down Your Weary Tune' – and I wish to make further reference to *King Lear*.

Lear's initial response to Goneril and Regan's filial ingratitude is burning anger and, more potently, a disturbance of mind produced by profound sorrow, pain, and grief. He wonders that his heart doesn't burst:

> O sides, you are too tough
> Will you yet hold?[34]

The pain – 'sharper than a serpent's tooth' – at being rejected by a daughter is in fact brought out in the first stanza of a later Dylan song, 'Tears of Rage'. But Lear's tears of rage and grief provoke a state of self-pity at his own misery which is moving for being so unbecoming:

> You see me here, you gods, a poor old man
> As full of grief as age, wretched in both.[35]

---

[34] *King Lear*, 2.4.
[35] Idem.

Later, he addresses the tempestuous heavens:

> Here I stand, your slave,
> a poor, infirm, weak, and despised old man.[36]

But feeling sorry for himself because he is cold and wet, having been cast out of symbolic as well as literal house and home, Lear comes to realise that the heavens are not simply crashing their thunderbolts and deluging their waters over his head alone. Every creature, man and beast, out in such a storm is suffering as he is suffering. He first recognises this in the uncharacteristic whimperings of his Fool, and his 'wits begin to turn':

> Come on, my boy. How dost, my boy? Art cold?
> I am cold myself.[37]

It is then that his sensibilities go beyond his immediate fellows – Kent, the Fool, Gloucester – to all who are, like him, cold and wet on such a night. Lear prays:

> Poor naked wretches, whereso'er you are
> That bide the pelting of this pitiless storm
> How shall your houseless heads and unfed sides
> Your looped and windowed raggedness, defend you
> From seasons such as these?[38]

The main point here is that, although Lear calls the storm 'pitiless' he acknowledges that man may exist *in* the universe, but he is not necessarily *of* it. He is facing up to the truth that, where he once believed in the grand concept of order, he must now come to accept chaos.

It seems to me that 'Chimes of Freedom' comes remarkably close to Lear's prayer, quoted above. The song finds the narrator – Dylan himself undoubtedly, but speaking in a recollected plural – caught in the kind of storm which raged above Lear's head on the heath. Admittedly there is an urban doorway to duck into by

[36] *King Lear*, 3.2.
[37] Idem.
[38] *King Lear*, 3.4.

way of escape, but the experience of the thunderstorm becomes, by observation, mystical.

The crashing thunder peals out like 'majestic bells' that are symbolic of a universal freedom – an escape into nature for those who are exposed to the storm including 'each and every underdog soldier'[39] the 'misdemeanour outlaw' and 'the outcast'. But the bells also toll for a long list of society's unfortunates: 'refugees', 'the luckless, the abandoned and forsaked', 'the deaf an' blind … the mute', 'the searching ones … the aching ones' and finally, 'the countless, confused, accused, misused strung-out ones'.

The experience is a religious one – the imagery conveys this. The chimes are the desolation of 'wedding bells', the hammering of the hail is 'mystic', the bells are 'church bells', there is the 'wild cathedral evening', but the introduction of the concept of the 'whole wide universe' at the song's conclusion is interesting because the chimes of freedom also toll for such diverse characters as 'warriors' – admittedly those rather inclined 'not to fight' – 'soldiers', 'rake' and even 'the guardians and protectors of the mind'. Indeed, perhaps there is only a short step from Dylan saying that the bells are tolling too for those whom he formerly accused as well as championed – certainly the 'guardians and protectors of the mind' sounds a little ominous in that direction. But maybe I'm stretching this a little too far. Suffice to say that the song barely approaches 'protest', save perhaps that the prostitute is 'mistreated … mistitled' or that many gentle souls are 'misplaced inside a jail' and, after all, in the fourth stanza the rain unravels tales for 'the disrobed faceless forms of no position'.

Now these may be the 'poor naked wretches' of Lear's prayer, but 'disrobed' seems to suggest that the characters may well have more than a little in common with 'the guardians and protectors of the mind', even though Dylan denies them the authority

---

[39] It's of interest here to recall Edward Thomas's 'The Owl' – a poem which has obvious affinities both with the storm in *King Lear* and with Dylan's 'Chimes of Freedom'. In 'The Owl', Thomas reflects from the warmth and comfort of his inn upon the night which has been 'quite barred out'. He is reminded of 'what I escaped and others could not' by the 'melancholy cry' of the owl, which he hears 'speaking for all who lay under the stars, soldiers and poor, unable to rejoice'.

to which their robes, when they wear them, entitle them. In a later song, 'Drifter's Escape', the judge, in an apparent fit of compassion, 'cast his robe aside', whereas the guardian of the law in William Zanzinger's trial for Hattie Carroll's murder 'spoke through his cloak', using the robe, which is the symbol of his office and thus the authority he commands, as a barrier from behind which he is capable of committing a travesty of justice without fear of reproach, for the authority which he wields has been invested in him by society, which he serves.

In *King Lear*, clothes and garments are indicative of social position. They are not 'natural' but assumed, and often used to conceal vices which 'tatter'd clothes' all too easily reveal:

> Robes and furred gowns hide all. Plate sin with gold
> And the strong lance of justice hurtles breaks;
> Arm it in rags, a pigmy's straw does pierce it.[40]

But the chimes of freedom are tolling for 'every hung up person in the whole wide universe' including those 'countless confused, accused ... ones' and Dylan had, in the past, done more than his fair share of accusing.

If there is a natural mysticism experienced and recorded in 'Chimes of Freedom', Dylan conveys a development of this kind of awareness in 'Lay Down Your Weary Tune'. Theodore Ziolkowski wrote:

> Many writers of the twentieth century might be called, as Hugo von Hofmansthal styled himself, 'mystics without mysticism' – writers keenly sensitive to the discongruities of life, who longed for a resolution of conflict here on earth and not in a transcendent realm of the future or beyond. They are mystics inasmuch as they wish to pierce through the veil of apparent conflict but without mysticism inasmuch as their resolution is immanent, not transcendent.[41]

---

[40] *King Lear*, 4.6.
[41] From *The Novels of Hermann Hesse*, Theodore Ziolkowski, Princeton University Press, 1967.

Steven Goldberg suggests that 'Lay Down Your Weary Tune' is the moment that Dylan moves 'from politics to mysticism'.[42] The song does mark the development of poetic thought in the way that 'A Hard Rain's A-Gonna Fall' had done before it. The mystical experience which is the song's subject matter grants the artist a pantheistic insight which is to affect, indeed re-direct, his art. The tune that the poet has been singing is seen to be a 'weary' one – in need of being laid to rest. The poet is granted a hearing of a universal music which man, in his inadequacy, is incapable of even approximating – having no 'hope to hum', let alone play or sing along with it. Yet seemingly all creation, save man, contributes to the orchestra which makes the music.

It is interesting to note the recurrence in 'Lay Down Your Weary Tune' of the main chorus rhyme – strum/hum. The chorus begins the song:

> Lay down your weary tune
> Lay down the song you strum
> And rest yourself 'neath the strength of strings
> No voice can hope to hum.

And it is sung after each stanza, except the next to last. In the last stanza, however, the strum/hum rhyme which had absented itself from the song for the first time, occurs twice:

> I gazed down in the river's mirror
> And watched its winding strum
> The water smooth ran like a hymn
> And like a harp did hum.
> Lay down your weary tune
> Lay down the song you strum
> And rest yourself 'neath the strength of strings
> No voice can hope to hum.

Here, Dylan quite clearly intends the rhyming syllable 'um' to dominate the sound at the song's conclusion, conveying, as it does, the sound made by the flowing of the river into which he

---

[42] Steven Goldberg, 'Bob Dylan and the Poetry of Salvation', *Saturday Review*, 1970.

is gazing. The syllable 'um' is a mantra used in meditation. It is uttered by the river at the crucial moment in the conclusion of Hermann Hesse's *Siddharta*. Its three letters A–U–M summarise all the power of the universe. At the end of the novel, Siddharta, having heard in the sound of the river every possible voice, finally perceives that they all blend together: 'the great song of a thousand voices consisted of one word: OM – perfection'. This same kind of perfection is clearly the subject of Dylan's song. In 'Lay Down Your Weary Tune', all the elemental forces – breeze, dawn, ocean, rain, trees, water – combine to produce sounds of harmony which Dylan's own vocabulary and store of imagery struggles to express. He has to resort to a sequence of similes – 'like a bugle … like an organ … like cymbals … like a trumpet … like a banjo … like a hymn … like a harp' – but it is also clear that these are not meant to be comparisons, as they fall short of what is required of them. The ocean may play 'like an organ' but of course an organ's majestic music would not come close to the sound that Dylan would like us to imagine we hear.

As he begins the last stanza and sings 'I gazed down in the river's mirror and watched its winding strum', it's significant that the river's music is made by the same means as the singer's own. He too is a 'strummer' and the river may serve him as a mirror in which he sees not himself but a reflection of his own artistic purposes. There is no mention of him seeing his own reflection here, because what would be reflected would be Dylan's own ego – that part of himself with which he consciously identifies. Yet the experience conveyed within this song is one which the sense of ego is lost. The first person 'I' occurs only three times in the song – once to establish awareness of what is symbolically a new state of being – 'Struck by the sounds before the sun, I knew the night had gone' – again in the last stanza in lines quoted above, but most significantly in the third stanza: 'I stood unwound beneath the skies and clouds unbound by laws'. 'Unwound' is a remarkable adjective, and it chimes in the assonance of 'clouds' and in the internal rhyme with 'unbound'. What has 'unwound' in the singer is the ego's part in the psyche. When the sense of ego is lost we forget who we are and where our physical and psychological boundaries are. Hence here the awareness of a universal freedom – the skies and the clouds are 'unbound by laws', the ocean is 'wild' in the sense of being ungoverned – and a freedom within the self, which one can only accept and 'rest 'neath' in the kind of state of forgotten identity which is only normally attainable for short spans of time.

Of course, everyone is capable of forgetting identity and boundaries temporarily – of entering an ego-less state of being, as in sleep, or in flights of fancy or under the influence of mind-altering drugs, or in the rapture of orgasm, but we return soon enough to ego awareness and to earth. In *Song & Dance Man*, Michael Gray makes some telling points at the beginning of the chapter in which he analyses 'Lay Down Your Weary Tune':

> Dylan is not a natural visionary in the sense that Blake is. Being an artist, he has vision beyond the scope of most of us, but that vision has not encompassed mysticism, as Goldberg says it has, unaided.

And then he comes directly to the point:

> For Dylan, 'the mystical experience' can also be called 'the acid experience'.

There can be little doubt that although Dylan must have been open to the influences of marijuana from the very beginnings of his creativity – one only needs to glance at Victoria Spivey's left hand in the photograph of her and the cherubic Dylan on the back cover of *New Morning*. 1964 must have brought him into closer contact with the effects of even more potent hallucinogens. The mystical experience of 'Lay Down Your Weary Tune' may be drug inspired but there is no doubt that Dylan's newly-discovered feeling of freedom from an ego-centred society owes more than a little to the drugs that were to open what Aldous Huxley termed 'the doors of perception'.

A song contemporary with 'My Back Pages' and 'Chimes of Freedom' and, like 'Lay Down Your Weary Tune', omitted from *Another Side of Bob Dylan* (and how telling that album title is) very deliberately by its author is 'Mr Tambourine Man'. But although 'Mr Tambourine Man' may well be the first overtly drug-influenced, drug-derived, drug-oriented Dylan song, the process of turning on had already been very specifically described for us in *Some Other Kinds of Songs*:

> first of all two people get
> together an they want their doors
> enlarged, second of all, more
> people see what's happenin an
> come t help with the door
> enlargement. the ones that arrive
> however have nothin more than
> "let's get these doors enlarged"
> t say t the ones who were
> there in the first place. it follows then that
> the whole thing revolves around
> nothing but this door enlargement idea.
> third of all, there's a group now existin
> an the only thing that keeps them friends
> is that they all want the doors enlarged.
> obviously, the doors're then enlarged.
> fourth of all,
> after this enlargement
> the group has t find
> something else t keep
> them together or
> else the door enlargement
> will prove t be
> embarrassing.

In 'Mr Tambourine Man', the feeling of being 'unwound', the experience of loss of ego-awareness is hauntingly portrayed in surrealistic imagery. Sensual perception of time and places, and psychological perception of self have all been blurred and destroyed. Dylan is standing (but only just) 'blindly':

> My senses have been stripped, my hands can't feel to grip
> My toes too numb to step.

He asks the dancing, swirling, Pied Piper of a Tambourine Man to 'take me on a trip' being 'ready to go anywhere ... to fade ... to go under' the 'dancing spell' which the Tambourine Man's 'magic' means of conveyance has to offer. The potential is one of boundless freedom – 'but for the sky there are no fences facin'' – beautifully summed up in the song's photographically triumphant closing lines: 'to dance beneath the diamond sky with one hand waving free, silhouetted by the sea'. Nevertheless, the song's final request, 'let me forget about today', jars slightly and almost imperceptible with an acknowledgement that even this almost ideal freedom is inevitably transient 'until tomorrow'.

There can be no doubt that with the songs discussed in this chapter, Dylan's poetic thought has reached a new stage in its development. Disillusioned by experience – of the kind recorded in 'Percy's Song' – the songs which continue to express optimism – 'When the Ship Comes In' and the turgid 'Paths of Victory' – do so more in desperation than anything else. By 1964, Dylan, influenced by perceptions loaned to him by hallucinogenic drugs which accelerated his spiritual development to the stage where he is able to perceive new truths about values of life and society and thus reject older ones as being at best 'weary', at worst 'lies', also begins to perceive the kind of direction which his art is to take. His task is no longer to accuse – 'crucify ... fight ... analyse ... define ... dissect ... inspect ... reject' (from 'All I Really Want to Do') – or to convert his audience by appealing to their sympathies or their own sense of moral or political right or wrong – 'I ain't lookin' for you to feel like me, see like me or be like me' – but to reflect in his art what he now perceives as truth about man, society and the universe of which he is a part. Dylan turns his eye first to America and its people, and if he doesn't like what he sees, all he can really hope to do is mirror reality rather than vainly attempt to change it. By being true to himself he will develop greater awareness of his role as artist, and thus ultimately of his own being.

5. The Titanic Sails At Dawn

> all is lost, Cinderella
> all is lost.

Thus concludes the poems on the back sleeve of *Another Side of Bob Dylan*. Neither desperation, nor pessimism particularly, but simply acceptance of a reality which can have no fairy-tale ending:

> I think also
> that there is not
> one thing anyplace
> anywhere that makes any
> sense, there are only tears
> an there is only sorrow.

The poems contain the initial impressions of a vision which is to become more and more nightmarish. One particular piece concluded with a passionate sketch of urban America that conveys the impression that its author is more sorrowful than disgusted. Certainly anger and youthful frustration have disappeared:

> boards block up all there is t see.
> eviction. infection gangrene an
> atom bombs. both ends exist only
> because there is someone who wants
> profit. boy loses eyesight. becomes
> airplane pilot. people pound their
> chests an other people's chests an
> interpret bibles t suit their own
> means. respect is just a misinterpreted word
> an if Jesus Christ himself came
> down thru these streets, Christianity
> would start all over again. standin
> on the stage of all ground. insects
> play in their own world. snakes

slide thru the weeds. ants come an
go thru the grass. turtles an lizards
make their way thru the sand. everything
crawls. everything . . . .
      an everything still crawls.

Dylan was to distil and encapsulate similar and further visions of American society – its values, its ills, its members, its institutions, its significance – in some of the songs that were to appear on his next three albums: *Bringing It All Back Home*, *Highway 61 Revisited* and *Blonde On Blonde*. Contemporaneous with the composition of these songs, Dylan was writing what was intended to be his first book, *Tarantula*. The final proof-reading was interrupted by Dylan's motorcycle accident in 1966 and the book's publication only came about in 1971 after galley proofs had been pirated and distributed unofficially.

Tarantula is, naturally, of great significance in any analysis of the development of Dylan's poetic thought, yet its format initially presents difficulties for the reader – difficulties that don't exist to anything like the same extent for the listener to the songs. Obviously the circumstances of the book's composition have affected its style. The book – a series of prose passages, letters, jokes, poems, statements, allusions – was written piecemeal whenever Dylan found the time to write in the months when his commercial success was skyrocketing. The glimpse of Dylan pounding his typewriter in a dressing room on his 1965 tour of England, featured in *Don't Look Back*, in itself goes a long way towards explaining why at times the book became a collection of tortured fragments that one might well re-structure and reorganise as one chooses. Indeed, save the important opening and closing sections, the remaining chapters may be dipped into at random and there will be no real loss of the book's overall impact.

The publisher's blurb – 'Filled with wordplay and fields of humour, *Tarantula* speaks of plain and complicated truths. It is both very sad and very funny, because it is a journey through our life and times' – is also fair comment. In *Tarantula* one may find some of Dylan's funniest writing as well as some of his most grimly serious, indeed pessimistic, statements. His love of language and ability to use it with remarkable originality is ever-apparent, as, notably, is his knowledge of literature. There are many punning allusions to other writers and other works – most notably T. S. Eliot and, prominently, Shakespeare.

Dylan's new stance as an artist is proclaimed in *Tarantula*'s pages, as are his audience's responses to it and his own feelings about it. Perhaps identifying early in the book as 'wandering Apollo' (an almost Keatsian identification) or 'Adam and Eve's minstrel' and finally as Prince Hamlet,[43] he reinforces this latter character's advice about art and the purpose of the artist quoted in Chapter Two:

> Yesterday I talked to Abner for forty minutes … he didn't talk to me – he talked into a mirror – I did not have the courage to crash or shatter myself.

Dylan was to use *Tarantula* to present a reflection of his own vision of urban America as Waste Land: 'i think i'm gonna do april or so is a cruel month & how you like your blue eyed boy NOW…?' he shouts to his audience. The question 'Don't you know no happy songs?' occurs early in the book and echoes an accusation aimed at Dylan in the fifth *Outlined Epitaph* – 'you sing such depressing songs'. But there's precious little to laugh at, save man's folly. *Tarantula* presents Bob Dylan 'sick with cavity … ludicrous, the dead angel, monopolising my vocal cords, gathering her parent sheep onward & homeward into obituary'. The time has come to 'learn new songs' and *Tarantula*'s author begins to reflect society's ills.

For Dylan in the 1960s, self-fulfilment was threatened by a dehumanized and dehumanizing world – a world of vulgar materialism, of spiritual poverty, a society without sustaining values. 'Money doesn't talk, it swears' – a neat epigram from 'It's Alright, Ma (I'm Only Bleeding)' – is a sentiment that emerges time and again in *Tarantula*. There seems little doubt that Dylan

---

[43] For an assessment of Dylan's identification with Prince Hamlet, see W.T. Lhamon Jr.'s 'Prince Hamlet and the Minstrel Boy' included in *Conclusions On The Wall: New Essays On Bob Dylan*, Thin Man, 1980.

sees money as a major root of social evil. One of the book's rare bald statements proclaims 'everybody knows by now that wars are caused by money and greed' and there is a picture of the average American 'nothing can reach those tens of thousands living behind the wall of dollar' and dollars may be 'pieces of paper' but the truth is 'people kill for paper'. The lure and sway of the mighty dollar is seemingly irresistible and there is a grim glimpse of Funky Phaedra who 'tries to outstare a bowl of money'. Although it may be argued that 'you can't buy a thrill with a dollar' even kids in school have been corrupted:

> 'does anybody wanna be anything out of the ordinary?'
> asks the instructor, the smartest kid in class, who comes
> to school drunk, raises his hand & says 'yes sir, I'd like to
> be a dollar, sir'.

And he's supposedly the smartest kid – though perhaps not as smart as 'a blond haired little boy in the first row' who, when asked 'are there any questions?' replies 'how far to mexico?'

But it's the dollar that fuels consumer society. All other values are cast aside: 'theyre putting up a supermarket across the meadow & that should take care of the farmer'. It's a grim pun on the way in which the appropriation of the meadow will 'take care' of him, of course. In a much later, unreleased song, 'Nobody 'Cept You', Dylan sings 'Everybody's got something to sell'. So, too, in *Tarantula*. The street cleaner who bumps into Jack amazes him by asking 'would you like to buy a pail?'

If Dylan expresses his own incredulity and dismay at the marketing of 'toy guns that spark' or 'hundred dollar plates' or 'flesh-coloured Christs that glow in the dark' in 'It's Alright, Ma (I'm Only Bleeding)', *Tarantula* offers 'a trick piece of puke which you put on the table and just watch the girls throw up' and 'Mrs Cunk who sells fake blisters at the world's fair'.

The means by which such commodities find their market is, of course, advertising, and this too is attacked in 'It's Alright, Ma (I'm Only Bleeding)'.

Advertising signs that con you
Into thinking you're the one
That can do what's never been done
That can win what's never been won.

In *Tarantula*, people are conned because they're taught to be gullible:

you can teach people to be beautiful
but dont you know that there's a
greater force than you that teaches
them to be gullible – yeah it's called
the problem force / they assign everybody problems.

An almost Joycean 'pot of golden rainbow' is promised, but it's the 'hospitable grave being advertised' and the greatest of crimes would seem to be 'persuasion, the crime against people, that be ranked alongside murder'.

Dylan brilliantly portrays the marketing business on both sides of the corporate desk. This is Syd Dangerous's letter to buzz:

dear buzz
    i want the bibles marked up thirty percent – to justify the markup, i want free hairbrushes given away with each bible – also, the chocolate jesuses should not be sold in the south...one more thing, concerning the end of the world game – perhaps if you had some germ warfare for it you could sell it for twice as much – things kinda stormy round here – office in turmoil – secretary wiped out recently – guess what happened to the pictures of the pres? yeah well some joker drew a earring on him in the original print & somehow it slipped by the production staff – needless to say, we couldn't get rid of any of them around here that's for sure, so we had to ship them all to puerto rico – thing worked out ok tho – distributors down there said they went like hot cakes...almost as fast as the red white and blue hamburger sets – oh – i meant to tell you, i think if you made the 'i voted for the winner' buttons triangle shaped, they might go a little faster...by the way, i did tell you to send the 'i'm a beatles eater' handkerchiefs to the dominican republic & Not to England – fraid you made a little mistake there, buzzy boy!

The whole piece is beautifully constructed and brilliantly executed in that breathless syntax of the pre-occupied big businessman, with a brain always at least one jump ahead of the consumer's. With such deviously imagined consumables as 'chocolate jesuses', 'end of the world games' complete with 'germ warfare' packs, and 'i voted for the winner' badges, the letter bears witness to Dylan's ability to unerringly penetrate the workings of minds supposedly totally alien to his own. While the satire contained within it is bitingly funny, the condemnation is total and bitter.

In contrast, notice how Dylan is able to strike a totally different register as he presents the view of a victim of such a person as 'Syd Dangerous', writing a baffled and bewildered cry for help, whilst not wishing to offend in any way the advertising company who have all but destroyed his life. It's a simple letter from a gullible man, Zorba the Bomb, but does it demand our compassion or our contempt?

> dear mister congressman:
> it's about my house — some time ago i made a deal with a syrup company to advertise their product on the side facing the street — it wasn't so bad at first, but soon they put up another ad on the other side — I didn't even mind that, but then they plastered these women all over the windows with cans of syrup in their arms — in exchange the company paid my phone and gas bill and bought a few clothes for the tots — i told the town council that I'd do most anything just to let some sun in the house but they said we couldn't offend the syrup company because it's called Grandma Washington's Syrup and people tend to associate it with the constitution… the neighbours don't help me at all because they feel that if anything comes off my house, it'll have to go on theirs and none of them want their houses looking like mine — the company offered to buy my house as a permanent billboard sign, but God, I got my roots here and I had to refuse at first — now they tell me some negroes are moving in down the block — as you can see, things don't look too good at the moment — my eldest son is in the army so he can't do a thing — I would appreciate any helpful suggestion — thank you.
> yours in allegiance
> Zorba the Bomb

There's enough in there to appeal to our sympathies – the corporate giant playing upon the individual's gullibility, hints of political corruption involving the town council, emotional blackmail, bribery, the selfishness of neighbours, isolation, helplessness – but there's that unavoidable touch of bigotry at the letter's end which makes us shift our opinion of Zorba enough for it to make a difference.

The corrupting influence of money extends even to art itself, which becomes just as much a marketable commodity as any other consumable. As Dylan wrote in 'It's Alright, Ma (I'm Only Bleeding)': 'It's easy to see without looking too far that not much is really sacred'.

Art for art's sake? Not a hope. Dylan savagely exposes the merchandise character of art in a capitalist society. Artistic achievement is commercially exploited and prostituted:

> Mr Clap – meantime – makes another visit to Freud 'only rich people can afford you' he says 'only rich people can afford all art – isn't that the way it is?' 'isn't that the way it always has been?' says Freud 'ah yes' says Mr Clap with a sigh – 'by the way – how's the mother?' 'oh she's ok – you know her name's art – she makes a lot of money.'

The capitalistic art consumer demands from the artist the production of 'pleasing' subjects and entertainments – splendour and glitter to conceal real horrors, pseudo-problems to distract us from fundamental social questions. Perhaps the most ironic cameo of all is the letter written by 'your fellow, kid tiger a protesty folksinger extraordinaire, recently triumphant at the vegetarian convention with my new song against meat'. Kid concludes his letter:

> got a new song against cigarette lighters. This matchbook company offered me free matches for the rest of my life, plus my picture on all the matchbooks, but you know me, it'd take a helluva lot more'n that before i'd sell out.

Yet kid is already obviously a sell-out; the song against cigarette lighters is already written. How long before kid tiger appears on matchbooks coast to coast? But kid's really just another victim of a system that sets the standards and seduces people into believing they must live by them. Life in mid-sixties America is a parade – a 'march where tab hunter leads with his thunderbird' – clean-cut kid and the American dream. The need for status extends through all the social strata. There's 'window-washer', for instance, who 'after once being pushed around happily and casually hitting a rock once in a while' (to remind himself of his own existence) is 'now bitter hung up on finding some inferior'.

Perhaps it all starts to go wrong with the schools and the educational system. Maybe it's the books they use:

> ok so you used to get B's in the ivanhoe tests
> & A minuses in the silas marners...then you
> wonder why you flunked the hamlet exams.

Or the questions they ask: 'who can tell me the name of the third president of the United States?' (Dylan derided the worth of 'memorising politics of ancient history' in 'My Back Pages'.) Or the instructor who asks 'is there anyone in class who can tell me the exact hour his or her father isn't home?' Perhaps there's little wonder that 'everybody suddenly drops their pencils and runs out the door'. Isn't that exactly what Dylan and many of his contemporaries were doing throughout the sixties?

The real stupidity of the system is summed up in a letter:

> to my students:
>   i take it for granted that youve all read and understand
> freud – dostoevsky – st. michael – confucius – coco joe
> – einstein – melville – porgy snaker – john zulu – kafka
> – sartre – smallfry – & tolstoy – all right then – what
> my work is – is merely picking up where they left off
> – nothing more – there you have it in a nutshell – now
> I'm giving you my book – i expect you all to jump right
> in – the exam will be in two weeks – everybody has to
> bring their own eraser.
>   your professor
>   herold the professor

The summary dismissal of a hotchpotch of names with the cursory 'all right then' is a typical teacher's phrase. For all his learning – what Dylan termed in 'Tombstone Blues' as useless and pointless knowledge – Herold can come up with nothing more original or expressive than 'your professor' to sign himself off. And the fact that Herold writes a letter to his students in itself suggests that there's more than a little lacking in the channels of communication. Maybe that's the point, though. There is also, at times, an unhealthy lack of communication in the world at large:

> i stayed awake three hours last nite with Pearl – she claimed to have walked by a rooming house i once lived in – we had nothing in common, me & Pearl – i shared her boredom & had nothing to give her.

Or the grimly ironic 'it pays to know who your friends are but it also pays to know you ain't got any friends' which later becomes 'all the friends have been taken'.

Dylan's artistic mirror reflects the bigotry that is rife in such a society. The truck driver who 'hates anybody that carries a tennis racket' has many potential allies for his hatred. In the first part of the section entitled 'Ape on Sunday', Dylan depicts the coming together of such characters who behave in sub-human ways. They trade insults on meeting and find they have something in common, at which:

> they go beat up some male secretary who works for a jockey... they walk thru the streets of France & poison the dogs.

The place that society holds for such Neanderthals whose sole raison d'être seems to be to hurt or to destroy is, ironically, in the vanguard of commerce. The two friends 'are invited to speak at religious and college gatherings & finally become board members of the rootbeer industry'.

'iron man' is another such character who has sprouted up 'from a dumb hill bully into a bunch of backslap'. We all know him, of course: 'he speaks to everyone as if they just answered the door'. But be careful not to openly identify him too closely with the apish friends – 'he don't like people that say he comes from the monkeys' – undoubtedly because he's a little closer than most. Nevertheless, although he is 'dull' and boring he is 'destroyingly' so – so watch out for the apes and 'iron man' and all the other 'meatheads' who sit around 'praising each other's power' because anyone with any kind of power is potentially dangerous.

Violence is never far below the surface of this society – 'go ahead, shoot! all you need is a license and a weak heart' – and the potential for violence is most often to be found in the hands of those whose social function is, in fact, to keep the peace. In 'Desolation Row', Dylan depicts a riot squad who are getting restless, in 'Stuck Inside of Mobile' a senator is waving a gun around, and in *Tarantula* there are so many different examples of such figures it's difficult to choose. How about this meathead who happens to be the chief of police:

> the chief of police holding a bazooka with his name engraved on it. coming in drunk & putting the barrel into the face of the lawyer's pig. once a wife beater, he became a professional boxer & received a club foot/ he would literally like to become an executioner.

Or the paranoia expressed in this letter:

> ok so i shoot dope once in a while. big deal. what's it got to do with you? i'm telling you mervin, if you dont lay off me, i'm gonna rip you off some more where that scar is, y'hear? like i'm getting mad. next time you call me that name in a public cafeteria, i'm just gonna haul off & kick you so you'll feel it. like i aint even gonna get angry. i'm just gonna let one fly. fix you good.

The letter is signed: 'better watch it, The Law'.

But as Dylan has already shown us in his earlier songs, there's really nothing that the individual can do to counteract this kind of mindlessness, when it is authoritarian and thus established by society as well as maintained and enfranchised by it. The result is 'blind allegiance to law fox … & the intoxicating ghosts of dogma' from some and apathy from others – 'all in all, nobody really cares' – and finally helplessness and despair from others: 'resign from mind the heart of light & approve the doom, the bending & the farce of happy ending'. Even the 'good samaritan' can't help, and finally falls prey himself to the violence of the world: 'he tells the senator to stop insulting the lawyer … the pig jumps on him & starts eating his face'.

Two final statements on the state of the world which is 'mad with justice' and 'run by those who never listen to music':[44]

> gangrene enthusiasm, ratfinks & suicide tanks from the pay phones to the housing developments & it usually starts to rain for a while

and

> a lifetime of goons & holes, company pigs & beggars & cancer critics … all being tossed in the river & combined in a stolen mirror.

I think these lines contain most of what Dylan is presenting in *Tarantula*. The first has sickness and suicide, money and the impersonality of development at the expense of the individual, and one of Dylan's recurring symbols for violence, the 'rain'. The second quotation contains the 'meatheads' and the emptiness, the mindlessness of big business and the victims of materialism, the destructive critics and finally the image of the 'stolen mirror' of Dylan's art; 'stolen' because Dylan's own symbol for himself as poet is 'thief'. Prometheus stole fire from heaven, the embodiment of aspiration towards the realms beyond the reach of mortals. Arthur Rimbaud and the symbolists were self-proclaimed Prometheans: 'Le poète est vraiment voleur de feu' ['The poet is truly the thief of fire'] wrote Rimbaud.[45] 'Yes I am a thief of thoughts not, I

---

[44] It may be interesting to recall Shakespeare's lines from *The Merchant of Venice* 5.1: 'The man that hath no music in himself, nor is not moved with concord of sweet sounds, is fit for treasons, stratagems and spoils. The motions of his spirit are dull as night.'
[45] Letter to Paul Demeny, 15th May 1871.

pray, a stealer of souls' wrote Dylan in his poetic manifesto, the eighth *Outlined Epitaph*.[46]

If 'all is lost' was the epitaph of *Some Other Kinds of Songs*, its equivalent in *Tarantula* is this: 'give up – give up – the ship is lost: go back to san bernardino – stop trying to organise the crew – it's every man for himself – are you a man or a self?'

While an extended study of *Tarantula* would need to take these points and many others put forward by the book in much greater depth, this last quotation sums up Dylan's own advice to himself. Attempts to 'organise the crew' are both foolish and vain – perhaps in both senses of the word – and Dylan has learned that much. In 'Desolation Row', Dylan uses the Titanic as his great symbol for America. 'The Titanic was the ship of the future, the "proof" of man's civilisation and progress, the unsinkable ship which, on her maiden voyage, sank.'[47] Nothing can stop her sailing, because everyone believes in her – save perhaps those with the vision to see beyond present consciousness. 'Are you a man or a self?' In such reflections, Dylan is coming closer to being a self, moving towards a clearer understanding of his own essential nature and of where he is in the process of personal unfolding.

---

[46] Dylan's 'Someday I may be hung as a thief' remark is relevant here. The aspiring artist wishes to be 'hung' as does a painter in a gallery – to have talents recognised and acclaimed. Thus the enigmatic phrase functions symbolically – Dylan is announcing that one day he will be accepted and recognised as a poet – a true 'thief' – even a 'master thief' which he acknowledges he isn't in 1965's 'Positively 4th Street'.

[47] Michael Gray, *Song & Dance Man*.

6. Desolation Row

Pain sure brings out the best in people, doesn't it?

— 'She's Your Lover Now'

What is this hell in myself? It is the religious term for the
conflicts arising from man's divided nature, for the chaos
of chthonic, inchoate forces in us which, as long as they
are not integrated in a controlled and controllable order,
exert a subterranean but no less tormenting tyranny over
us. In the exposition of this chaos and of the anxiety which
it breeds in us [the artist] has been untiring.

— Theodore Ziolkowski, *The Novels of Hermann Hesse*

By late 1964, Dylan's poetic consciousness had moved well beyond
feelings of anger and frustration as he progressed to an awareness
that the true function of his art was to be a mirror of society that
would reflect the reality of its values and priorities, or rather the
chaos that purports to be a civilised and ordered society.

This is not to say that Dylan became a realist. He is not, at
this time, the purveyor of cinéma vérité; neither *Tarantula* nor
the Tarantuloid songs of *Bringing It All Back Home* and *Highway
61 Revisited* could be honestly described as realistic. But neither
can the image in a mirror be truthfully described as being 'real'.
Hamlet's point, in defining the purpose of art as being 'to hold,
as 'twere, the mirror up to nature' was not to argue in favour of
kitchen-sink realism but that art should project the image of the
truth of reality. From 'My Back Pages' onwards, Dylan's artistic
direction demanded that he should not shirk reality but confront
it by new means. The old ways had foundered and failed, yet the
first criterion of his new approach was total honesty; Dylan began
again by accepting what he knew to be reality, or at least what he

could perceive to be reality. If that reality embraced only chaos, that was what his art should portray.

The means he adopted to reflect the perceived chaos was an apparently chaotic style. W.T. Lhamon likens Dylan to Hamlet and his adoption of the 'antic disposition';[48] he might also be compared to Lear's Fool, whose handy-dandy speeches present truth in terms of folly. Dylan's music became electrified and he pushed electricity and amplification as far as it could be pushed in the mid-sixties, playing, with his backing musicians, louder and harder than anyone had ever played before. He began to use his voice in quite extraordinary ways – in ways which no singer had ever contemplated, stretching words, slurring syllables and sounds, distributing stress and intonation in totally unexpected and unorthodox fashion, shouting and wailing and sighing and grumbling and crying – both on record and even more markedly in his concerts.

Dylan's use of language became similarly re-orientated. Words began to assume symbolic values in even more obtuse ways. Dylan began to exploit allusion to considerable effect – to literature, to rock music, to himself, to modern culture. Reality melted into surreality. The 'rules' of lyric composition were distorted. Impressions were intensified, but they always reflected the reality of the chaos.

'Farewell Angelina' illustrates the development of Dylan's imagery at this time and is ostensibly a valediction to a lover forbidding just about everything:

> There's no need for anger
> There's no need for blame
> There's nothing to prove
> Ev'rything's still the same.

On the inevitable parting, Dylan could just as well be singing to himself about the nature of his own responses to what he sees all around him. Society's values have been distorted by misappropriation: 'The bells of the crown are being stolen by

---

[48] In 'Prince Hamlet and the Minstrel Boy', *Conclusions on the Wall: New Essays on Bob Dylan*.

bandits'. There is a dimly perceptible requiem-type solemnity about the music that plays beneath a symbolically ever-darkening, ever-threatening sky, most markedly in an image of impending doom, whose impact lies in the fact that it is, rather than in what it does: 'Just a table standing empty by the edge of the sea'.

The courtyard, once full of life and action, is being 'forsaken' by 'fifty-two gypsies' who 'file past the guards' calmly and in orderly fashion, leaving the landscape to be occupied by characters who engage in apparently unconscious and certainly increasingly mad or chaotic pastimes. 'Cross-eyed pirates' – akin to the 'bandits' of the first stanza – are clapped and cheered as they shoot 'tin cans with a sawed-off shotgun'. On the rooftops, beneath the 'embarrassed' sky, 'King Kong, little elves … dance Valentino-type tangos' totally unaware of the death, doom and destruction all around. The climax comes as the song ends:

> The machine guns are roaring
> The puppets heave rocks
> The fiends nail time bombs
> To the hands of the clocks…
> The sky is erupting.

All that's needed here are 'some pillars and Cecil B. DeMille' to film the cataclysm. 'Farewell Angelina's sister-song is 'It's All Over Now, Baby Blue' which draws similar pictures of impending doom, and a rapidly approaching one at that, characters running away, lamenting their fate – like 'your orphan' who merely stands, 'crying like a fire in the sun' vainly, with pitiful futility – or else surrendering themselves madly to travesties of former preoccupations, as does the painter who is left behind 'drawing crazy patterns on your sheets'.

What they're running from is a society voyaging towards its iceberg. Dylan's subject matter on the *Bringing It All Back Home* and *Highway 61 Revisited* albums may be repetitive, but its impact is cumulative. The songs are expansions of ideas contained in *Tarantula*, and there's a good deal of cross-reference in symbolism and imagery. The following chapters are devoted to a closer examination of the content of fourteen of these songs, which present us with Dylan's expressionist reality of what is revealed to be more and more a chaotic nightmare world – what David Downing in *Future Rock* terms:

> Dylan's vision of human society as a vast tragi-comic fairground, a timeless, self-sustaining relativistic system … an electric carnival … an amphetamine Babylon.

Dylan sets his own scene in the sleeve notes to *Bringing It All Back Home*. He observes 'i'm standing there watching the parade'. But he soon discovers that the paranoia of the parade can easily engulf him as 'a middle-aged druggist, up for district attorney' begins to hysterically accuse him of being 'the one that's been causing all them riots over in vietnam'. And this guy isn't alone: 'i look around an all these people he's talking to are carrying blowtorches'.

In a 'pause', he voices some of his more private thoughts. In *Tarantula*, Dylan wrote: 'the world is run by those who never listen to music anyway'. Here he adds 'the fact that the white house is filled with leaders that've never been t the apollo theatre amazes me'.

Here is the new artistic stance – 'i have no arguments' – echoing 'Farewell Angelina' and 'i accept chaos'.

Dylan was performing 'It's Alright, Ma (I'm Only Bleeding)' in the fall of 1964 and it marks a transition in both the poetic thought and, indeed, in its poetics. But it is the idea of acceptance that should concern us. Dylan catalogues aspects of society that deserve anger, accusation or protest, but then refuses to grant them their deserts. Instead, he simply *accepts* them, since there is 'no use in trying' to understand them. Words are 'wasted', and when there are 'waterfalls of pity', the sympathies of the individual are almost insignificant – 'just one more person crying'. Certainly one interpretation could be that Dylan's own words have become 'disillusioned', and so he withdraws, making gestures of resignation:

I got nothing, Ma, to live up to

or

Who really cares?

or

Okay, I've had enough

and finally

It's life and life only.

Dylan originally used the last phrase as the song's title. But if Dylan now thinks there's 'no sense in trying' to 'understand', there has been a major shift in perspective – a shift confirmed in a letter to Ralph Gleason in 1964 in which he wrote, 'I've conceded the fact there is no understanding of anything.'[49]

David Downing, quite rightly I think, ascribes this particular change in Dylan to Dylan's interest in Zen Buddhism at this time. Certainly the influence of Zen is evident in *Tarantula*, which is liberally sprinkled with Zen 'solutions':

> first bachelor, Constantine, he winks at second bachelor, Luther, who immediately takes off his shoes & hangs them around his neck.[50]

It was also found in Dylan's own responses to would-be interviewers at this time, much to their bafflement. Dylan's use of the symbol of the lightbulb for spiritual enlightenment emerges around this time too. The opening shots of *Don't Look Back*, where Dylan arrives in London bearing an enormous lightbulb are worthy of note.

David Downing on 'It's Alright, Ma (I'm Only Bleeding)' in *Future Rock* is worth quoting at length here:

[49] Quoted in 'Bob Dylan: The Children's Crusade', *Ramparts*, March 1966.
[50] Dylan would later restructure and rewrite this passage as the sleeve notes to *John Wesley Harding*.

Life is only meaningless to those who seek meaning. Zen Buddhism ... does not so seek. The song begins with a neat inversion of the famous Zen-poem line – 'at midnight the bright sun'; the line 'there is no sense in trying' could have been taken from a Zen primer. Not because things do not change, but because 'trying' in itself embodies that split in the mind between thought and expression which the Zen experience seeks to heal, and so restore to the individual his natural spontaneity. A Zen Buddhist would find the society portrayed in 'It's Alright, Ma' just as distasteful, but would not 'try' to change 'it' in any conventional sense. To change it you would have to be part of it; to be part of it would prevent you from changing it.

'Subterranean Homesick Blues', a title used for one of *Tarantula*'s sections, could itself find a home in the book's pages. It's an amphetamine trip through the urban wasteland, full of the main preoccupations of *Tarantula* but with a neat touch of self-parody in its early picture of Dylan on the streets 'thinking about the government'. Money is prominent – both the 'man in the coon-skin cap' and the 'man in the trench coat' are making financial demands; it's 'hard to tell if anything is gonna sell' though the ironic advice to the 'kid' is that if he's going to survive in a society where getting hit by 'users, cheaters, six-time losers' is pretty much inevitable, he'll need to play the game and 'please' as many people as he can by buying gifts.

There're plenty of other thing to 'look out' for too: 'phone's tapped anyway', 'watch the plain clothes', 'don't follow leaders', 'they keep it all hid', and 'try to avoid the scandals'. But after all that, unless the kid gets wise and lights himself a candle he's going to be sucked right in: 'twenty years of schoolin' and they put you on the day shift'.

The awful inevitability of that is like the forty-four word life-history of Fringe in *Tarantula*:

> Fringe is born – he wears short pants – goes to college – gets a job for a war magazine – he marries a nice plump girl whose father is a natural winner/ Fringe meets more & more people – he goes on a diet & then he dies.

Perhaps jumping down a manhole isn't so crazy after all.

'Maggie's Farm' is narrated by one who seems to have made up his mind to opt for the manhole. It's a neat allegory of course for America, where the true potential of the individual often goes unrecognised, and 'it's a shame' that one who has 'a head full of ideas' should be made to 'scrub the floor'. The trap of the vicious circle of a capitalist society is presented in the second stanza where nickels and dimes handed 'with a grin' to the worker, are immediately snatched back on rather doubtful pretexts; authoritarianism, the institutions of 'God and law' are used to ensure that the 'servants' know their place. But Maggie's pa is viciously and motivelessly aggressive and Maggie's ma is a patent deceiver. Finally, there is the point that such a society sets out to deny the individual personal identity. Individuality is something to be discouraged – hence the kid in 'Subterranean Homesick Blues' is advised not to wear sandals – too eccentric/bohemian – but encouraged to 'chew gum' and thus be like everyone else in America: 'Well I try my best to be just like I am, but everybody wants you to be just like them'.

Again there's a useful parallel in *Tarantula* where 'All Petered Out' has a problem with his chick, who's doing her best to be just like she is, but her attempts look like they're doomed to failure too:

> dear Sabu
> it's my chick! she tells me that
> she takes long walks in the woods.
> The funny thing about it is that
> i followed her one nite, & she's
> telling me the truth. i try to
> get her interested in things
> like guns and football, but all
> she does is close her eyes &
> say "i don't believe this is happening"
> last nite she tried to hang herself …
> i immediately thought of having her
> committed, but goddam she's my chick,
> & everybody'd just look at me funny
> for living with a crazy woman.

perhaps if i'd bought her her own car,
it would help…

The passage evokes tremendous sympathy for the girl and total contempt for the unfeeling writer and his selfish incapability of understanding or love. His surprise at her telling him the truth is self-condemnatory.

'Maggie's Farm' isn't humourless, of course, and Dylan laughs a lot in *Tarantula*. 'Bob Dylan's 115th Dream', as it appears on the album, begins with uncontrollable laughter as musicians apparently miss their cue on an earlier take. Dylan continues to laugh all the way through the song at the crazy situations the 'hobo-sailor' narrator, a Chaplinesque figure, finds himself in a land he quite spontaneously decides to call 'America'. Yet what is confronted isn't that funny, really. Captain Ahab's worst impulses are excited on landing, and he immediately sets about 'writing up some deeds', intending to 'start buying the place'. Things don't quite go as Ahab and the boys think they might, though. A cop, 'crazy as a loon', has them arrested for doing what comes naturally to whaling sailors – 'carryin' harpoons'. But doing what comes naturally is unlikely to gain much credit in the city. When the hobo-sailor goes into a bank for money for bail: 'They asked me for some collateral, and I pulled down my pants'.

The guy's naive enough to believe that he can get something for nothing, naive enough to fall for the old French girl and 'friend' trick, which costs him his boots, naive enough to believe that the house with the US flag on display will be able to offer him friendship and succour in time of need: 'The man says "Get out of here I'll tear you limb from limb"'.

There's a less aggressive response from the man in the funeral parlour. The innocent abroad is becoming disheartened – the funeral parlour is just about his last hope. As he delivers his story one last time, with a weary and disillusioned 'sigh', the owner simply responds as a businessman: 'He gave me his card. He said, "Call me if they die"'.

After being cursorily assaulted by a bowling ball and a pay phone, he becomes 'fed up' and tosses a coin to decide on his direction. Although the coin comes up tails, which rhymes with jail and thus determines his return to Ahab, the sailor finds a rhyme with 'sails' and thus decides that the omen agrees with his own estimation of the situation.

After one last encounter with an officious but gullible coastguard who has expressed his authority by nailing a parking ticket to the *Mayflower*,[51] he pulls out, offering a heavily ironic 'Good luck' to Columbus, who just happens to be sailing in.

This is a more light-hearted view of a familiar parade of capitalism, inverted values, and non-humanity in a society that lacks compassion, sympathy, and sustenance, and which has only materialism, aggression, ignorance, or repressive authority to offer.

The songs on *Highway 61 Revisited* take everything just a little further down the line, and again the sleeve notes function as a way in to the songs. The notes contribute *as much* to Dylan's overall contemporary vision as do individual songs or sections of *Tarantula*. The characters function symbolically – the 'hundred Inevitables' might just as well be called the Predictables. They are characterless nonentities, fashioned and accepted by the society that elsewhere is Maggie's Farm and here the 'Insanity Factory'. They might well be 'made of solid rock & stone' for all they have in common with what is truly human. But what is 'truly human' remains the problem, and by now it is a problem Dylan is far more inclined to accept than to attempt to resolve. Few of the other characters seem particularly nice to know. Cream Judge is, as his name suggests, an 'authority' figure who might well have been one of Herold the professor's students. He is 'writing a book on the true meaning of a pear – last year he wrote one on famous dogs of the civil war'. The Cream Judge was introduced to Savage Rose and Fixable by a mutual friend – Lifelessness. The sleeve notes tell us that 'Lifelessness is the Great Enemy' and Savage Rose and Fixable seem literally intent on introducing Lifelessness to White Heap by 'kick[ing] him in the brains'.

The 'Insanity Factory' is an apt name for this society. If you

[51] Dylan uses parking tickets and parking meters as symbols of society's obsession with official restraint in other songs too – 'Subterranean Homesick Blues' is a notable example.

want to know where to find it 'take two steps to the right, paint your teeth & go to sleep'; in other words, you can't miss it. The Insanity Factory is bought, owned and operated by the WIPE-OUT GANG, whose very name proclaims their significance and function. But it is the final paragraph that bears the most interesting statement:

> I cannot say the word eye any more ... when I speak this word eye, it is as if I am speaking of somebody's eye that I faintly remember ... there is no eye – there is only a series of mouths – long live the mouths.

The Shakespearean pun I/eye[52] only reveals itself in the gaps between page and eye, and eye and mind. One must read 'eye' as 'I'. Dylan is speaking of the movement of his ego-consciousness. Whereas 'I' was omnipresent at one time in Dylan's songs, the first person artist/narrator has given way to the impressions, expressions, reflections of personae. Dylan has, by and large, freed himself from his former ego-centricity and claimed a new artistic objectivity through which he can see both his world and, importantly, himself, in a much truer perspective. Hence the 'series of mouths' which are heard in the songs and the ego which has been left so far behind – 'I was *so much* older then' (my italics) – that it can now be only dimly perceived as 'somebody's eye that I faintly remember'.

Of *Highway 61 Revisited*, Irwin Silber wrote:

> Listening to *Highway 61 Revisited* one realises more clearly than ever before the essentially existentialist philosophy that Dylan represents. Song after song adds up to the same basic statement: life is an absurd conglomeration of meaningless events capsuled into the unnatural vacuum created by birth and completed by death; we are all living under a perpetual sentence of death and to seek meaning or purpose in life is as unrewarding as it is pointless; all your modern civilisation does is further alienate man from his fellow man and from nature.[53]

[52] See *Romeo and Juliet* 3.2.
[53] In *Sing Out!*, March 1966.

'Tombstone Blues' is set on Maggie's Farm or Highway 61 or Rue Morgue Avenue or what will ultimately be defined as Desolation Row. Its indefinite setting defines the reality of what happens within it, while a parade of pathetic, inhuman, dangerous, lifeless and sometimes holy characters passes through without direction or certainty, whirled along by the perfectly synthesised circus sound of the accompanying music.

If Dylan's lyrics are once removed from realism on *Bringing It All Back Home*, they are twice removed on *Highway 61 Revisited*, and nowhere more so than in 'Tombstone Blues'. Just as Dylan stretches and elides his syllables and stresses, pushing his music where none has gone before, so the surreality of his figures, metaphors and symbols moves towards Dadaism. But nothing has altered, save the perspective, and that has only become just a little more oblique. Dylan still paints his lurid picture of a topsy-turvy, handy-dandy world of inverted values and priorities. Jezebel is a nun. The head of the chamber of commerce – respectable institution as it is – is Jack the Ripper. John the Baptist is a torturer. The king of the Philistines fattens his slaves. And so on. There is perhaps a subliminal flash of Vietnam's continued presence with Gypsy Davey, who 'burns out ... camps' with a blowtorch 'to win friends and influence his uncle'. The National Bank continues to justify its own existence as the home of America's true spirituality by selling 'road maps for the soul', 'at a profit' of course, to 'the old folks' home and the college', which, by this time might well be one and the same place.[54]

And perhaps again there's an attempt to speak directly to his audience, explaining and justifying himself as Dylan always very consciously and very deliberately has tried to do at each stage of his career:

> Now I wish I could write you a melody so plain
> That could hold you dear lady from going insane
> That could ease you and cool you and cease the pain
> Of your useless and pointless knowledge.

[54] In the *Playboy* interview of 1966, Dylan said: 'Colleges are like old-age homes; except for the fact that more people die in college than in old-age homes, there's really no difference.'

The lines are significant initially in that they are expressed in an almost totally non-melodic song that drives and thrashes its way along at breakneck speed – a song that could never hope to 'ease' or 'cool' or 'cease the pain' of the listener's knowledge of what is being expressed. But then again, such knowledge is ultimately 'useless and pointless', as perhaps is all knowledge. As Dylan said in 1965, 'We all think we know things, but each of us really knows nothing.'[55]

Whatever, there seems to be no hope of preventing the oncoming insanity as life gives way to lifelessness. This particular aspect of 'handy-dandy' is pointed out by Laurence Gonzales:

> Throughout the song there are references to death and dying, the city fathers, the nun, the members of the Chamber of Commerce are all stereotypes of lifelessness, the living dead, representative of the life that shocks one into senselessness. Paul Revere and Jack the Ripper are monuments to great scenes of dying ... and for Dylan's population the ultimate success is to die spectacularly 'ever after'.[56]

In the album's title song, Dylan reflects the same ills in much the same terms, but the song begins with the striking suggestion that even God is caught up in the whole insane merry-go-round, as Dylan produces a beat version of the story of Abraham and Isaac. If God's initial demand of Abe – 'kill me a son' – takes him by surprise and stretches not only his credulity but his faith, God follows up by threatening violence, at which Abe complies, as he knows he must.

Georgia Sam, another character likely to be black without being defined as such, enters with 'a bloody nose' – the product, no doubt, of the kind of violence God had in mind for Abraham. Sam is running scared and finding, ironically, no help from society's charity; Sam is finally shown the only place he can go from here by 'poor Howard', who may be 'poor' in material or

[55] In *Don't Look Back*.
[56] Laurence Gonzales, 'Persona Bob; Seer and Fool', *Essays in English and American Language and Literature*, 1972.

spiritual terms, but who clings to the only thing which can help him to survive – his gun.

Syd Dangerous and Buzz reappear in the third verse in the guises of Mack the Finger and Louie the King – shady underworld entrepreneurs with tacky consumer goods to dispose of. I suppose 'forty red white and blue shoestrings' might appeal to someone – perhaps the Puerto Ricans who snapped up the pictures of the President with the earring and, indeed, the red white and blue hamburger sets in *Tarantula* – but 'a thousand telephones that don't ring'? Mack asks if Louie can help him unload them – 'Easily' says Louie, but then again, perhaps that shouldn't be too surprising in a society whose shops are stocked with plastic or chocolate Jesuses, fake blisters and presumably pet rocks too.

The final stanza presents the 'very bored' gambler who's 'tryin' to create a next world war' and takes his idea to a promoter. The promoter's response parallels that of Abraham to God in the opening stanza and thus rounds off the song's structure. But just as Abraham eventually comes round with a positive response, so does the promoter who says 'I never engaged in this kind of thing before, but yes I think it can be very easily done'. He'll even sell tickets; and thus sanity is once again sacrificed to the great God Dollar.

In *Bob Dylan and the Pastoral Apocalypse*, Gregg Campbell sums up the song as being a comment 'on the total absurdity of a society in which hype, manipulation and cupidity are the norms'.

In 'Just Like Tom Thumb's Blues', Dylan speaks in the voice of, and simultaneously addresses, the persona of one who tried to 'jump down a manhole' and find his way off of Highway 61. The fact that the guy chose the wrong manhole is unfortunate, because he's become the victim of what he saw as his way out, and I think there's little doubt that this particular hole is in his arm.

When he 'started out' he may well have been the 'blond haired little boy' in *Tarantula* who asked 'how far to mexico?' But whether Juarez is a real place or a state of mind, it seems likely that they only issue one-way tickets and once you're there, you're 'lost', 'your gravity fails and negativity don't pull you through' and the next place you'll find yourself is 'Rue Morgue Avenue'.

Dylan adopts the first person in the second verse, suggesting that Rue Morgue Avenue is only a couple of blocks away:

> I cannot move…
> I don't have the strength
> To get up and take another shot.

Perhaps 'Sweet Melinda' is a personification of whatever he cannot get up to take another shot of. Certainly the Juarez peasants don't find her so attractive – 'the goddess of gloom' – and presumably aren't enticed so easily 'up into her room'. Quite right too: 'she takes your voice and leaves you howling at the moon' or 'screaming' as Dylan sometimes sings. This seems to be a pretty bad state to be in; a glimpse back towards Housing Project Hill, though, reminds him that there's nothing of value to go back to:

> It's either fortune or fame
> You must pick up one or the other
> Though neither of them are to be what they claim.

The guardians and protectors of Housing Project Hill's society are busy asserting that they are the society and not its servants: 'The cops don't need you and man they expect the same' and 'all the authorities, they just stand around and boast'. So the choice would seem to be either Scylla or Charybdis, Housing Project Hill or Rue Morgue Avenue. Choose the latter and you'll end up like Angel 'who looked so fine at first but left looking just like a ghost' – in fact probably left *as* a ghost and the 'joke' was very definitely on her. Die here and you die alone. The speaker is already following in Angel's footsteps – 'I started out on burgundy but soon hit the harder stuff' – though the will to survive, it seems, is still strong enough for him to make the decision with which the song concludes – 'I'm goin' back to New York City I do believe I've had enough'. Knowing when you've 'had enough' is all very well, but perhaps there is enough in those final lines to suggest that at least he won't fall into the hands of the 'hungry women' on Rue Morgue Avenue. Not just yet anyway.

Miss Lonely in 'Like A Rolling Stone' and Mr Jones in 'Ballad of a Thin Man' are both addressed directly with thinly-veiled contempt and venomous ridicule. Mr Jones is looking for answers, just as the young Bob Dylan was in 'Mixed Up Confusion'. But he doesn't seem to have learned any lessons from whatever experience he may have had, which the song implies must be precious little anyway, for Mr Jones, who walks in clutching his pencil, is plainly an observer of, rather than a participant in, life. He tries 'so hard' to understand what he sees all around him but he fails. His questions are met with questions and 'the geek' – the furthest out of all far-out eccentrics and oddities who bites heads off live chickens in fairgrounds and side-shows – regards *him* as the 'freak'.

Mr Jones is a dealer in 'facts'. He's been through the educational system, yet his academic success is, in the end, 'useless and pointless' and his efforts to seek to know make him look ridiculous and vulnerable:

> You walk into the room
> Like a camel and then you frown
> You put your eyes in your pocket
> And your nose on the ground.

But he'll never be able to sniff out any answers – 'It's Alright, Ma (I'm Only Bleeding)' already told us that there's 'no sense in trying' to understand. But Mr Jones, spending his time discussing 'lepers and crooks' and reading the complete works of F. Scott Fitzgerald, obviously never got to hear that song. He probably reads *Ivanhoe* and *Silas Marner* too, and thus is doomed to failure in his attempts to 'understand' what's happening, for it is precisely attempting to understand that prevents him understanding.

In his essay 'Bob Dylan and the Poetry of Salvation', Steven Goldberg writes that 'Like A Rolling Stone' 'is addressed to a victim who has spent a lifetime being successfully seduced by the temptations that enable one to avoid facing his own existence'.

Yet the acceptance and indeed possession of those 'temptations' is 'once upon a time' as the song begins – part of a fairy-story that must now give way to the harsher truth of reality. Stripped of all her defences – her pride in education (at the 'finest school'), her status at the pinnacle of society ('Princess on the steeple'), her material possessions ('diamond ring'), her expensive car ('chrome horse'), her fine friends (the 'pretty people' who think 'they got it made', the 'diplomat' who carries his own snob symbol, the 'siamese cat' on his shoulder[57]) – she's left 'invisible', without identity, without locus, having to face those she once regarded with disdain and contempt. These include the 'mystery tramp', 'the jugglers and the clowns', and 'Napoleon in rags' – each of whom 'amused' her; the first because she paid them and 'Napoleon' because of his quaintness which she felt she could patronise. All she has left is an isolation which is total. But then again, how far is that true of each member of Dylan's audience at this time, or even of Dylan himself?

Queen Jane (in 'Queen Jane Approximately') might well be a prelapsarian Miss Lonely, suffering 'the fashionable ennui that periodically affects us all'.[58] She's tired of herself and of everything she does; she can no longer find clowns to entertain her, she wants someone she 'doesn't have to speak to' but she seems to find Dylan in a much gentler and compassionate mood than Miss Lonely did in her demise. But if this is the ennui that 'affects us all', the song seems to be referring to Dylan himself. 'Queen Jane is a man,' Dylan revealed in August 1965.[59] Perhaps he does tire of himself and all off his 'creations' at times; certainly he knows how it feels by now when 'all of your children start to resent you', having experienced audience hostility at Newport. The 'clowns' and the 'bandits' he has left behind to fight on in their own battles have either disappeared or come back to hound him with complaints, and the 'advisers' who think his 'conclusions should be more drastic' throw his old records at his feet in an effort to convince him of the 'pain' they think he should still be capable of expressing. They don't recognise that

[57] Dylan uses the pedigree cat as snob symbol on the cover of *Bringing It All Back Home*. In Guy Pelleart's *Rock Dreams*, the painting of 'Superstar Bob' has Dylan in a limousine, in an expensive fur coat, clutching a pedigree cat.
[58] Steven Goldberg, 'Bob Dylan and the Poetry of Salvation'.
[59] In an interview conducted by Nora Ephron and Susan Edmiston, held in the office of Dylan's manager Albert Grossman, New York, August 1965.

it's simply expressing itself somewhat differently now, perhaps more acutely than ever.

The album's final song, 'Desolation Row', is:

> The culmination, an overtly drawn collage of the apocalypse. From the opening line – 'They're selling postcards of the hanging' – through ten verses, Dylan recites a society out of control, mostly blind to the portents of its doom.[60]

Almost all the songs discussed in this chapter and indeed *Tarantula* and the sleeve notes can be seen to be harbingers of this epic song. The song is cast in the form of a dramatic monologue, narrated by one who is a part of the society he is describing, yet who has sufficient detachment to allow his prospect of the parade to be objective. As Laurence Gonzales observed:

> One of the things that makes 'Desolation Row' so much more polished than previous songs is the fact that Dylan has taken a step back from the material to become a little more detached, a little less bitter, a little more humorous.[61]

All that has been said about *Tarantula*, 'Tombstone Blues' or 'Highway 61 Revisited' may be said again about 'Desolation Row', in which Dylan defines and refines his political analysis of America – its culture, its people, its society, its values, its significance – in an effort to see it more clearly and reflect more faithfully and truthfully. Here it's a chaotic parade of the handy-dandy infected values of disorder, soullessness, lifelessness and social sickness. The fact that Dylan succeeds in producing a song of such significance that he suggested it should be adopted as the national anthem and learned off by heart by every child[62] is testament in itself to the progress which Dylan recognises his art to have made:

> Emerson remarked that it is a good thing now and then, to take a look at the landscape from between one's legs.

[60] David Downing in *Future Rock*.
[61] In 'Persona Bob: Seer and Fool'.
[62] In *Playboy*, May 1966.

Although this stunt might seem pointless when things are already topsy-turvy, it can be the more helpful then. One may say that what this chaotic world needs first of all is more *dis*-sociation; by breaking up factitious alliances and oppositions, one may get at the deep uniformities.[63]

The song opens with the setting of the scene. It is night – a spiritually dark time, a social, symbolic darkness that is all the more dark as 'the moon is almost hidden' and the 'stars are beginning to hide'. Much of the imagery contributes to the pervasive feeling of impending doom. The fortune-telling lady has 'taken all her things inside' – at least she has foreseen that there is no future to be foreseen. But many others – those not making love – are said to be 'expecting rain', a recurrence of Dylan's often used symbol for violence, catastrophe or cataclysm. The Good Samaritan is 'getting ready for the show' and they're 'getting ready for the feast' across the street, where they've 'nailed the curtains' – a disturbingly final action.

'The Titanic sails at dawn' the ninth stanza announces; but the ship would seem to be timetabled – its sailing a daily event, which should be borne in mind. 'Desolation Row' isn't announcing the imminence of a once-and-for-all conclusion, as some have argued. Dylan isn't singing 'A Hard Rain's A-Gonna Fall' again, with a new tune and different words. Catastrophe is about to happen, it's true, but then again it's happening and it has happened. It's ongoing. Doom is continuous. Michael Gray makes a valid point in *Song & Dance Man* about the contribution of the song's structure to this impression:

> If it wasn't for the last verse, with its different function, the song could be circular, which is to reassert that the parade could pass not once, or even several times, but endlessly, timelessly. The very lengthiness of the song enforces this impression, as it is meant to, and so does the long and rather formless instrumental section which comes between the penultimate verse and the last. A variant effect, though a closely connected one, of this instrumental section is to

[63] Herbert Muller quoted in Walker Gibson's *The Limits of Language*, Hill and Wang, 1962.

117

take the last verse away from the circular plane of the rest and set it aside. Only on the page does it 'follow on' from the other verses; in reality it is off to one side, a satellite, alone but with a special focus which can be brought to bear on the rest at any point. When people consequently say that 'Desolation Row' has two endings, they could more usefully say instead that it doesn't have an ending at all.

The fact that there isn't an ending is where the awfulness enters the song. It's enough to provoke a panic-stricken 'There must be some way out of here', or a painful 'Can this really be the end?' from 'All Along the Watchtower' or 'Stuck Inside of Mobile' respectively – both relevant songs that we'll get to in due course.

Meanwhile, back in the 'part surrealism, part impressionistic metaphor, part allegory and part riddle ... anti-logic nightmare', which in truth, rather than in art, is all too much of a waking dream, lifelessness goes on. The 'authority' figures are here: the commissioner is blind, hypnotised and walking a very precarious tightrope; the riot-squad, who seem to want to provoke riots rather than suppress them, are restless; Einstein, an intellectual authority, is a bum;[64] and 'all the agents and the superhuman crew' emerge at midnight to 'round up everyone that knows more than they do'. This is state suppression of the individual thinker. If the system is to maintain itself, it should not allow its authority to be questioned but should do its utmost to perpetuate the ignorance of, and thus its own acceptance by, the people. The crew's powers of persuasion are greatly augmented by their access to 'heart-attack machines' and 'kerosene' as well as by the massive impregnability of their Kafka-esque castles, in which their 'persuasions' are, it would seem, none-too-gently ministered.[65]

Against this kind of established system, the individual is powerless. All he can do is play out his role as appropriately – or, in this topsy-turvy world, perhaps as inappropriately – as he can. Thus Cinderella continues 'sweeping up', Romeo moaning,

[64] 'Amidst the reality of chaos, his intellect is so irrelevant that he has to re-learn the alphabet', David Downing, *Future Rock*.
[65] The situation is very reminiscent of that depicted in Ray Bradbury's short story 'The Pedestrian' – a story which undoubtedly inspired Paul Simon's 'The Sound of Silence'.

Ophelia peeking – and her 'lifelessness' has her so completely in its grip that her particular way out, 'death', is seen to be 'quite romantic', and so on, it would seem, ad infinitum. The effect is cumulative, the nightmare inescapable. Ezra Pound and T. S. Eliot – poets who should be seers – are fighting (presumably over opposed views of the downfall of Western culture) 'in the captain's tower'– the very bridge from which the ship's course should be directed. It is ironic, though, that they should fight over which course the ship will take when the Titanic can only sail to its destruction, no matter the route.

The final 'satellite' stanza shifts perspectives and gets us to see some of the things that are going on on Desolation Row in a different light. The narrator of the monologue is speaking from *inside* Desolation Row. He is not simply an observer but a participant, just as much as the Good Samaritan or T. S. Eliot or Ezra Pound. Naturally he too experiences the generally pervasive gloom. After the superb bathos of 'Yes I received your letter yesterday (About the time the doorknob broke)' we get the acknowledgment of such feelings: 'When you asked how I was doing, was that some kind of joke?'

It isn't a joke to ask such an inappropriate question of an inhabitant of Desolation Row but a symptom of what Michael Gray calls the 'lethal unawareness' of just about everyone to what is really happening. You'll never understand if you try to understand. You'll never understand if you don't become a part of what it is you're trying to understand, or, as Alan Wall puts it:

> Desolation Row is certainly no place to live, but unless you've been there then you have no right to speak with authority about anything.[66]

The song ends:

> Right now I can't read too good
> Don't send me no more letters, no
> Not unless you mail them
> From Desolation Row.

[66] Alan Wall, *The Passage of Bob Dylan*, New Blackfriars, 1973.

Desolation Row will never be seen to be Desolation Row until its inhabitants recognise that it is Desolation Row. But as long as 'nobody has to think too much', it will never be other than it is. Is it reassuring or depressing that on such a night only two people seem to be looking out from Desolation Row?

7. Blonde On Blonde: Bob Dylan's Nigredo

> The breaking down of substances into the *prima materia* would bring about the stage called the *nigredo* which is characterised by the utter blackness of the original chaos. It is a period of destruction and despair, and it is absolutely essential to the process. It has its parallel in mystical literature as 'the dark night of the soul' ... The nigredo is akin also to what is experienced by an individual as deep depression, either suffering a physical illness or beset by a disease, a weariness of soul. It is the bottom of the pit, where disorientation and weakness and hopelessness are the quality of life.

— June Singer: *Androgyny: The Opposites Within*[67]

Although it is tempting to draw an alchemical parallel between the sequence of processes in bringing about the *prima materia* and Bob Dylan's poetic processes in producing *John Wesley Harding* from *Blonde On Blonde* through the touchstone of *The Basement Tapes* songs, I'll leave the prima facie relevance of the above quotation to speak for itself for the time being. If Dylan's depiction of ever-darkening chaos was finally stretched and defined with 'Desolation Row', what more can he hope to achieve by pursuing that particular artistic direction? The answer is precious little, and it would be unfair to say that *Blonde On Blonde* takes up where *Highway 61 Revisited* leaves off, for in truth it doesn't. There's only one song on this double album that looks at society from the same perspective as the songs discussed in the last chapter: 'Stuck Inside of Mobile with the Memphis Blues Again'. Like Juarez or Highway 61 or Desolation Row, Mobile is more of a social abstraction than a geographical location.

The narrator is an uneasy resident of Mobile, restless, depressed, and very much aware that he's trapped, even though it's very

[67] June Singer, *Androgyny: The Opposites Within*, Routledge & Kegan Paul, 1977.

painful to have to admit it: 'deep inside my heart I know I can't escape'. He's trapped in his wretchedness in a society that has nothing to offer him but its lack of coherence, and though he feels desperately the need to communicate, there seems to be neither anyone with whom he can communicate, nor any means by which he might. The song opens with the 'ragman' trapped in the cycle of his own pointless and humdrum existence, drawing circles that symbolise his inescapable and inexpressible fate: 'I'd ask him what the matter was, but I know that he don't talk'. In the second stanza, there's another situation in which the speaker feels the need to 'send a message' to a French girl who's been speaking to Shakespeare (who is dressed appropriately as an entertainer). Whereas there was no point in trying to speak to the ragman, there are no means of communicating with the girl: 'The post office has been stolen and the mailbox is locked'. The repetition of the song's chorus builds up the despondency of the speaker until you'd almost think it was despair.

In the seven stanzas that follow, the narrator allows us glimpses of some of Mobile's other citizens and his encounters with them. At least they speak to him, each in his or her own way and for his or her own purposes. Our hero – to his credit – continually attempts to learn from them. But the situations he gets himself into almost always backfire. Mona's advice about the railroad men seems well-intentioned and we've already heard that 'the ladies treat me kindly'. Perhaps it's his vulnerability, his wide-eyed innocence, his openness to influence, his childlike bashfulness or coyness – he's a beautiful loser. 'Oh I didn't know that' he says to Mona, in accents that really do need to be heard, and then gives a perfectly non-grudging account of previous mistreatment at the railroad men's hands.[68]

Reactions to Grandpa's death mark him out as being different, in his receptiveness, from everybody else. The gun-toting senator handing out free tickets for the 'wedding of his son' – perhaps even forcing them on people to ensure a good turnout – seems to have omitted our hero, who nearly gets busted for being ticketless.

[68] The railroadman 'smoked my eyelids an' punched my cigarette' is an example of the inverted epithet of which Dylan Thomas was so fond.

The preacher offers only curses in response to the kid's questions – and the narrator does come across as a kid, though perhaps it's the innocence or the kind of naivety we encountered in the hobo-sailor. Certainly it's 'innocent abroad' time again and he falls for all the tricks – the 'games' people play, which, in 'It's Alright, Ma (I'm Only Bleeding)', we were advised to dodge.

The 'rainman' is a pusher whose wares are mixed 'like a fool' by the narrator, with predictably bad results:

> It strangled up my mind
> An' now people just get uglier
> An' I have no sense of time.

Delectable Ruthie, the jet-setting, waltzing, sexual sophisticate, attempts her own form of seduction, brushing away his shy 'Aw come on now' with a man-eating:

> Your debutante just knows what you need
> But I know what you want.

So the song reaches its conclusion. The kid seems to have come through another day in Mobile. He's been frustrated, used and abused as usual, but in a city of 'neon madmen', at least he's survived and just about kept his sanity. He's also kept his openness and his integrity – rare enough qualities – and has even clung to his sense of humour. His whispered response to the preacher – 'You see, you're just like me, I hope you're satisfied' – bears witness to that. Yet by the song's last stanza he's still 'stuck'; he still has the 'Memphis Blues' and will have them 'again' and 'again' until he's able 'to find out what price you have to pay to get out of going through all these things twice'.

The idea of paying a price is appropriate enough. This is another song with an inevitable cyclical quality about it, but unlike 'Desolation Row', there's no real let-up. Again the song's length suggests its endlessness – here is where reading the words from the page and listening to the record bring out totally different responses. When *heard*, the song has an added effect, for whereas we can see when the song will end on the printed page, in performance we never really know how long we will have to endure Mobile, or its inhabitants. It would make even more sense if the song were put in the form of a mobius strip or a tape loop, with the ragman and his circles reappearing right on cue after the kid's dreadful thought of having to go through the whole thing again.

King Lear springs to mind again here. The play's last act, and indeed, last scene, shows Shakespeare playing these kinds of tricks with his audience. He provides his play with several false endings, fooling his audience and characters into believing their experience within the play has been completed before introducing another ending, and then another – each more depressing than the last.

As Act 4 begins, Edgar thinks he has been 'blown unto the worst' of his fortunes. On cue, his newly-blinded father, his eyeless sockets still bleeding, is led on stage. Edgar comments grimly:

> And worse I may be yet. The worst is not
> So long as we can say 'This is the worst'.

Finally, in Act 5 Scene 3 when Lear enters with Cordelia dead in his arms, Kent and Edgar, almost in a fit of wishful thinking as much as desperate incredulity, ask:

> Kent: Is this the promised end?
> Edgar: Or image of that horror?

But it is neither the end nor the image of the end of the world or of the play; Lear's own broken-hearted death succeeds it.

'Visions of Johanna' is the only other song on *Blonde On Blonde* that concerns itself primarily with a depiction of society and its parade of characters, but its tone is unique and its intended effect is very different from 'Memphis Blues Again', 'Desolation Row' or the other 'Insanity Factory' Hieronymus Bosch-type collages.

The electric circus with its shattering multiplicity of sounds and its flashing Day-Glo colours and kaleidoscopic images begins to wind down. The fairground merry-go-round with its seemingly endless cycle of mythical, historical, surreal, allegorical, symbolical characters decelerates. 'Visions of Johanna' – 'Johanna' having Hebraic connotations of some kind of 'end' – presents a view of the weary, weak, disorientated, hopeless 'end' the kid in Mobile must have dreaded in his very worst nightmares, and which can justifiably be described as the 'disease, weariness of soul' state of the alchemical nigredo.

The narrator's sensibilities have been shattered, debilitated by his experience of urban chaos. He becomes infected with Baudelaire's 'spleen' – insidious, nauseous, exhausting. 'Visions of Johanna' is a brilliant evocation of modern man in the very heart of his wasteland. Dylan has never evoked atmosphere better. The song begins with a hot, stuffy, sleazy, tawdry boredom – a soul-devouring ennui, nausea, spleen. Hopelessness and frustration – even despair – have been left far behind. The 'we' – an interesting collective persona – who 'sit ... stranded' are simply 'trying to be so quiet' – attempting to attain a state in which they might just be able to deny their own existence. Louise tempts them to 'defy' the 'handful of rain' she offers. But no one seems to have the energy, let alone the will to 'defy it'. 'There's nothing, really nothing to turn off.' It's an 'everybody's making love' (or at least Louise and her lover are) situation behind nailed curtains. But the hustle and bustle of shifting preparation evoked in 'Desolation Row' is completely absent. Everyone is 'quiet', the radio 'plays soft', the all-night girls 'whisper', the night watchman's flashlight 'click[s]' and is heard through the silence. No sound, no life. The landscape of desolation presents, in Alan Wall's words:

> An arid area of betrayal and frustration ... all the characters
> are placed in abstract relationships, and one never finds out
> the cause of the betrayal.[69]

'Little boy lost' 'brags', 'speaks' and finally mutters consciously of his 'misery', unconsciously of his uselessness, in 'small talk' which is merely aimed at 'the wall' – maybe literal, maybe the figurative wall of silence, for he can expect no response

[69] *The Passage of Bob Dylan.*

being like the thin man, beyond the reach of explanation. He merely represents an annoying interruption of the silence of the meditation upon Johanna which continues to occupy everyone's mind. Johanna has conquered the mind of the narrator; the visions 'kept me up past the dawn'. In Louise, the visions of Johanna have taken the narrator's place.

The 'visions of Johanna' seem to be a contemplation of infinity, towards which all minds are turned. The only existential equivalents of the abstractions of 'salvation' or 'infinity' are the museums, in which man's culture is preserved as timelessly and as eternally as is possible in temporal existence. But Mona Lisa's smile is one of spleen, and there is the folly and materialism of humanity on display. Art is valued just as jewels are, in monetary terms. The following comment from Dylan's interview with Ephron and Edmiston in 1965 is pertinent here:

> Great paintings shouldn't be in museums. Have you ever been in a museum? Museums are cemeteries … Great paintings should be where people hang out … You pay half a million and hang one in your house and one guest sees it. That's not art. That's a shame, a crime … it's not the bomb that has to go, man, it's the museums.

The binoculars symbolise man's mulish attempts to see beyond the boundaries of his finite perception, and inevitably 'these visions of Johanna, they make it all seem so cruel' or ridiculous, pointless, vain. Life, that is.

The individual can only sit and wait and contemplate. Social interaction simply calls up pretence or deception, parasitical behaviour, vanity, selfishness – all evoked in the final stanza. All that remains is the close observation of self-degeneration – 'we see this empty cage now corrode' – which is enough to explode the consciousness of the individual – as 'we' changes to 'my' – leaving the grimly mortal pun of the harmonica's discordant funereal music in 'skeleton keys and the rain', and the visions of Johanna which continue to exist, even though the consciousness which conceived them, or attempted to perceive them, has dissolved into infinity. The visions remain because they are ideas or archetypes which existed before the machinery of man's consciousness or perhaps even of Divine consciousness capable of attempting to attain perceptions of them, came into being.

Dylan was to find that the further into objectivity he journeyed, the more isolated he became. He began to reflect a world that demanded nothing – no sacrifice, no heroes, no dedication. This led consequently to the emergence of feelings of being 'lost', 'stranded' or 'stuck' in a society or a relationship, with no sense of belonging and no trace of satisfaction.

'Visions of Johanna' is a key song in the *Blonde On Blonde* collection and demonstrates why *Blonde On Blonde* isn't simply *Highway 61 Revisited* revisited. The other songs bear this out, for although many contain glimpses of the urban and human chaos Dylan came to accept with *Bringing It All Back Home* and its successor, almost all are concerned directly with oppressive and unsatisfactory sexual relationships. ('Rainy Day Women #12 & 35' is the remaining exception.) They are Dylan's 1966 equivalents of the 'love songs' that were sprinkled sparingly through his songs from 1962 onwards, and which this book has not yet considered. The time has come now to see how this particular aspect of Dylan's poetic art progresses.

8. Songs of Love and Hate

So far, I've tried to trace Bob Dylan's attempts, through his art, to come to terms with the part of the psyche that is normally beyond the perception of the ego-conscious individual. I've examined the development of his poetic thought in his songs, poems and the 'novel' – a thought that concerns itself with man and his part in, and relationship with, society. By analysing the shifts in Dylan's conception and understanding of these aspects of human existence, I hope I've shown the development of his awareness of his own significance – an awareness brought about with the development of his art.

But the songs that deal with personal rather than social relationships are just as important in their contribution to the artist's intellectual and psychological development. Bob Dylan's awareness of self, in other words, depends just as much upon his coming to terms with his sexual identity as it does upon his understanding and acceptance of his social identity.

It's a well-known Dylan 'fact' (and Dylan facts are made up generally of one part truth, two parts half-truth, four parts myth and two parts lie) that his first song, at least the first singable piece of work not dedicated to his mother, was written to Brigitte Bardot. Unfortunately, or more probably fortunately, this isn't extant, but 'Girl of the North Country' takes the credit as the first published Dylan – for want of a better term – love song. It's strictly autobiographical in concept, dedicated on the Oscar Brand Show, in an expansive gesture, to 'all the North Country girls'. The song seems to be a token just to say that he hasn't forgotten his girl since he's been away, but that's not quite how it comes out. The singer tells the potential traveller to the North Country to 'remember me to one who lives there', which could be taken to imply 'make sure she remembers me' as much as 'tell her I've not forgotten her'. But I may be doing

Dylan a disservice there. Still the fourth stanza leans more in that direction:

> I'm a-wonderin' if she remembers me at all
> Many times I've often prayed.

What is of prime importance to the singer is not the girl, but himself. He's prayed 'many times … often … night … day' that she remembers him. It's important to his ego that he should be remembered not so much *to* her as *by* her. In the second stanza, the traveller is asked to make sure that she has 'a coat so warm' – a subconscious expression of the feeling that without his being there, the girl is much more exposed to the world's hostilities than she was when he was there to 'keep her from the howlin' winds'.

There's a set of songs that are the product of Bob Dylan's New York love affair with Suzie Rotolo, the girl walking arm in arm with him on the cover of *The Freewheelin' Bob Dylan* album. When Suze travelled off to Italy on 8th June 1962, her absence provokes a couple of lover's laments in 'Down the Highway':

> Lord I really miss my baby
> She's in some far-off land

and later

> The ocean took my baby
> My baby took my heart from me
> She packed it all up in a suitcase
> Lord, she took it away to Italy, Italy.

Though 'Bob Dylan's Blues' gives us a flash of former happiness:

> I got a real gal I'm lovin'
> And Lord I'll love her till I'm dead.

But it's all very twee, very adolescent – 'a real gal' – and clichéd pop, and should really be beneath our consideration, save that again it bears witness to Dylan's overriding concern for his own feelings, from the indulgent self-pity of 'Down the Highway' to the jump for joy in 'Bob Dylan's Blues'.

'Don't Think Twice, It's Alright' is certainly a little more substantial. It's the first of many love songs to have an acidic edge. And a little more than that, for when Dylan wants to hurt, he can hurt and hurt again. Hence this isn't just a 'farewell and I'll be gone' song, but a song in which the speaker announces his departure and then continues to yell over his shoulder all the way down the road, so the girl will have to acknowledge that:

> You're the reason I'm trav'lin' on…
> We never did too much talkin' anyway…
> I can't hear you anymore…[70]
> Goodbye's too good a word, gal.

And the unkindest cut of all:

> You just kinda wasted my precious time.

It's also the first of a number of songs in which the speaker expresses the desire not to get too deeply entangled in the affair, even though the temptation to do so is real enough as he turns over memories of former affairs:

> I once loved a woman, a child I'm told
> I give her my heart but she wanted my soul.

Even with this newly deceased affair there's the half-wish that:

> There was something you would do or say
> To try and make me change my mind and stay.

But the singer reminds both the girl and himself not to think too much about it: 'it don't matter … it's alright'.

'Hero Blues' anticipates 'It Ain't Me, Babe'. In each song, Dylan depicts a woman whose ideals cannot be met by what he has to offer. Each woman wants something that just isn't there

---

[70] To be echoed in 1974's 'Idiot Wind'.

to be had. The consequent disappointment may be painful, but it's also foolish – the woman's wishes having been misdirected in the first place. The light-hearted 'Hero Blues' presents a woman who wants a hero for very selfish reasons: 'so she can tell all her friends'.

To have a hero, a fighting hero, for a lover, may do wonders for the woman's own ego – which needs feeding here – but not much for the lover who cannot meet these expectations:

> You need a different kind of man, babe
> You need Napoleon Boneeparte.

The girl in 'Hero Blues' is shallow-minded and has thus been affected by what she has read in books or seen on the screen. The problem is an old one and Dylan can be seen to be restating the problems faced in Sheridan's *The Rivals* by Jack Absolute, who has to contend with a novel-addict whose ideas about what life should provide are coloured by romantic novels: 'She reads too many books, she's got new movies inside her head' writes Dylan in the printed version of the song.

'It Ain't Me, Babe' is a later and more fully realised version of the same idea, but with more tenderness and compassionate understanding than flippancy, at least in the first two stanzas. Demands for someone 'never weak but always strong' are unfair in themselves and can serve only to bring out feelings of inadequacy in the person who cannot meet them. But the unreasonableness goes further; she wants him to 'protect' her and 'defend' her whether she is 'right or wrong', and that's a neat insight into the personality of the woman he's finishing with. The repeated 'it ain't me, babe' and the insistent 'no, no, no' seem to be counteracting her protests of which the song doesn't grant us a hearing, though their nature is implied clearly enough.

The second stanza begins by asking her to 'go lightly', the singer wishing to avoid as much of the inevitable unpleasantness at parting as possible. 'I will only let you down,' he sings, and again we're given the impression that it's the commitment demanded to which he cannot reconcile himself. He cannot bring himself to respond positively to someone who demands that he 'close his heart' completely.

The tone of the third stanza is different; the apologetic, even sympathetic register of the first two stanzas hardens by necessity. If gentle persuasion doesn't convince, maybe coldness and hardness will. 'Everything inside is made of stone' he says, and then an even crueller remark: 'anyway I'm not alone'. There's an even coarser sexual joke at the end of the song; set against her storybook romanticism of wanting 'someone to gather flowers constantly' or 'a lover for … life' is the basic truth of her wanting someone to 'come each time you call' – a very deliberate innuendo.

'Tomorrow Is a Long Time' offers a tender tribute to an absent lover, particularly in its final stanza where her beauty is claimed to go far beyond that of anything found in nature, though that's pretty much poetic stock. Otherwise, the song is again egocentric, being far more concerned with the singer's own feelings of wretchedness and loneliness – particularly the grossly self-indulgent middle stanza where he seems to assert that he's become one of the living dead in her absence. Whether the fineness of the song's melody saves the entirety from being maudlin, however, is doubtful.

In the final *Outlined Epitaph*, there's a brief contemplation of loneliness:

> lonely? ah yes
> but it is the flowers an the mirrors of flowers that now
> meet my loneliness
> an mine shall be a strong loneliness
> dissolvin deep
> t the depths of my freedom
> an that, then, shall
> remain my song.

The assertion that it shall be freedom rather than loneliness that he will ultimately acknowledge is a very positive one, though there's a hint that its strength is more than a little forced. What will occupy his loneliness is his art – the 'mirrors of flowers' which are the artistic equivalents of the flowers themselves.

By this time, Dylan's affair with Suze Rotolo was at an end. In a heavy waft of nostalgia and self-pity, Dylan chronicles his memory of her and of their parting in the tenth *Outlined Epitaph* and in 'Ballad in Plain D'. Both pieces are poorly conceived and badly executed; sexually, Dylan doesn't seem to have progressed beyond the adolescent perspective. If the experience itself was one of immaturity, the fact that his reflections of the experience are themselves immature simply compounds the problem.

Here's an extract from the poem to Sue – 'the true fortuneteller of my soul':

> I think of Sue most times
> beautiful Sue
> with the lines of a swan frightened easy
> as a fawn in the forest
> by this time deep in dreams
> with her long hair spread out
> the colour of the
> sun soakin the dark
> an scatterin light
> t the dungeons of my constant night.[71]

It's schoolboy stuff.
'Ballad in Plain D' begins:

> I once loved a girl, her skin it was bronze
> With the innocence of a lamb, she was gentle like a fawn
> I courted her proudly but now she is gone
> Gone as the season she's taken.

It proceeds to document the circumstances of the 'timeless explosion of fantasy's dream' (the end of the affair!). True, Dylan acknowledges his own immaturity, mentioning 'the changes I was going through' in passing and on the record at least, referring to his 'young summer's youth'. That particular verbal monstrosity has been eradicated in the printed version, substituted by the equally thoughtless, and indeed less sensible, 'young summer's breeze'.

[71] cf. Robert Frost's 'Birches'.

'Boots of Spanish Leather' is a much neater and more satisfactory end-of-the-affair account, cast unusually, and thus interestingly, in dialogue form for its first six verses before he-who-has-been-left-behind completes the song, having realised the falseness of she-who-has-left. His part of the dialogue serves to stress the integrity of his love but a couple of lines may betray the slightest hint of part of the reason he was being left.

In the second line of verse two, the idea of 'ownin'' comes in, and is repeated in the fourth verse: 'your sweet kiss ... that's all I'm wishin' to be ownin''. Maybe it's this possessiveness that she's running away from. Certainly that would go some way towards explaining her attempts to buy him off with things he can own – 'something fine ... of silver or of golden' – and indeed this is finally borne out at the song's conclusion when, realising that he can't have her, he settles for 'Spanish boots of Spanish leather' – at least taking something from the foundered affair.

'One Too Many Mornings' also presents a love relationship in which something's been lost, or rather in which the narrator realises the lack of something that was never there. It's a time of crisis, and yet the crisis is internal – 'inside my mind'. This time there's a pained resignation about it all; no one's to blame, it's the way it is:

> When ev'rything I'm a-sayin'
> You can say it just as good
> You're right from your side
> I'm right from mine.

The fact that there are sides at all indicates the affair's conclusion. As Dylan puts it in a much later song, 'Shelter from the Storm':

> Now there's a wall between us
> Somethin' has been lost.

In a lecture entitled 'Is This Really The End', Christopher Ricks pointed out that even in this song which suggests absence of fault or blame, the middle stanza sees Dylan totally preoccupied with himself, striking attitudes, feeling self-pity, wallowing in his own emotion. Ricks's complaints are just but the song ultimately survives it, though the point does need to be acknowledged. A more blatant testimony to this all-consuming ego is to be found in the conclusion of 'Denise, Denise', where it would take a metaphysical mind to see traces of John Donne or William Shakespeare!

> I'm looking deep in your eyes, babe
> And all I can see is myself.[72]

Dylan is making progress by now though. The more Dylan experiences women, however, the more bewildered he becomes. 'I Don't Believe You' is the classic example, of course, when the morning after the night before 'she acts like we never have met'. It's a lovely, funny song, full of truth, convincing incredulity, amused bafflement. The sensual passion of the night's sexual adventures is neatly conveyed – 'the wild blazing nighttime … the night ran swirling an' whirling … her mouth was watery and wet' – but the fickle about-turn the following morning has left him feeling like a baffled child 'facing the wall … if I have done something wrong, I wish she'd tell me what it is, I'll run an' hide'.

By the time of his writing 'If You Gotta Go, Go Now' and 'Mama, You Been On My Mind', Dylan is more in control of situations – of his attitudes towards women, towards his relationships with them, and towards himself. The first song is a witty attempt at sexual manoeuvring which is as honest:

> I am just a poor boy, baby
> Lookin' to connect

as it is amusing:

> It ain't that I'm wantin'
> Anything you never gave before
> It's just that I'll be sleepin' soon
> It'll be too dark for you to find the door.

---

[72] cf. John Donne's 'The Good-Morrow' – 'My face in thine eye, thine in mine appears' – and Shakespeare's *Merchant of Venice* 5.1 – 'I swear to thee, even by thine own fair eyes, wherein I see myself.'

The second song is a declaration of a feeling that defies definition – of an attachment that lies beyond friendship or sexual interest but isn't simply affection, though it falls well short of love. One thing's for certain, the immature poses of the past are seen now for what they were:

> I am not pleadin' or sayin', 'I can't forget'
> I do not walk the floor bowed down an' bent...

He's not about to argue that it's 'love' that's made his mind go 'hazy' – 'maybe it's the weather' – and there's certainly neither possessiveness and its petty jealousies – 'it don't even matter where you're wakin' up tomorrow' – nor the demand for commitment – 'I am not askin' you to say words like "yes" or "no"'. Perhaps this time around there's a feeling that he's met someone who can give as good as she can take, whose feelings for him coincide with his feelings for her. The song was reputedly written the night before it was sung in duet with Joan Baez at the Hallowe'en Concert at New York's Philharmonic Hall in 1964.

The man who can handle that can certainly handle any number of Ramonas who come crying to him. In 'To Ramona', Ramona comes running for help; mistreated, half-destroyed by the influences of others around her, she's a victim, and maybe a naive or gullible one at that, of 'a dream, a vacuum, a scheme', of 'a world that just don't exist'. She's been fooled, her head 'twisted' by worthless things she's been told. She doesn't know where to go or what to do. The advice her sympathetic listener offers is sound, but Ramona herself has the key to her own problems. The sooner she gains self-awareness, the sooner her 'sadness shall pass'. The only things now working against her are 'the thoughts of yourself feeling bad'.

He's able to root out the cause of her sorrow:

> From fixtures and forces and friends
> Your sorrow does stem
> That hype you and type you
> Making you feel
> That you must be exactly like them.

136

As Dylan came to realise in his analysis of his relationship with society – of which he found himself inescapably a part – sorrow or anger or self-pity are of no value. We might briefly glimpse back to *King Lear* and the old man's experience of these emotions before he stripped himself naked in search of his true self: 'Who is it that can tell me who I am?' Lear cries.[73]

The starting point for Dylan in his artistic relationship between self and society, for Lear in his search for identity and locus after casting off his kingly persona, and now for Ramona, is knowledge of oneself. 'There is no help I can bring', Dylan sings to Ramona, emphasising that there is 'no help'; she must 'just do what you think you should do'. Earlier he observed:

> I've heard you say many times
> That you're better'n no one
> And no one is better'n you.

Ramona must begin again with an awareness of what is – not a dream of 'a world that just don't exist'. Lear too must face up to his own existence and acknowledge that he's given his crown away – this is the Fool's lesson to Lear, taught over and over until learned. Lear must recognise what he is, not what he was, nor wants to be. At the time of writing 'To Ramona', Dylan was also writing 'My Back Pages' and 'It's Alright, Ma (I'm Only Bleeding)', similarly coming to terms with what is, seeing the futility of anger or self-pity and recognising the value of acceptance:

> Everything passes
> Everything changes
> Just do what you think you should do.

The lesson is addressed to more than just Ramona, of course. Before we get back to *Blonde On Blonde*, there are three other songs about women in which Dylan attempts to paint honest pictures of emotional realities. David Downing draws a parallel between Dylan's poetic art of this time and the art of the

[73] *King Lear*, 1.4.

Expressionist painters at the beginning of the twentieth century. He says this of them in *Future Rock*:

> Since their art was an expression of their own feelings and experiences, they could avoid the rules of perspective, proportion and colour, normally used to mirror the actual world. Colour was used symbolically, proportions were distorted, surface beauty replaced by the inner beauty of emotional intensity. Familiar objects were juxtaposed in unfamiliar situations. All this to serve that internal truth which was now valued more than visual harmony.

The three songs in question are 'Spanish Harlem Incident' from *Another Side of Bob Dylan*, plus 'She Belongs to Me' and 'Love Minus Zero/No Limit' from *Bringing It All Back Home*. Dylan introduced this last song in 1965 concerts with the words: 'I think of this song as a painting in purple'[74] or 'This is a painting in maroon and silver'.[75]

'Spanish Harlem Incident' is a remarkable piece. It is addressed to a 'gypsy gal' whose sexual energy makes her 'too hot for taming'; this impression of an animal passion is reaffirmed by the description of her 'wildcat charms'. The first verse is more than anything else given over to an evocation of heat. The song begins:

> Gypsy gal, the hands of Harlem
> Cannot hold you to its heat.

These lines have several effects. Firstly Harlem itself exudes heat – the heat of the city and the air is stifling, yet the gypsy gal's heat is even greater and transcends that of her environment, like Cleopatra on the barge at Cydnus. Secondly, Harlem is subtly personified – the gypsy gal is too hot to be held *by* Harlem, which brings in an impression of physical contact that is so important to the song's effect; the gypsy gal's sexuality is such that it demands to be touched, held, caressed. Thirdly, the alliteration in the lines gives the impression of panting breaths – both because of the temperature of the setting and the girl,

[74] Santa Monica Civic Auditorium, 27th March 1965.
[75] Sheffield City Hall, 30th April 1965.

whose 'flaming feet are burning up the street', and because of the speaker's desire for her:

> I am homeless, come and take me
> Into the reach of your rattling drums.

The speaker's 'homelessness' is not literal but an implicitly sexual homelessness, which becomes explicit in his plea. 'Reach' brings back the idea of physical contact – the speaker wants to be 'taken', later 'swallowed' by her devouring sexuality. The abstraction of her 'rattling drums' summons up images of beating pulses and thickening blood, before the girl's gypsy soul is invoked as the verse concludes:

> Let me know, babe, about my fortune
> Down along my restless palms.

The 'fortune' he wants to know of is the immediate future, and her response to his plea. His 'restless palms' unite the fortune-telling idea with the previously mentioned desire for physical contact which the girl apparently demands simply by being what she is.

In the second stanza, the speaker admits that he's already 'fallen far beneath' her sexual allure; he's 'swallowed' in his desire for her. The Dylan Thomas trick of inverted metaphor[76] or rather transferred epithet in 'pearly eyes' and 'diamond teeth' is totally appropriate in this context. Her eyes are potentially dangerous for the casual or rash gazer – 'fast and slashing' – yet unavoidable. She seems to be a part of the 'pitch black' night with which the speaker's own 'pale face' contrasts rather obtrusively. The recorded version of the song has a slightly more specific reiteration of the plea – 'Come an' make my pale face fit into place' – that's followed by the ecstatic and appealing 'ah please!' before the demands of the printed lines:

> Let me know, babe, I'm nearly drowning
> If it's you my lifelines trace.

[76] cf. 'And Death Shall Have No Dominion'.

Finally the very fact of his being in her presence is sexually fulfilling: 'You have slayed me, you have made me' and the remarkable line 'on the cliffs of your wildcat charms I'm riding' combines impressions of her sexuality, the subtle feelings of danger, and the sexually ambivalent 'riding'. The song ends with its singer laughing in an ecstatic delight at the privilege of this non-experience experience before the final wishful-thinking expression of maintained desire. The printed version of these closing lines lessens the effect of those which are sung on the official recording. In *Writings and Drawings*, Dylan writes:

> I got to know babe, will I be touching you
> So I can tell if I'm really real.

On the record, he sings:

> I got to know babe, will you surround me?
> So I can know if I'm really real.

While 'touching' conveys something of the contact pleaded for in the song, 'will you surround me' is a far more erotic plea, whose tenor is much more in keeping with the sexually ambivalent vocabulary of 'come and take me', 'swallowed', 'riding' or his 'restless palms'. Either way, a sexual adventure with this woman would be one means of establishing the singer's own reality to his satisfaction. It hints at the idea of the search for identity through an overtly sexual relationship which might by necessity involve some kind of self-sacrifice, but which will ultimately contribute towards attainment of self.

The 'gypsy gal' is what Ramona has the potential to become if she could cast off the repressive influences she has fallen victim to. Ramona has her own sexual allure for the singer – her 'magnetic movements … capture' him. 'She Belongs to Me' and 'Love Minus Zero/No Limit' paint pictures of similar ideals – or maybe a similar ideal woman. The perfection of the object of the first song is absolute, from the opening line – 'She's got everything she needs' – to her power to increase and reduce male stature at will.

Dylan forms a complete spiritual identification with the woman and all she immediately represents – the spontaneity of the child, life, love, beauty, the intuitiveness of the female as mother and as sister. She is beyond the law, beyond possession, beyond reproach. She has a magical quality by which her own energy is transferred to the ring she wears; finally she demands and deserves only our supplication and tribute.

In the tenth *Outlined Epitaph*, Dylan writes:

> you ask of love?
> there is no love
> except in silence
> an silence doesn't say a word.

He's saying here that the more such an emotion or collection of emotions as is summarised by the word 'love' is spoken of, the further away from its true meaning the words, the speaker and the listener are taken. Again we have a kind of Zen double-bind situation. Love is, but if we speak of what it is when we attempt to understand or define or investigate or express what it is, the more impossible the attempt becomes. Thus Dylan's response to society and to love develop in parallel. His earlier songs attempt to investigate, assess, express and understand aspects of society – particularly those aspects that deserve condemnation. But the more his poetic thought develops, the further away from this early stance his art moves. So it is with the love songs. By now the kind of poetic thought that produced 'Tomorrow Is a Long Time' or 'Ballad in Plain D' has been left behind; 'ideals' or romantic clichés such as 'faithful', 'roses', 'valentines', 'promises' or 'perfection' are of no use or value to the woman exalted in 'Love Minus Zero/No Limit'. The very title makes its own point: love, end of statement – save perhaps for 'absolute' or 'infinite'.

The woman's truth or faithfulness is not something that needs to be spoken of at all, by herself or by his song. Because she is true – true to him, true to herself – she doesn't have to say it to him or to herself. John Donne found himself a similar woman in the early seventeenth century and his own words of praise were similarly acknowledged to be superfluous. He contented himself with the statement: 'Thou art so truth'.[77]

All romantic paraphernalia are seen as superfluities to be laughed at, and she laughs 'like the flowers', naturally, unselfconsciously, completely herself. And her elemental truth – 'she's true like ice, like fire' – is a truth of simply being what you are, not what you would like to be or what you would like others to think of you as. It's the same exhortation that Ramona needs to heed and the gypsy gal has no need of whatsoever.

In John Donne's 'The Sun Rising', the feeling of all-consuming importance with which love endows lovers, and the insignificance or irrelevance of everything or everyone else that lovers experience, is brilliantly expressed. The lovers are elevated, in their own estimation, to the point where the bed in which they lie becomes the very centre of the universe, while the remainder of life and human activity is either forgotten or reduced to such insignificance as to touch the contemptible.

Dylan attains a similar effect in the remaining verses of 'Love Minus Zero/No Limit'. The significance of all human activity is reduced simply by the existence of 'she'. The city is represented as a collection of 'dime stores and bus stations', politics becomes 'talk', academic study a repetitive and futile occupation, its product as insignificant and as transient as graffiti. Ambition is summarily dismissed: 'There's no success like failure and failure's no success at all'.

The mysteries of religious and civic ceremonies, conveyed in the surrealistic third stanza, are similarly reduced. The solemnity and grandeur of such 'ceremonies' is punctured by the mention of the 'pawn' who plays his part begrudgingly. Symbols of cultural achievement are similarly insignificant. The 'statues' that celebrate greatness in life and art are 'made of matchsticks' and, like the colossus of Ozymandias, will in time 'crumble into one another', whilst 'she' will remain forever herself, paying no heed, knowing too much 'to argue or to judge'.

[77] John Donne 'The Dream'.

All these elements are combined in the first half of the final stanza:

> The bridge at midnight trembles
> The country doctor rambles
> Bankers' nieces seek perfection
> Expecting all the gifts that wise men bring.

The men are only 'wise' because they know what 'gifts' are likely to win such prizes as bankers' nieces, presumably 'roses', 'valentines' and 'promises by the hour' should do the trick. The other spheres of human activity are represented in the dismissive image of the aimless ramblings of the backwoods 'country doctor'. The significance of society is reduced to the image of the shaky bridge – which might even be the 'captain's tower' on the Titanic – before the song's impressive, if enigmatic, conclusion:

> The wind howls like a hammer
> The night blows cold and rainy
> My love she's like some raven
> At my window with a broken wing.

Certainly the first two lines take us back to the elemental truth of the woman; the wind, the night and the rain simply are, and their elemental strength (brilliantly suggested in the physical and forceful simile 'howls like a hammer', which is as unexpected as it is evocative) is what it is. The simile accorded to the woman – 'like some raven at my window with a broken wing' – has its own kind of elemental value. Dylan often uses the image of his 'window' symbolically. It is through his window that he perceives the world and its inhabitants. The window, like a door, can close and can open. It can be enlarged and reduced. It can supply or deny access or communication. It denies it in 'It Ain't Me, Babe', where it is necessary as a barrier between himself and his former lover, and it remains firmly shut. His departure may be observed through the window in 'Don't Think Twice, It's Alright'. In 'Can You Please Crawl Out Your Window?' and in 'Tell Me Momma' the window is the means by which experience may be enlarged; it provides access to a wider and more fulfilling world, if the characters in each song would only acknowledge it as such.

At the end of 'Love Minus Zero/No Limit', the window is all that stands between the singer and the elemental forces of nature. It shields and protects him. The raven needs him, needs his help, but to open the window would be to admit forces that are well beyond his potential to control. The song reveals the awe in which the singer holds the woman who is the song's subject. Admittedly, the raven at the window is maimed, but this is perhaps not surprising. The woman is an idealisation who bears little relation to reality; she is a 'dream of woman', and such a dream would inevitably find it difficult to exist in its ideal state in the imperfect world of rain and wind – hence the 'broken wing'. But the question with which the song leaves us is whether the singer has the strength to admit his ideal to his own perceived reality. For him, the window is protective and a creature of such elemental truth is awesome, maimed or not. The song's conclusion does not resolve the question.

9. She's Your Lover Now

Don't ask me nothin' about nothin'
I just might tell you the truth.

— 'Outlaw Blues'

If Bob Dylan's marriage to Sara Lownds on 22nd November 1965 goes some way towards identifying the subject of such a remarkable tribute as 'Love Minus Zero/No Limit', it doesn't help us too much in any analysis of motivation for the composition of the songs on *Blonde On Blonde* – or then again maybe it does. After such positive tributes to a woman, awed celebrations even, as 'Love Minus Zero/No Limit' and 'She Belongs to Me' on *Bringing It All Back Home*, *Blonde On Blonde* is almost entirely without equivalent songs. Instead, we get a number of songs expressing a negative attitude towards sex and love – a word which is only used here in its sexual sense – or towards women. A number of songs express a need, but it's a shallow need – sexual rather than spiritual.

If there is an exception, it is the difficult 'Sad-Eyed Lady of the Lowlands'. The song may be described as 'difficult' because of its abstract, surrealistic and sometimes non-cohesive imagery, and because its impact belies the importance attached to it by the fact that it occupies the entire final side of the double album. It's a long song that doesn't hang together too well, despite being anchored by a five-line chorus, repeated five times:

Sad-eyed lady of the lowlands
Where the sad-eyed prophet says that no man comes
My warehouse eyes, my Arabian drums
Should I leave them by your gate
Or, sad-eyed lady, should I wait?

The woman is all-but-unapproachable, guarded by 'sad-eyed prophets' who ward off would-be suitors; Dylan is suppliant and offers wide-eyed admiration and tributes to her, humble as they might be, in the hope of being granted admission to her presence. The lines from the 1975 song 'Sara' – 'Stayin' up for days in the Chelsea Hotel, writin' "Sad-Eyed Lady of the Lowlands" for you' – a last gasp attempt to persuade his wife not to leave him, give us an uncharacteristically clear steer on its intent. In 'Sara', Dylan originally expressed the sentiment that Sara possessed 'strength that belonged to the gods'. If he sees his 'mystical wife' in terms of Isis – the eternal feminine, the great Mother – perhaps this 'unapproachable goddess' idea isn't too inappropriate. Certainly, the song presents its fair share of religious imagery in the description of the sad-eyed lady:

> With your mercury mouth in the missionary times
> And your eyes like smoke and your prayers like rhymes
> And your silver cross and your voice like chimes.

Later there are her 'gypsy hymns', her 'holy medallion' and her 'saintlike face'. The song argues that no one can 'bury … carry … outguess … impress … resist … mistake … persuade … employ … destroy' her. Even the 'kings of Tyrus' – a phrase that summons up, unaided, impressions of great wealth, opulence and power – are reduced to waiting meekly and subserviently 'in line for their geranium kiss' though they desire more than 'just to kiss' this imposing lady.

Stock similes cannot do justice to her physical beauty, so Dylan turns to the extraordinary to present a picture-collage – 'eyes like smoke … flesh like silk … face like glass' – and through such transparency her 'gentleness … can't help but show'. Her values are not those of the 'farmers and the businessmen' – 'how could they ever mistake you?' he sings. But she stands statuesquely, archetypically beyond their pettiness.

Of the other songs on the album, no less than seven express attitudes towards love, sex and women that may be generally termed 'negative'. Two of the songs already discussed – 'Memphis

Blues Again' and 'Visions of Johanna' – convey the feeling of being lost, 'stuck' or 'stranded' and suffering a debilitating loneliness.

Taking the album as being three-sided, given that 'Sad-Eyed Lady of the Lowlands' stands apart, it begins and ends with two laments of loneliness. It opens with 'Rainy Day Women #12 & 35', a ragged lament of one who is permanently 'stoned' – a neat pun of course – as a victim of society and as one who takes refuge from that society in drugs. Both ways, loneliness is the main point and gives rise to the appeal 'but I would not feel so all alone, everybody must get stoned'. Dylan may well have been influenced here by 'Get Drunk!', a prose poem by Charles Baudelaire:

> One should always be drunk. That's all that matters; that's our one imperative need. So as not to feel time's horrible burden that breaks your shoulders and bows you down, you must get drunk without ceasing. But what with? With wine, with poetry or with virtue, as you choose. But get drunk.

The closing song of the album's third side, 'Obviously Five Believers', comes with another appeal – this time to an absent lover:

> Please come home
> Yes, I could make it without you
> If I just did not feel so all alone.

Between these songs, loneliness pervades all the other tracks, and drugs – one means of temporary escape – permeate much of the imagery. The loneliness is partly social, but primarily sexual. 'Obviously Five Believers' pathetically and maybe hopelessly expresses the plea of sexual loneliness:

> Don't let me down…
> I won't let you down…
> No I won't…
> Please come home.

'Temporary Like Achilles' is similar in its intent. The distance between the speaker and his 'honey' is emphasised over and over. There's another symbolic 'window', a 'second door', someone who's sent out 'to have me barred' – 'Achilles' in fact, a forbidding 'guard' – a 'velvet door' and the singer's attempts to 'lean' or 'rush' 'into your hallway' come to nothing. All he can do is plead – again pathetically and hopelessly. He ends up 'kneeling ... helpless'. In 'She Belongs to Me' there is a prophetic observation that, with this kind of woman, 'you will wind up peeking through her keyhole down upon your knees'. But did he really anticipate falling so far?

> Like a poor fool in his prime
> Yes, I know you can hear me walk
> But is your heart made out of stone, or is it lime
> Or is it just solid rock?

The reiterated chorus lines emphasise the distance that keeps heart from heart:

> You know I want your lovin'
> Honey why are you so hard?

The abandoned, still faithful lover persona reappears in 'Absolutely Sweet Marie'. He's separated this time by a 'railroad gate' and complains 'you know I just can't jump it'; he later laments that he can't unlock her house either: 'You see, you forgot to leave me with the key'. But we know that Marie almost certainly didn't 'forget' when she left him. Again, the incapacitating loneliness and emptiness is expressed with more than a hint of sexual frustration in the innuendo: 'I'm just sitting here beating on my trumpet with all these promises you left for me'. There are the pleas of faithfulness – 'I waited for you when you hated me' – but that last phrase gives away the hopelessness. The song ends with an image of degraded, desperate loneliness:

> And now I stand here lookin' at your yellow railroad
> In the ruins of your balcony
> Wond'ring where you are tonight, sweet Marie.

Throughout the desperation there's just one hint of bad feeling towards her, though even that could just be self-pity as much as malice or spite: 'not too many can be like you, fortunately'.

This pleading, down-on-my-knees posture, however, is not the type of supplication present in such songs as 'Pledging My Time', 'I Wanna Be Your Lover' or 'I Want You', where the strength of the speaker's position seems much more assured, and where less seems to depend upon the response, or lack of it, to the questions posed. There's desperation in 'Temporary Like Achilles', 'Absolutely Sweet Marie' and 'Obviously Five Believers', but there's a nonchalance – conscious but unaffected – in these other songs. Not much really depends on the outcome of the question from 'Pledging My Time':

> Won't you come with me, baby?
> I'll take you where you wanna go.

The request is not for a relationship but for a sexual encounter: 'And if it don't work out, you'll be the first to know' says the speaker, dismissively and unemotionally. And though he's making the sacrifice of spending a few minutes on the preamble, his lack of enthusiasm doesn't really augur well for his chances of success. Indeed, he's probably anticipating the inevitable with that earlier 'if it don't work out' statement. There's a cheapness about the whole affair.

The mindlessness of the reiteration of 'I wanna be your lover' in the song of that title (not included on *Blonde On Blonde*) is a long way from the thoughtfulness of 'I Want You'. Perhaps Dylan only really discovered what he'd put into 'I Want You' in 1978 when his concert performances of it brooded and ached and yearned with an emotion that was both painful and heartfelt.[78] On the record, the happy-go-lucky rhythms seem to belie this interpretation, though the printed lyrics tell a different tale on the page.

The would-be love affair is set against the wasteland society devoid of spiritual value that was evoked so effectively in 'Visions

---

[78] Dylan may have been influenced by Bruce Springsteen's slow solo piano version of this song as performed in concert in 1975.

of Johanna'. It is a society whose inhabitants can only lament their own existence, their own lifelessness. The images presented in the opening lines are derived from Charles Baudelaire – a poet with whom Dylan admits identification:[79]

> The guilty undertaker sighs
> The lonesome organ grinder cries
> The silver saxophones say I should refuse you
> The cracked bells and washed-out horns
> Blow into my face with scorn.

Dylan already alluded to Baudelaire's *Spleen* (beginning 'Pluviôse…') in 'A Hard Rain's A-Gonna Fall'. The state of 'spleen' conveyed in some of Baudelaire's poems is not simply world-weariness or disillusion – feelings that are often expressed in the stock Romantic form of 'ennui' – it embraces ugliness and disgust, restlessness and indolence, stifling lethargy and dreary emptiness. Baudelaire conveys spleen often through the objects of the everyday world that grate on the nerves, and Dylan's superb opening lines in 'Visions of Johanna' – the coughing heat pipes, the bland music station on the radio – begin with Baudelaire. In the opening lines from 'I Want You', the 'undertaker sighs', the 'lonesome organ grinder' (an obvious sexual innuendo[80]) cries, 'mothers weep', politicians take the usual (and socially acceptable) escape route into alcoholic oblivion. The material aspects of the society are 'cracked … washed out … broken' and there seems to be precious little hope of immediate redemption because 'the saviours … are fast asleep'.

The means of escape or salvation for the singer is the woman to whom the song is addressed, and the need for her is conveyed emphatically enough in the repetitions of the chorus:

> I want you
> I want you
> I want you so bad
> Honey I want you.

[79] In the sleeve notes to *Planet Waves*.
[80] cf. 'I Shall Be Free' (recorded version) with its sexually licentious woman who is described as a 'meat grinder'.

If we were to interpret this or respond to it as we do to, for example, the love affairs of Antony and Cleopatra in Shakespeare's play or of Bracciano and Vittoria in Webster's *The White Devil*, our sympathies would undoubtedly lie with the lovers. In both of these plays, the metaphysical qualities of a passionate love affair enable the lovers to achieve a kind of spiritual salvation and avoid despair in societies that are devoid of the humanistic or spiritual values of which the lovers would appear to be in need.

But the love of Antony and Cleopatra or Bracciano and Vittoria may be argued to be what they claim for it – spiritually based and capable of elevating them beyond the plane of otherwise despicable humanity – though society brands it as being base and wilful and merely the manifestation of inordinate lust or sexual desire in each case. The speaker in 'I Want You' doesn't make any such claims for the quality of the love he offers or searches for. In fact, he admits that he's often chastised by women because, when it comes to 'true love' – notable by its absence from society anyway – 'I don't think about it'. He admits he is in pursuit of merely sexual fulfilment, and no matter with whom – the Queen of Spades[81] or the chambermaid[82] – it's all one, though the chambermaid gets her own tribute:

> She is good to me
> And there's nothing she doesn't see
> She knows where I'd like to be
> But it doesn't matter.

Each of those first three lines has its own sexual value. The further the song goes, in fact, the further away from the plea of 'I Want You' we move. By the time we arrive at the strange final stanza – the value of which lies more in how it sounds than what it says[83] – there's a hardness, even a viciousness in the intonation which seems to be directed less at the memory of the speaker's mistreatment of the 'dancing child' and more to the woman

[81] A character who, more than coincidentally, makes an appearance in the same *Spleen* by Baudelaire.
[82] Dylan prints 'my chambermaid' but has sung 'her chambermaid'.
[83] Dylan did not include this stanza in his 1978 concert performances of the song.

herself. The spitefulness of 'No, I wasn't very cute to him was I?' is aimed at her, as if by spoiling the child's enjoyment – by a mean, low and despicable act of taking away the child's source of joy and Blakeian innocence, his flute – the singer attempts to, and probably succeeds in, hurting the woman. By the song's conclusion, although he's still mouthing the same 'I want you', he's really saying 'I don't want you at all' and feeling disgusted that he ever felt the need to make the plea in the first place; maybe the chambermaid will do just as nicely.

If this interpretation of the feeling behind the song is acceptable, it tallies with much of the feeling expressed in *Blonde On Blonde's* other songs. These are very much songs of sex. There's the undeniable need, so strong as to be capable of making a man kneel and demean himself. But this comes with disgust, and the supplication, the flattery, all the armoury of seduction, give way to contempt and hateful condemnation of the women for ever possessing that original power over him, and even to a disgust for sex itself, with its irresistible yet degrading force.

'Fourth Time Around' depicts a sexual encounter that produces exactly these responses in its narrator. We don't have to read too much into the song to understand that the speaker solicits a woman into having sex with him, possibly unconscious of the fact that she's a prostitute. His attempted words of affection or feeling, which are not quoted, are brusquely and unsympathetically dismissed by the woman – 'don't waste your words, they're just lies' – and she simply proceeds about her business in a clinical and abruptly efficient way. Time's money after all and when she's through with him – in the superb pun of 'breaking my eyes' – and comes out with the really humbling 'What else you got left?', which suggests pitiful inadequacy and would surely crush its recipient, as it is meant to, she demands her payment.

As she's 'straighten[ing] her suit' – and it's probably hardly been disturbed – the speaker strikes a Chaplinesque stance, feigning bewilderment:

> So I forced my hands in my pockets
> And felt with my thumbs

And gallantly handed her
My very last piece of gum.

Whether or not he really did go into this whole thing with no inkling of the fact that 'everybody must give something back for something they get' and that 'gallantly' maybe does attest to his innocence, he soon learns the harsh reality:

She threw me outside
I stood in the dirt where ev'ryone walked.

His return to the woman's house in search of his forgotten shirt sees him pondering his experience – 'I tried to make sense' – before introducing a third person into the song, another woman, 'you' as opposed to 'she'. After finally infuriating the woman so much as to render her senseless, he leaves, turning to the second woman, who is apparently sexually crippled, paralysed, having both wheelchair and crutch, but who is able to offer him something of far greater value than sex – 'And you, you took me in, you loved me then'. As the song ends, sex is left far behind and the speaker asks, again with a superb pun, that the matter should not be allowed to impinge upon, and therefore by implication soil, a perfectly good relationship:

And I, I never took much
I never asked for your crutch
Now don't ask for mine.

Disgust for sex is, I think, fairly obvious in this song. It's there too in the final stanza of 'Leopard-Skin Pill-Box Hat', which is an extended joke at the expense of a woman whose absurd hat bears witness to her absurdly small mind. The song is a consistent, though admittedly fairly good-humoured, put-down. She probably deserves our pity as much as our scorn. But the cheapness of the sex-for-sex's sake encounter comes across at the end of the song:

Well, I see you got a new boyfriend
You know I never seen him before

> Well, I saw him
> Makin' love to you
> You forgot to close the garage door.

In those lines Dylan employs two euphemistic clichés – 'boyfriend' and 'makin' love' – brilliantly, and the offhand reference to the 'garage' brings out the sordid reality as well as any extended description could have done.

If *Blonde On Blonde* is a product of Bob Dylan's period of poetic and personal development, which is perfectly caught by the alchemical concept of 'nigredo' – 'a weariness of soul ... where disorientation and weakness and hopelessness are the quality of life' – this sexual disgust appears to be a major symptom. Maybe it's no coincidence that as Lear experiences his 'nigredo', he too sickens himself with thoughts of human sexuality:

> The wren goes to 't, and the small gilded fly
> does lecher in my sight...
> To 't, luxury, pell-mell!...
> Behold yond simpering dame,
> Whose face between her forks presages snow,
> that minces virtue, and does shake the head
> to hear of pleasure's name.
> The fitchew nor the soiled horse goes to 't
> with a more riotous appetite.
> Down from the waist they are centaurs,
> though women all above:
> But to the girdle do the gods inherit;
> beneath is all the fiends'.
> There's hell, there's darkness, there's the sulphurous pit –
> burning, scalding, stench, consumption!
> Fie, Fie, fie, pah! pah![84]

The 'simpering dame' held in such contempt here, could well be wearing her leopard-skin pill-box hat or could just as equally be Baby in 'Just Like A Woman'.

'Baby' – and what a sickeningly appropriate name that is – is just like the 'simpering dame' whose face 'minces virtue' and yet whose external appearance conceals a nature which is very

[84] *King Lear*, 4.6.

different. She adorns herself 'just like a woman' with all the paraphernalia of 'new clothes ... ribbons ... bows ... pearls' and even her 'amphetamine' as well as her fog – perhaps her unsuccessful attempt to assume a mystique, or maybe just the vagueness of mind which seems to go with all the other stuff. Dylan is coming down very hard here on women who play at being women and who thus deny all that the heroine of 'Love Minus Zero/No Limit' asserted. Not only are the adornments – curls as well – contributing elements to a fake picture, so are all her actions. Everything she does is not done as she herself does it, but very self-consciously as a woman does it, including making love and aching as well as taking and ultimately, tellingly, faking.

If Dylan's message to Ramona was to be true to herself, and if 'Love Minus Zero/No Limit' presented an idealised picture of a woman who had an elemental truth to her own nature, 'Just Like A Woman' presents Baby as the antithesis. Baby's propensity for faking it makes it impossible for her to realise her own nature:

> Baby can't be blessed
> Till she sees finally that she's like all the rest.

Only when she can acknowledge her common humanity, and thus move some way towards self-identification, will Baby finally be blessed with self-knowledge. Meantime, the speaker has involved himself with Baby who took him in when he'd fallen on hard times, when figuratively 'it was raining ... and I was dying of thirst ... I was hungry', but has now come to feel stifled by their apparently loveless sexual relationship. Baby, it is assumed, is no more capable of offering 'true love' than she is of anything else that could be described as 'true'. When the time has come for the speaker to 'quit', another woman – 'Queen Mary' (an equivalent to 'I Want You's Queen of Spades), who seems capable of offering something that cannot be faked, friendship – is there to be turned to, rather like the unidentified 'you' in 'Fourth Time Around'.

The two remaining songs on *Blonde On Blonde* are songs of parting, though the speaker's feelings are very different in each case. 'Most Likely You Go Your Way (and I'll Go Mine)' has elements of scornfulness and derision and generally bad feeling towards the woman, and the decision to end the affair is quite clearly the speaker's. We're given the woman's side of the 'discussion' only through him, though she seems to do her own share of pleading, at least until the last stanza. Tacked on to her reported words are caustic responses, designed to condemn her and the supposed truth of her pleas, whilst asserting the speaker's own strength of position and belief in himself:

> You say you disturb me
> And you don't deserve me
> But you know sometimes you lie
> You say you're shakin'
> And you're always achin'
> But you know how hard you try.

Her behaviour, in other words, is just like Baby's. The song may well begin where 'Just Like A Woman' leaves off. The sequence and continuity of thought is neat enough. The speaker has made his decision – 'I'm gonna let you pass' – pointing out that even if she can stoop to the pretence of pleading, he cannot any longer:

> I just can't do what I done before
> I just can't beg you anymore.

If she can lie and fake it, he cannot: 'Sometimes it gets so hard to care'. The final stanza indicates a change of tack by the woman. If lies can't persuade him to stay, maybe honesty will prevail. But truth and untruth have become so blurred that by now he just doesn't know what to believe:

> You say you're sorry
> For tellin' stories
> That you know I believe are true.

When she confesses that she has 'some other kinda lover' and tells him that his (the speaker's) kisses 'are not like his' (the other lover's), there's a double ambiguity. Firstly, the 'other kinda lover' implies in one way that he's not *really* a lover, only a 'kinda' lover – perhaps someone with whom she's had casual, non-committal sex – but the phrase can be heard as 'some other kinder lover'. In what way his kisses are different is open to the interpretation of the speaker or of the woman. It's all very much in keeping with the duplicity of her nature. Even when she is telling supposed truths – confessing – there is ambiguity, and when she's confessing to untruths, she may well be lying. The decision has been made though, and her efforts to retain his presence, let alone his affection, come to nothing. In the chorus with which the song concludes, the speaker is fully confident of his own strength – 'time will tell just who has fell and who's been left behind' – fully convinced, it would appear, of his own righteousness.

The same is true of the speaker in 'She's Your Lover Now'. This great (and unfortunately unreleased) song has an extra touch of complexity in that it is addressed to two people simultaneously – the singer's ex-lover and her new boyfriend. The woman is trying to make it up with the singer, who tries to put the break-up of their affair into some kind of perspective whilst the other man, who cuts something of an absurd figure throughout, does nothing to restrain her, but seems to smile complacently and apathetically. Having come to realise just what he's taken on, the new lover probably hopes that the singer will take her back. There's little chance of that, however, and the singer continues to remind him of his obligations – 'she's your lover now!' – with a grin of his own non-involvement.

It begins with the singer's memories of their parting: 'The scene was so crazy, wasn't it?' It was painful enough, and the singer adds, cynically, 'Pain sure brings out the best in people, doesn't it?' The responsibility is equally shared, it appears. The singer admits that he contributed to the affair's destruction, but asks:

> Why'd you have to treat me so bad?
> Did it have to be that way?

He then turns his attention to the other lover, pointing out that the woman is 'comin' on so strange', that 'she's got her iron chain', and adding that 'somebody had better explain' but that it's no longer his responsibility. As the song reaches its (printed) climax, the woman begins to run her finger up his sleeve and again her new lover simply disregards it. 'Ain't there nothin' you can say?' the singer yells, warning him that her behaviour is going to get stranger and stranger the more he fends off her advances: 'You'd better do something quick, she's your lover now'.

It's a delightful, funny song, full of closely observed truths about human behaviour and human nature. But it doesn't totally fit with the tone of the songs included on *Blonde On Blonde*. Its (probable) place was occupied instead by a song that shares some common elements of structure and tune – 'One of Us Must Know (Sooner or Later)'. David Downing's comment on this song in *Future Rock* is telling:

> Between these two who think they know it all, and those who know they know nothing, there are the two lovers of 'One of Us Must Know', both caring, both trying to get close to each other, but both blind to the other's experience. Magritte painted a picture of a couple kissing, hoods over their heads, and called it *The Lovers*. Dylan's couple are likewise unaware of the hoods covering them, and it is this unawareness which destroys their relationship.

Whether or not the speaker meant to behave as he did towards her, her desertion of him is implicitly justified, even though he claims that she over-reacted. What she took 'so personal' was an apparent affront; 'I didn't realise how young you were' he sings, somewhat condescendingly. But although he may have 'never really meant to do you any harm', the 'really' indicates that games are being played, which is borne out by a line from the chorus: 'You just did what you're supposed to do' (just as Baby would have done). While he still claims 'I really did try to get close to you', there's enough in the song to suggest that he too was playing a game – a kind of jealousy game – that backfired:

> When I saw you say 'goodbye' to your friend and smile
> I thought that it was well understood

That you'd be comin' back in a little while
I didn't know that you were sayin' 'goodbye' for good.

If 'regret' doesn't come across too strongly here, hidden beneath the words is 'loneliness', the symptom and product of yet another failed relationship. Not seeing beyond yourself is a problem. As long as you remain a prisoner of your own ego, then the other person remains a projected fantasy (Jung's 'anima'), which is a part of you; your self-preservation depends on your control of such fantasies. In its depiction of possessiveness, jealousy, and unreality, 'One of Us Must Know' shows two people seeking to control their own fantasies in order to preserve their egos.

Which leaves us, and Bob Dylan, precisely where? Well, it leaves us with an album that exhibits pictures of the emptiness, pain, bewilderment, lack of spiritual value, lack of love, disgust, contempt, duplicity, pathos, bathos and above all the loneliness that can exist within relationships in the same way that they exist within society.

Blonde On Blonde presents reflections of a society that lacks value or direction, and which confines the individual whilst denying them their individuality – a society that confronts Dylan with chaos rather than order and forces him to accept its chaos, while offering nothing to believe in. It's a whirlpool of madness, the only escape from which seems to be in the temporary refuges of drugs or sex. Drugs demand their own price. 'Pledging My Time's singer has 'a poison headache ... I can hardly breathe', while he can say 'I feel alright' and, if things get so bad that the ambulance is called, well, 'somebody got lucky'. The kid in Mobile has his mind 'strangled up', 'Absolutely Sweet Marie's narrator finishes up with 'the fever down in my pockets' and eventually in jail, and so on. The drug references are scattered liberally throughout almost all of the songs.

Sex offers no solutions either, merely presenting more problems and a different kind of soul-destroying trap. The album is without love. It presents sexuality from different angles but consistently as a source of dissatisfaction. Many songs express a contempt for women, but the contempt is the product of self-disgust. The songs present relationships breaking up for many and various reasons: lack of communication, lack of understanding, lack of sympathy, lack of compassion, lack of value and, most of all, lack of love. Many songs present the distances that exist between lovers and between former lovers. There is an all-pervasive loneliness, which is almost a sickness.

Blonde On Blonde is an album of sickness and in its songs Dylan portrays his own sickness, which his art set out to accept and reflect. His growing belief in his ability to transcend the ego has come to nothing for he's as self-conscious as ever. The album needs to be considered against the biographical background. With the development of his wild, whirling images and his mercury music, amplified to distortion just as the words are sung and stretched to distort their sound and the language is hammered and forged to present an antic perception of reality, Dylan seems to set himself on Arthur Rimbaud's path, which demanded:

> d'arriver à l'inconnu par le dérèglement de tous les sens. Les souffrances sont énormes, mais il faut être fort.

> [Reaching the unknown by the derangement of all the senses. The sufferings are enormous, but one has to be strong.][85]

Dylan took his songs and musicians on exhausting tours, first in America, then in Australia and Europe. To keep going, he relies on amphetamines and turns to mind-altering drugs to expand his consciousness. He pushes himself to the point of mental breakdown and physical exhaustion, driving himself head first into the twilight zone where the boundaries of sanity and insanity are lost. He becomes a victim of his own visions.

Furthermore, he becomes trapped by the role his audience have forced upon him. He surveys the world from a 'bubble of ego'[86] which has been formed by his star status. Rather than run from it, he has run straight into it, as he unconsciously presents in his songs. Dylan is given the role of a twentieth-century messiah,

[85] Letter to Georges Izambard, 13th May 1871.
[86] Joan Baez's phrase from her book *Daybreak*, Dial Press, 1968.

a bearer of truth, delivering his own parables, offering insight without salvation or promises of paradise. The chaos without becomes a chaos within. The Titanic sailing at dawn now applies to Dylan's own lifestyle. In his biography of Dylan, Anthony Scaduto quotes 'an Australian actress':

> Something was happening to him that was beyond his control. I think he was frightened by what people expected of him, what they had begun to think of him.[87]

David Bowie's *Rise and Fall Of Ziggy Stardust* presents a perceptive cameo of the process which Dylan became a victim of:

> Making love with his ego
> Ziggy sucked up into his mind
> Like a leper messiah.

By mid-1966, Dylan's audience was anticipating the inevitable, and Dylan had never been further away from realisation of his inner self, nor had he ever been so powerless to do anything about it.

[87] Anthony Scaduto, *Bob Dylan*, Abacus, 1972.

10. A Painted Face on a Trip Down Suicide Road

> I was on the road for almost five years. It wore me down.
> I was on drugs – a lot of things ... and I don't want to live
> that way any more ... I'm just waiting for a better time.

— Bob Dylan, *Rolling Stone*, 29th November 1969.

Before going on to consider the songs written in the months after Bob Dylan's motorcycle accident, and the songs that were to make up the *John Wesley Harding* album of 1968, I'm going to return briefly to *King Lear* and then take two songs – 'Dirge' and 'Shelter from the Storm' – out of chronological context. Both songs are pertinent here, for both are retrospective analyses of Dylan's situation by the summer of 1966. But first back to Shakespeare.

At the play's beginning, Lear knows exactly who he is: King of Britain, not simply by right of inheritance but by Divine Right, a theory still accepted by Shakespeare's audience. His words, actions and decisions are to be accepted by his court and people because his authority is beyond human question. He is an absolute monarch who has been absolute monarch for almost all of his long life. But Lear is old – fourscore and upward – and, it must be admitted, a little foolish. His power still manifests itself in flashes of majestic authority; in the opening scene he divides his kingdom into three pieces merely by drawing his finger across a map. He is further able to banish – in this case, his daughter and his most faithful retainer – with a word and a wave of his hand.

But the major action of the opening scene is not the division of land nor the banishments that succeed it, but Lear's abdication. Lear has his reasons: he is old and weary of the burdens of kingship. He tells his court that his predivision of his kingdom into three not-quite-equal parts is so 'that future strife may be prevented now'. This in itself is evidence of his folly, but the main point is this: Lear is 'King Lear'. A king is the archetype of human potential. In renouncing his kingship, Lear renounces his identity. As he hands over the 'coronet' that symbolises his monarchy, he insists 'only we still retain the name, and all the additions to a king' and announces that the 'sway, revenue execution of the rest' is now equally shared by Cornwall, Albany and their wives – Lear's daughters Regan and Goneril.

Lear is attempting to do something that, by definition, cannot be done. If he is king, he cannot both give away his right to authority – to respect and obedience – and yet retain them: he cannot give away his kingship and continue to be 'King Lear'. Yet this is what he attempts to do. Lear is to become painfully aware of the folly of such a scheme as events unfold, but the major consideration that causes him as much discomfort as any other – including even his daughters' ingratitude – is that he abdicates not just power, but with it locus and, the main point here, identity.

Lear was born to be 'King Lear'. Take away the 'King' and what is left? It's a question asked of him by his Fool in an attempt to get his master to face the truth, painful as it may be:

> Now thou art an O without a figure. I am better now than thou art. I am a fool, thou art nothing.[88]

The lesson comes hard:

> Does any here know me? Why, this is not Lear. Doth Lear walk thus? Speak thus? Where are his eyes?

With an identity crisis exacerbated by confrontations with his daughters whose sole intent is to deny the power Lear considers it his right to retain, Lear is pushed further towards madness. His daughters effectually banish him to endure a storm of such elemental ferocity that is as bad as anyone can ever remember. Even the wild beasts are in shelter. Lear is exposed ranting and raving, suffering but learning, coming to terms with the extent of his power, with the true nature of his relationship with nature, understanding gradually who he is if he is not king. Stripping

[88] *King Lear*, 1.4.

himself, he discovers that he is mirrored by Poor Tom, the naked Bedlam beggar, as he recognises essential humanity in Tom and in himself:

> Thou art the thing itself: Unaccommodated man is no more but such a poor, bare, forked animal as thou art.[89]

It is the first time in Lear's life that he must acknowledge that he is a human being and recognise what it is to be one. Reality has previously been concealed by his 'clothing', which symbolically indicates status or role, while concealing the truth of nature. Lear's role as king fed his ego; total obedience is its own form of flattery, which begets pride, which often begets folly. But folly must remain beyond the criticism of all but the licensed Fool, as Kent discovers to his cost.

Lear's role as king meant that he was consumed by his monarchic ego-consciousness. His essential nature remained hidden from him until the kingship, flattery and ego were removed. The purgation in *King Lear* does not result from the storm, which simply wets and freezes him, but coincides with the worst the storm can inflict upon him.

As has been argued, in 1966, at the time of his composition of the songs for *Blonde On Blonde*, and during his world tour, Dylan was having his own identity problems. The situation had become almost schizophrenic. An initial problem of identity came with Dylan's denial of his background. Robert Zimmerman became Bob Dylan when he became a performer. In the first part of 1964 – the year in which his popularity began to skyrocket, helped along by his guest appearances before Joan Baez's ready-made and receptive audiences – Dylan wrote, 'I "expose" myself every time I step out on the stage.'[90]

But later that year, when Dylan became established as a solo performer, he began to acknowledge a dichotomy between his 'true' identity and what he presented to his audience – or perhaps what was perceived by his audience. After performing 'Gates

---

[89] *King Lear*, 3.4.
[90] *Some Other Kinds of Songs.*

of Eden' in his Hallowe'en concert in 1964, Dylan announced, 'Don't let that scare ya! It's just Halloween. I have my Bob Dylan mask on.' The comment brought laughter and applause, but few, if any, could have realised its importance. Dylan must have already felt that the process that was to make him a star through the next eighteen months – a process Dylan willingly accepted and which Scaduto, somewhat facilely, argues was the main force driving Dylan on at this time – was beginning to take control, not just of his career, but of his very identity. As time passed, as Dylan achieved more and more success, earning more money, critical acclaim, respect and gaining more influence and power, his ego became dominated by the persona of 'Bob Dylan – the star' and the essential 'Bob Dylan – the alter ego' became recessive.[91]

A myth grew around Dylan as 1965 became 1966. A star who had been hailed as a poet and a prophet became a 'messiah' in the media and consequently in the public eye. The greater the deranging influence of touring and drug-taking became, the more the myth took control. To all intents and purposes, the alter ego ceased to exist and Bob Dylan's sole identity became the ego-dominated 'star' persona, 'Bob Dylan – the messiah'.

'Dirge', a song from the 1974 album *Planet Waves*, is an interesting autobiographical retrospective on the situation in 1966 after Dylan's world tour. The eight years of hindsight allows Dylan perspectives that maybe even the songs on *The Basement Tapes* lacked, even though these songs, as I will argue, attempt to summarise and analyse the process, and its effects, which (almost) claimed Dylan as permanent victim.

A 'dirge' is a funeral song, sung in commemoration of the dead. The 'dead' subject of Dylan's 'Dirge' is the star-persona of 1966 – an incarnation that caused Bob Dylan to approach the brink of self-destruction:

> I hate myself for lovin' you and the weakness that it showed
> You were just a painted face on a trip down Suicide Road.

---

[91] Dylan explores this dichotomy in his film *Renaldo and Clara*, where the characters of Renaldo and Bob Dylan represent these two selves respectively, Renaldo being played by Bob Dylan himself.

In *Modern Man in Search of a Soul*, Jung wrote, 'A great work of art is like a dream; for all its apparent obviousness, it does not explain itself and is never unequivocal.' 'Dirge' is far from being unequivocal. It can be heard as a song to Sara – the reverse side of the coin to 'Wedding Song'. Nevertheless, the 'painted face' recalls the idea of identity concealed by the mask of the performer, and there are several images of public performance in the song: 'The stage was set, the lights went out' and 'the curtain fell' or 'I went out on Lower Broadway' or 'man … acting out his folly'. 'On a trip' is deliberately ambivalent, conveying both the sense of 'heading towards' as well as alluding to the drugs that were keeping Dylan on course down 'Suicide Road' in the middle of 1966.

Dylan speaks of 'loving' the role that demanded the 'painted face', though in retrospect this was symptomatic of 'weakness'. Time has brought both recovery and experience, following escape from what can now be seen as a 'foolish game we played'. 'I'm glad the curtain fell' he sings, for what was abandoned was a 'hollow place' devoid of substance and spirituality, a place of martyrs lamenting the folly of their own demises, and of those who have yet to achieve martyrdom – 'angels' who continued to 'play' the 'foolish game' 'with sin'.

The process that brought Dylan, and *so* many others, to the 'hollow place' began worthily enough with 'songs of freedom' which attempted to expose the 'naked truth' of 'man forever stripped'. But the singer of the songs of freedom became 'a slave in orbit', trapped in processes beyond his control. The 'orbit' – the eternal cycle of the existence of the public performer, of the star-persona on the endless round of concerts, interviews, sessions – is portrayed at length in *The Basement Tapes* songs. It is inescapable, or at least seemingly so, and not only takes away and continues to deny the freedom of the artist, but stifles his creative power and represses his energies: 'Like a slave in orbit, he's beaten 'til he's tame'.

Such a price is too great for what, after all, is only 'a moment's glory'. 'It's a dirty, rotten shame' is not simply dismissive; each word – dirty, rotten, shame – should be taken at face value and not heard simply as constituent parts of a clichéd phrase.

Escape from the 'orbit' and its slavery was achieved – though at a cost. The price is high – 'loneliness', 'solitude', the traumas of alienation from self – but the expenditure is justified: 'At least I'm out of debt'.

The star doesn't make himself, of course. He is produced by the acclamation of the audience. But he who has escaped the shackles of stardom has no thanks for his former audience – he is strangely devoid of any kind of feeling for them; in fact:

> Can't recall a useful thing you ever did for me
> 'Cept pat me on the back one time when I was on my knees
> We stared into each other's eyes 'til one of us would break
> No use to apologise, what difference would it make?

It is a great stanza – an unparalleled expression of the relationship between performer and public, who in their praising are contributing to the destruction of the artist, just as the flatterers in Lear's court produced the foolish egoism that proved the king's undoing. In David Bowie's *Ziggy Stardust*, it was, in truth, the 'kids' who 'killed the man' – though he is identified by the media as a 'rock'n'roll suicide'. The stanza quoted above is far from unequivocal and could be heard as Dylan coming face to face with himself – looking into the mirror and seeing the past not that darkly: 'We stared into each other's eyes 'til one of us would break'.

The lines could refer to the emotional nightmare he encountered at the time – the conflict of a personality split, of a superstar who was meant to be an anti-hero figure, not a personality cult. Such conflict, in conjunction with the exhaustion of the 'race', brings Dylan to his knees, physically and mentally. The image is to recur in 'Please, Mrs. Henry': 'I'm down on my knees'.

'Dirge' concludes with a reiteration of the opening line – 'I hate myself for loving you' – and the singer ends with 'but I should get over that', the self-hatred, that is, not the self-love, which he has, thankfully, already gone well beyond.

In 'Shelter from the Storm', a song from the 1975 studio album *Blood on the Tracks* that Dylan introduced in 1978 concerts as 'the story of my life', Dylan employs the image of the 'storm' to express the state of 1966 existence – the madness of the inescapable 'orbit' of the touring rock'n'roll star. As persona took the identity of person, 'Bob Dylan' became 'a creature void of form' with neither shape nor home, wandering alone in a cold and hostile 'world of steel-eyed death' (on the points of silver needles). At times he becomes the hunted – the 'wanted man' – the outlaw pursued remorselessly, just as Poor Tom is 'whipped from tithing to tithing and stock-punished and imprisoned' in *King Lear*, forced 'through fire and through flame, through ford and whirlpool, o'er bog and quagmire' and exposed to 'the pelting of this pitiless storm':

> I was burned out from exhaustion, buried in the hail
> Poisoned in the bushes an' blown out on the trail
> Hunted like a crocodile, ravaged in the corn.

The 'crocodile' simile is striking. In ancient Egyptian mythology, the crocodile god Sebek was the symbol of maximum creative energy. Clearly there is a correspondence with the image of artist-creator as 'misdemeanour outlaw, chained and cheated by pursuit' (from 'Chimes of Freedom'). The pursuit is ironically led by those who would acclaim him, though whose praise and flattery would force an identity on to the unsuspecting artist they would have as a messiah:

> In a little hilltop village, they gambled for my clothes
> I bargained for salvation an' they gave me a lethal dose
> I offered up my innocence and got repaid with scorn.

Dylan uses the 'hilltop' image of achieved success here as he does in many other songs (including 'It Takes a Lot to Laugh, It Takes a Train to Cry', 'Minstrel Boy' or 'When I Paint My Masterpiece', as well as others). Success brings adulation which is destructive – the image of spoon-fed 'poison' is reiterated; that which is offered to feed or nourish is the source of demise. The artist, who has only 'innocence' to offer in his pursuit of eternal truth or beauty, is abused and mistreated. He is stripped of his innocence and exposed to forces beyond his control, which hinder his artistic progress and clog with 'mud' the road of excess which leads to the palace of wisdom, or to individuation. The same forces invert values – 'blackness' becomes 'a virtue' – and are ultimately capable of overwhelming a creature whose 'form' they have already annihilated.

The song's main purpose is to speak of the part played by Sara in his escape from 'the storm' and of the subsequent breakdown of his relationship with her, and I'll return to it later.

The 'way out' of the storm of the madness of rock superstardom in 1966 was provided by Bob Dylan's motorcycle accident on 29th July 1966. The lyrics of 'Pledging My Time' proved to be ironically prophetic: 'Somebody got lucky, but it was an accident'.

Whether Dylan 'got lucky' or not is a matter of definition. The accident certainly allowed him – forced him – to stop the merry-go-round, cut down the drug intake and recover the strength to begin again to find himself. Just as Hamlet faced death on the ship to England, escaped it through 'providence', and returned to Denmark with new perspectives on his own significance, Dylan reached the edge of the abyss of his own life in 1966, peeked over the edge and 'got lucky' just before he plunged into the waters of oblivion.

The songs written and performed with The Band in 1967 whilst Dylan was recuperating from the injuries sustained in the accident – and the effects of his lifestyle immediately before it – are meditations upon and reflections of that lifestyle, its values and its effects on him. It's as if, through these songs and those on *John Wesley Harding*, Dylan needed to put the past into some kind of perspective to prepare himself to make progress in his art and efforts to reach, through that art, an understanding of himself. The songs are a part of Dylan's own purgation. In ridding himself of former values, now recognised as false, and of the ego-centric star identity, Dylan also sheds the sound of his electric music. If *Blonde On Blonde* or the 1966 concert music was the music of excess which failed to take Dylan to the palace of wisdom, all superfluities are disposed of on *The Basement Tapes*. Just as Lear stripped in order to recognise himself, so the Basement songs present Bob Dylan standing naked and ashamed, as a man who 'betrayed both himself and his audience in pursuit of the chimera of success amidst corruption'.[92]

'Minstrel Boy', possibly a later song but included with the Basement songs in *Writing and Drawings*, offers a glimpse of Dylan as 'minstrel boy' at the time of *Blonde On Blonde*. Ironically naming himself 'Lucky', the second verse is literal enough:

> Lucky's been drivin' a long, long time
> And now he's stuck on top of the hill
> With twelve forward gears, it's been a long hard climb
> And with all of them ladies, though, he's lonely still.

The word 'stuck' is a familiar reflection of the 'exitlessness' already spoken of as a feature of the 1966 songs. 'Top of the hill' as an image of the summit of ambition is an old friend too, having been anticipated in 'It Takes a Lot to Laugh, It Takes a Train to Cry'. There Dylan considered the ominous possibility of 'dying' on top of the hill but expressed consolation in the feeling that at least his music – his 'baby' – would survive him. The phrase 'it's been a long hard climb' reappears in 'When I Paint My Masterpiece' – another retrospective career-analysis song – while the fourth line quoted above relates exactly to the themes expounded in the songs on *Blonde On Blonde* – 'all of them ladies' and yet still the pervading loneliness and soul-devouring spleen.

The Basement songs proper, though, present a portrait of the manic months 'on top of the hill'. 'Million Dollar Bash' sets the scene: its lunatic parade of characters, Bob Dylan included, tear down the road in pursuit of fame and fortune. Life is hectic and meaningless, yet the lure of the 'million dollar bash' always produces squeals of delighted anticipation ('OOH baby! OOH-EE') and the chase continues. For Dylan the chase was the life of a rock star on the road, with its absurd yet seemingly interminable round of concerts, interviews, recordings, photographs – 'Don't forget to flash!' (smiles for the camera) – personal appearances, the eternal 'orbit' of slavery sung of in 'Dirge', a life that deprives the

---

[92] David Downing, *Future Rock*.

singer of home, the realities of friendship, trust, faith and almost, eventually, sanity. There's an awareness here that the demands of such an existence are too great. The singer acknowledges, 'I'm hittin' it too hard' then gives us an understanding of what's involved:

> I get up in the mornin'
> But it's too early to wake
> First it's hello, goodbye
> Then push and then crash.

There may well be a cynical smile with the last word quoted above, but the lure of that ultimate gig, the last word in a star's ambition, and the million dollar bash is too great to be resisted. The burden borne down this road to madness includes a whole host of hangers-on – 'everybody from right now to over there and back' – and if Dylan has already hinted at his awareness of his inability to survive these kinds of pressures, the final verse presents the first indications of the inevitable insanity amidst the turbulence and traumas of striving after goals that are ultimately to be recognised as false:

> Well I looked at my watch
> I looked at my wrist
> Punched myself in the face
> With my fist
> I took my potatoes
> Down to be mashed
> Then I made it over
> To that million dollar bash.

'Long Distance Operator' presents another view of the insufferable pressures that accompany international fame. Here Dylan uses a metaphor, a symbol, of which he's particularly fond: the telephone represents his role as communicator – as a poet, as a writer of songs and as a performer. Unhappily, Dylan's attempts to communicate have produced results that, if not entirely unexpected or indeed unlooked for, are nevertheless almost impossible to come to terms with: 'there are thousands in the phone booth, thousands at the gate'. The pressures build, 'this phone booth's on fire, it's getting hot inside' and 'everybody wants to be my friend', until finally he loses control of his own destiny: 'I believe I'm stranglin' on this telephone wire'.[93]

Elsewhere Dylan voices the complaint about the demands the public place on him. 'Mixed Up Confusion' shows a very early awareness of the fact that 'there's too many people and they're all too hard to please' – a sentiment that recurs in the foreword to *Writings and Drawings*:

> If I can't please everybody
> I might as well not please nobody at all
> There's but so many people
> An' I just can't please them all.

The extent to which an artist has to compromise in his private life as well as in his public one is ironically portrayed in 'Don't Ya Tell Henry'. 'Henry' both here and in 'Please, Mrs. Henry'[94] is a symbol for Dylan's public, and the 'image' of the Bob Dylan they know must be permanently maintained. The alter ego – Bob Dylan the ordinary human being who is just like anyone else, who has simple pleasures and occupies himself in doing 'normal' things with his time – must be suppressed and kept from the public at all costs, lest the image be tarnished or destroyed:

> I went down to the beanery at half past twelve
> A-lookin' around just to see myself
> I spotted a horse and a donkey too
> I looked for a cow and I saw me a few
> They said, 'Don't ya tell Henry...'

---

[93] 'It Takes a Lot to Laugh, It Takes a Train to Cry' also concerns itself with this communication breakdown. The singer has something simple to communicate – 'Wintertime is coming, the windows are filled with frost' – but there is a barrier between himself and his audience: 'I went to tell everybody but I could not get across'.

[94] David Bowie also uses 'Henry' in this sense on his *Rise and Fall of Ziggy Stardust* album in conjunction with the aforementioned symbol of the telephone. As the pressures of fame build, Ziggy the star cries: 'Oh leave me alone ... Oh Henry get off the phone' in 'Suffragette City', which helps to reinforce the links between the character of Ziggy Stardust and Dylan in 1966.

Dylan being forced to be 'lookin' around just to see myself' is thus expressing what I've referred to as his identity crisis – a state of affairs that in 1975 Dylan analysed profoundly and wisely in *Renaldo & Clara* in which he plays Renaldo and in which Ronnie Hawkins plays 'Bob Dylan'. The film shows the process of the separation of these identities and the problems which thus arise.

'Please, Mrs. Henry' and 'Yea! Heavy and a Bottle of Bread' express a plea and a yearning respectively for the release from the demands placed upon Dylan, and contain glimpses of those pressures. In 'Please, Mrs. Henry' he has enough awareness to be able to admit that he's taken it all too far:

> I've been sniffin' too many eggs
> Talkin' to too many people
> Drinkin' too many kegs.

And again there's that vital awareness of the inevitable consequences:

> I'm groanin' in a hallway
> Pretty soon I'll be mad.

The 'hallway' is the twilight zone, where a decision about future direction has to be made. There's no doubt that he's pleading to be allowed to disentangle himself from the pressures of the mayhem he had so fervently embraced: 'I'm down on my knees' both in pleading and in exhaustion, 'there's only so much I can do'.

'Yea! Heavy and a Bottle of Bread' presents a sketch of the endlessness of the road. The repetition of the first verse as the last conveys the infinity of the circle. From a town that is 'just brown' to Wichita, to California and then back on the bus – a 'heavy' existence and the 'bottle' and the 'pipe' and the 'bread' to keep the show on the road. 'Don't be slow' is repeated, as are all the final lines of the verses, indicating the repetitiveness of the process, or the fact that no one is communicating too well. Certainly the 'poor little chauffeur' can't stand the pace.

'Lo and Behold!' takes us further down the road, to 'San Anton' ... Pittsburgh ... Tennessee ... back to Pittsburgh' and Dylan's 1971 retrospection 'When I Paint My Masterpiece' broadens the horizons as far as Rome and Brussels. But even if the towns are different, the situation is always the same: groupies in hotel rooms, each with her own claim to fame ('Botticelli's niece'), hours spent 'dodgin' lions' – possibly from martyrdom – or 'wastin' time' or being wasted. The 'lions' that need to be dodged might well be those voracious newspapermen who have 'to be held down by big police', but there's no escape from the public. Escape from one place, arrive in another and 'everyone was there to greet me when I stepped inside'. The song has its own lament:

> Sailin' round the world in a dirty gondola
> Oh, to be back in the land of Coca-Cola!

It's an acknowledgment of the fact that the road to fame and fortune leads only to dissatisfaction, offering false values – 'I ran on the hilltop following a pack of wild geese' – and even despair – 'I almost cried'. The song's title, and the concluding 'Someday, everything is gonna be different' may sound like optimism, but beneath the surface there's an awareness that the 'masterpiece' never will get painted. It's a neat touch to conclude *Writings and Drawings* with the song's lyrics.

As Dylan sang in 'Minstrel Boy' and later in 'Tangled Up in Blue', each year finds him 'still on the road',[95] the idea of never being able to escape – that wherever he happens to be there'll be newspapermen or clergymen or young girls or big police – is beautifully captured in another, later song, 'Wanted Man':

> If ever you see me comin' and if you know who I am
> Don't you breathe it to nobody 'cause you know I'm on
> the lam.

'Wanted Man' takes us on a whirlwind tour of the United States, listing the towns where the singer is 'wanted' and, wherever he is,

[95] The line 'me, I'm still on the road' in 'Tangled Up in Blue' is lifted straight from 'Train to Anaheim,' a 1973 song by David Blue which has a great deal in common with Dylan's.

'there's somebody set to grab me anywhere that I might be'. It's a neat presentation of the outlaw rock-star persona.

Two further laments in the Basement collection are 'Tears of Rage' and 'I'm Not There'. In 'Tears of Rage' the lament is twofold; each verse concludes 'we're so alone' or 'we're so low'. The song also contains the question 'Why must I always be the thief?', another example of Dylan's 'poet' symbol.

'I'm Not There' is remarkable. Available only as an unofficial recording, it is a Dylan 'work-tape'. Dylan improvises only vaguely realised lyrics against a hauntingly beautiful melody. The remarkable thing about it is that even though, for the most part, the lyrics are not lyrics at all but sounds, the performance is moving and emotionally overflowing. It is Dylan's saddest song, and one of his greatest vocal performances, for he catches feeling without words. From the lyrics that can be made sense of, it is possible to understand that the song is an expression of grief at the fact that the singer's lifestyle, ever hurrying, ever moving on, has taken its toll of very valuable personal relationships. There may be autobiographical glimpses at the girls he was forced, by the demands of his career, to leave behind him – Suze Rotolo, Echo Helstrom, Joan Baez – and though it all comes with the acknowledgment 'I'm not there, I'm gone', it's Dylan who has left and there's nothing he can do about getting back, except wish:

> I wish I was there beside her...
> I wish I was there to help her...

There are brief eulogies – a girl who was his 'prize forsaken angel', and one who is 'gone like the rainbow that was shinin' yesterday' – but the truth is that he can't stay behind: 'The race is much too fast to stay on'. If he remembers that on his leaving 'she cried both day and night', it only makes the pain harder to bear. But the race towards that million dollar bash was 'all about temptation' and his final piece of advice is merely 'don't trust anyone'.

In three of the Basement songs, Dylan presents cynically comic self-portraits of the super rock star, the character whose ego dominates to the exclusion of all other awareness, until he is blind to his own folly and pride and he believes in his own myth – that his powers are messianic. 'Tiny Montgomery' is about to hit town:

> Now ev'ry boy and girl's
> Gonna get their bang
> 'Cause Tiny Montgomery's
> Gonna shake that thing.

The swagger and the sexual cock-sureness here comes across not only in the lyrics but in Dylan's superb drawling delivery of them. Just for Tiny to 'say hello' is something for which the audience should be eternally grateful:

> Tell everybody
> Down in ol' Frisco
> That Tiny Montgomery's comin'
> Down to say hello.

The fact that the song's subject is enormously 'tiny' is a neat joke, but the madness, aimlessness and futility of the road he's on is presented in a long list of imperatives:

> Take it on down
> And watch it grow
> Play it low
> And pick it up
> Take it on in
> In a plucking cup.

In 'Lo and Behold!', Dylan becomes a little more complex. There are two distinct voices representing the two aspects of identity that are at war within. The swaggering, boastful, egocentric performer who can afford to bestow liberal gifts with the money he's made – 'a herd of moose' for example – blows into town in true Tiny Montgomery fashion. There's even an arrogance in the tricksy rhyming:

Now I come in on a Ferris wheel
An' boys, I sure was slick
I come in like a ton of bricks
Laid a few tricks on 'em.

Simultaneously, there's the voice of the alter ego who sees through the vainglory and falseness and desires to rid himself of the lifestyle and his other 'self', of whom he is ashamed. The 'shame' is expressed when this character is asked his name, which would identify the star-persona of which the alter ego is ashamed. The pleas, heard elsewhere, become a little more impassioned as the chorus concludes 'get me outta here'.

The goals the song lists are recognised as false and afford no kind of satisfaction; no squeals of delight here for the idea of the million dollar bash, merely contempt: 'Gonna save my money and rip it up!' And there's a yearning to return to a humbler but presumably more meaningful way of life: 'I'm goin' down to Tennessee, get me a truck 'r somethin''.[96]

The song ends with the statement of intention to slow down, to take a rest – 'count up to thirty' – but the idea of escape becomes temporary and the final 'gonna thread up!', which takes us back to the drugs imagery, comes across as a boast that should appall rather than impress. Thus the ego regains its ascendancy.

The singer's awareness of the folly of a crazy, drug-driven lifestyle is admitted once more in 'Goin' to Acapulco', but the admission is accompanied by an acknowledgement of the inherent difficulties of breaking away: 'It's a wicked life, but what the hell'. Acapulco represents the 'fun' of life in the fast lane: 'Goin' to Acapulco, goin' on the run'. The singer uses his 'fast white faithful steed' to get there too – very ominous.

The 'Tiny Montgomery' character – the 'painted face' aspect of Dylan's personality that has almost completely taken over from the inner, more spiritually inclined persona – is portrayed again as the mighty 'Quinn the Eskimo', who seems to have the potential to rid everybody of their 'despair' simply by his arrival in town. 'Every girl and boy' reappear – they're clearly big Quinn/Dylan

[96] Lines which refer to Elvis Presley's occupation before he got caught up in the pop process.

fans. Quinn is presented as a messiah: 'everybody's gonna jump for joy' when he 'gets here', the 'pigeons gonna run to him', and 'everybody's gonna wanna doze' or possibly a 'dose' of what he's offering. What he's offering is salvation from the despair of a meaningless existence – 'building monuments ... jotting down notes ... feeding pigeons'. The narrator is just one of the masses – 'I like to do just like the rest, I like my sugar sweet' – very ordinary. But Quinn represents the extraordinary. He's a character they'd all like to be and who is worshipped for *what* he is, not who: 'You'll not see nothing like the mighty Quinn'.

If some of the Basement songs portray the mania of life 'on the road' – the futile quest after false ideals, the endless, hectic pursuit that will only result in the traps of dissatisfaction, shame and nausea – and if other songs voice the alter ego's pleas for release or hopes of escape and alternative, more meaningful lifestyles, there are a couple of others that suggest the whole bizarre trip is going to provide its own conclusion, which will be sudden and final.

'This Wheel's On Fire' and 'Down in the Flood' are both expressions of this idea. The latter begins with predictions of the 'catastrophe' that will put an end to it all: 'crash on the levee'. The 'crash' will effectively remove everybody's 'best friend' and the song emphasizes both the inevitability and the finality of such a conclusion:

> You're gonna have to find yourself
> Another best friend, somehow.

'This Wheel's On Fire' has an even more appropriate image of the 'crash':

> This wheel's on fire
> Rolling down the road
> Best notify my next of kin
> This wheel shall explode!

'This Wheel's On Fire' is of further interest in that it goes some way towards indicating, through a complexity of tenses, some kind of regenerative experience that will follow the explosion.

In writing the song, Dylan looks back on something that has already happened, yet the persona who narrates the song is looking forward to when it will happen. In the first stanza, the lines 'You know that we shall meet again, if your memory serves you well' are antithetical and apparently paradoxical. How can a future meeting be foreseen by remembrance? The question takes us to the wheel motif again, a symbol that has parallel literary occurrences, of which the most significant is in T. S. Eliot's 'The Waste Land', though the fiery wheel occurs in *The Family Reunion* too:

> It was only reversing the senseless direction
> For a momentary rest on the burning wheel.

King Lear expresses something similar in his personal vision of hell:

> I am bound
> Upon a wheel of fire that mine own tears
> Do scald like molten lead.[97]

Dylan also has alluded to this image before: 'Don't speak too soon for the wheel's still in spin' (from 'The Times They Are A-Changin''). But in 'The Waste Land', Eliot has a broader concept in mind, which Dylan refers to in 'This Wheel's On Fire'.

The wheel has strong affinities with Samsara, the wheel of becoming or rebirth. In Rudyard's Kipling's *Kim*, the Lama says, 'I go to free myself from the Wheel of Things by a most broad and open road.' In both of the major Buddhist schools of thought, the Theravada and the Mahayana, the wheel plays a vital part in the idea of rebirth and the journey towards Nirvana. In 'The Waste Land', the narrator, bound upon the wheel, is imprisoned in flesh:

> I have heard the key
> Turn in the door once and turn once only
> We think of the key, each in his prison.

---

[97] *King Lear*, 4.7

These lines have affinities with sentiments expressed in 'I Shall Be Released' and in the later 'George Jackson':

> Sometimes I think this whole world
> Is one big prison yard
> Some of us are prisoners
> The rest of us are guards.

In the cyclic quality of Buddhism, the wheel pursues its inexorable course, mixing 'memory' of former existences and 'desire' (tanha) for life which necessarily will prolong the period on the wheel. The exploding of the ever-rolling human wheel to which fates and existences are bound signifies a dramatic change in existence. For Dylan, this clearly came about as a result of the explosion of his own 'wheel', to which he found himself 'bound' and 'rolling down the road' out of control.

'Open the Door, Homer' is a real oddity in that Dylan sings 'Open the door, Richard' throughout, although he prints 'Open the door, Homer' in *Writings and Drawings*. This may be to avoid too personal a reference, for 'Richard' was a real person – Richard Fariña, long-time friend of Bob Dylan's from his Cambridge days.[98]

Given that Dylan and his wife and friends were wise enough to see that by the summer of 1966 Dylan was rolling down the road to self-destruction, and given Dylan's recognition – voiced in the Basement songs – of the need for a way out before exhaustion, insanity or death from overdose claimed him, the form that a way out could take would present its own problems. For a star of Dylan's popularity, a sudden and premature 'retirement' would only have resulted in his being subjected to siege by the media, and the entire crazy, hectic scene enveloping him from without, rather than from within. The motorcycle accident provided something to hide behind as all but the most insensitive pressmen or critics would be expected to leave a badly injured celebrity the time and grace to recuperate, and illness of any kind is generally unlikely to affect a career in the public eye as much as a sudden and willful 'opting out' might.

[98] Dylan recorded with Fariña and Eric Von Schmidt in London in January 1963.

Dylan used the accident as an inducer of myth. Rumour spread that the crash was far worse than initially reported and that Dylan would be a vegetable and never sing again. This not only gave him the opportunity to dry out but, as a spinoff, greatly increased his mystique – a mystique that has clung to him ever since.

'Open the Door, Homer' recounts 'certain things' – mainly life advice – that its singer has learned from others:

> 'Take care of all your memories'
> Said my friend, Mick
> 'For you cannot relive them.'

Maybe Dylan learned these 'lessons' from the finality of Fariña's tragic death in a motorcycle crash in April 1966, only three months before Dylan's own crash. It was perhaps the memory of this that finally 'opened the door' for Dylan's exit:

> Open the door, Richard
> I've heard it said before
> But I ain't gonna hear it said no more.

Having discovered and accepted the looked for escape, Dylan has time for reflection, which emerges in songs in which his former values are reassessed and seem to come to nothing. In 'Nothing Was Delivered', the reflective, released persona addresses the ego-dominated star-persona. In other words, the newly regenerated Dylan speaks 'truth' untainted by 'spite or anger' to the old Dylan, whom he feels has been guilty of taking but not giving. The past has only come up with 'all those lies', and what is needed now are some answers because 'what you sell has not been received':

> It's up to you to say
> Just what you had in mind
> When you made ev'rybody pay.

The time's come to not waste words – 'someone must explain'. The advice of the chorus is 'take heed of this and get plenty of rest'

– presumably to build up enough strength to be able to give 'back all of what you owe' and to use art to speak again what is 'simply' true without concern for egocentric hang-ups and problems.

'Too Much of Nothing' is also a reflective song about being misguided in the past and becoming so vain and full of himself that he felt capable of 'abus[ing] a king'; he could 'walk the streets and boast like most' – an attitude that is certainly depicted in the Basement songs. But after all the boasting, 'he wouldn't know a thing'.

Again there's the impression that belief in false values 'can turn a man into a liar'. The chorus announces the same intention to change and adopt new priorities in a similar vein to 'Lo and Behold!'. Valerie and Vivian, and presumably Turtle, Gorgeous George and T Bone Frank as well as the other liggers, are to be said 'hello' to, but the final request is telling:

> Send them all my salary
> On the waters of oblivion.

Maybe the only thing that has surprised Dylan is just how long it's taken him to realise the error of his ways. 'Too Much of Nothing' makes it plain that 'it's all been done before, it's all been written in the book' – lines that, with the chorus, surely point towards the Bible, in which Dylan was known to be immersing himself at this time:

> In the day of confession
> We cannot mock a soul.

The source of Dylan's possible redemption, or salvation, is increasingly seen to be a spiritual one. In 'I Shall Be Released', a song that pleads for release from a 'lonely crowd' of lost souls, Dylan expresses his hope in a 'light' that points him towards the East:

> I swear I see my reflection
> Some place so high above this wall.

Alan Wall comments:

> The voice that emerges from this song comes recognisably from the *inside* of an asylum and it rejects all forms of mythic self-protection, and calls out for a kind of grace which will free the singer from his intolerable imprisonment.[99]

Dylan's eyes turn towards heaven, towards God who made man in his own image, and indeed towards Christ, for in the lyrically undeveloped worksheet that is 'Sign on the Cross', Dylan's chorus is the most stable part of the song: 'It's that ol' sign on the cross that worries me'. For Dylan, a Jew, the sign above Christ's head – 'King of the Jews' – is a matter for meditation that will occupy him through consideration of his own Jewishness and an exploration of his spiritual consciousness that will lead him eventually to convert to Christianity and, thereby, to an apparent resolution of the search for identity and affirmation of destiny.

[99] From *The Passage of Bob Dylan*.

11. Drifter's Escape: A New Kind of Innocence

> I know it from my own experience and from the
> documents of many other souls. Always, at all times in
> history and in all religions and forms of life, we find the
> same typical experiences, always in the same progression
> and succession: loss of innocence, striving for justice under
> the law, the consequent despair in the futile struggle to
> overcome guilt by deeds or by knowledge, and finally the
> emergence from hell into a transformed world and into a
> new kind of innocence.
>
> — Hermann Hesse, 'A Bit of Theology' (1932)

It's very likely that the emergence of Bob Dylan's star-persona, his dominant identity in 1966, separated him from the rest of humanity – as Quinn the Eskimo was something remarkable compared with everybody else – with the consequence that 'Bob Dylan the artist' began to be unable to feel, while 'Bob Dylan the human being' became unable to love. This would account for the content of the songs that made up *Blonde On Blonde* where Dylan showed himself to be growing more petty and disillusioned. The voice in these songs is of an egotist committed to triviality, particularly with regard to the seemingly endless games of sexuality or the pursuit of fame and fortune.

I've argued that *Blonde On Blonde* is Bob Dylan's nigredo. It is a testament of spleen, of spiritual despair concealed by the adoption of a mocking superiority towards other people, especially women; the songs are 'expressions of discontent … of displeasure, of idleness, of lovelessness', and Dylan paints himself as a victim of the 'soul sickness of the rich'.[100] Dylan's retrospective self-disgust, expressed in passing in the Basement songs, is more prominent on *John Wesley Harding* – an album that 'charts a search through

[100] Hermann Hesse, *Siddharta.*

various ineffective mythologies'[101] and contains expression of the despair, transformation and 'new kind of innocence' spoken of by Hesse in the quotation above.

Here Dylan's emotions rest somewhere between the troubled, as he thinks of his former existence, and the relieved, as he thinks of his new condition. By this time, he journeys through at least two public selves whilst trying vainly to hold onto his private self. The first public self was that of the crusader, the bard shouting from the bow of the ship of the future, the voice of those who took a stand against injustice, inequality, racialism, war, poverty and every social evil. He discarded this identity in 1964 with his realisation that things simply were and should be simply accepted as 'life and life only'. Dylan tries to clarify this point through characters such as Mr Jones in 'Ballad of a Thin Man' and Ramona in 'To Ramona', self-seekers like Dylan, but who failed to see that self and the world, or indeed the universe, were not two different things. If Mr Jones would simply accept, and if Ramona would simply 'be herself', their search would end.

Dylan's second self had gone beyond the control of his private self. The 'thief' became performer, became star, became prophet, became messiah. He was swallowed by his own myth. His self became dominated by ego and the alter ego became recessive. But this second self was burnt-out in the madness of a pursuit that the alter ego recognised as empty and futile.

Stripped of his two spurious selves, Bob Dylan's private soul comes to the fore in the *John Wesley Harding* songs as he reflects upon the follies of the past and the new beliefs upon which the future would rest. On *John Wesley Harding*, Dylan comes nearer to erasing the sense of difference between self and society from his psyche, and nearer to appreciating the futility of trying to understand what can only be experienced. As Dylan moves into his third self, love becomes the most important aspect of experience and inspires the songs of *Nashville Skyline*, providing Dylan with the belief that there is some sense or pattern in the universe.

[101] Alan Wall, *The Passage of Bob Dylan*.

The process of coming to terms with the unconscious forces within the individual psyche occupies Dylan for almost three years and the struggle is expressed in many songs. At least Dylan had favourable conditions for his regeneration. Woodstock provided the necessary seclusion, and his friends from The Band, his wife Sara, and his growing family provided some of the necessary grace. At last, Dylan could conceive of something new and discard the rock star-persona he had allowed to dominate the 'moderate man' he speaks of as his true self.

Dylan actually writes of the process of these two 'selves' coming to terms with each other in 'The Ballad of Frankie Lee and Judas Priest', 'All Along the Watchtower' and in the album's sleeve notes. In other songs, Dylan looks back at himself as he was, but as he no longer is. One thing that Dylan has rediscovered, as the sleeve notes *Three Kings* point out, is his sense of humour.

Dylan's opposed selves – the public and private personae – are represented in the notes. The public persona, 'Mr Dylan', has 'come out with a new record … [which] of course features none but his own songs' – a delightful parody of the publicity handouts that accompany albums sent to reviewers. Three seekers after truth, the 'three kings', are in search of the key to 'unlock' the meaning of the new songs. By making these characters 'three kings', Dylan points to their conception of 'Mr Dylan' as a messiah who has the ability, in his songs, to make them whole, for are all in need of regeneration. The third king hits on the idea of the 'key' to the songs being 'Frank', who symbolises Dylan's 'true' persona, his private self which has been repressed for so long; in 'The Ballad of Frankie Lee and Judas Priest', this same persona is represented by 'Frankie Lee'.[102]

As the kings arrive to question Frank about the new album, they find him engaged in unremarkable, 'ordinary' activities: 'sweeping up, preparing the meat, dishing himself out...' Frank

---

[102] It's incidentally interesting that *Self Portrait*'s 'Little Sadie' has Dylan exclaiming 'Oh yes, sir, my name is Lee'. There's a further parallel in the song when Frankie is identified as 'Frankie Lee the gambler whose father is deceased'. In the *Rolling Stone* interview of 29th November 1969, Dylan, speaking of Toby Thompson's *Village Voice* articles, said, 'I don't like the way this writer talked about my father who has passed away.'

has a wife, Vera, and is embarrassed as kings crawl into his presence on their hands and knees. The first king asks about the new record in 'the most meaningful way' and Frank readily admits that he is the key to the songs – that they're all about him. The king is excited and asks Frank to 'open it up for us':

> 'And just how far would you like to go in?' he asked, and the three kings all looked at each other. 'Not too far but just far enough so's we can say that we've been there.'

This kind of foolish shallowness that Dylan appears to depict as the attitude of some of his public towards his work may be taken in more than one way. But Frank meets folly with apparent wisdom, offering the kings a remarkably energetic Zen solution to their question. As the story concludes, the kings are more than satisfied, even though their responses to Frank's solution range from apparent comprehension to bewilderment to silence; all are 'mysteriously' made whole, blowing horns and celebrating their happiness, but it is Vera's comment that really provides the 'key' that the kings came in search of:

> 'Why didn't you just tell them you were a moderate man and leave it at that instead of goosing yourself all over the room?'

The whole piece is a parody of attitudes. The kings' satisfaction is a false one, though they believe it to be true. The truth about the songs on the new record seems to be that he is Frank – just a 'moderate man'. He no longer believes himself to be a messiah, but if he can help others with what he has to say and without being hurt or giving up his pursuit of the direction he has determined for his life – a 'moderate', ordinary, unremarkable course – perhaps everyone might achieve some kind of happiness. This is the 'moral' of the entire collection.

Lyrically, Dylan speaks in parables. The songs are almost all narratives and the style is bereft of most of its former surrealism. There's little figurative language. The music is similarly reduced, mostly pared down to acoustic guitar, bass, harmonica, drums and a little piano, with pedal steel coming in at the album's conclusion.

'The Ballad of Frankie Lee and Judas Priest' is by far the album's longest cut. In it, Dylan presents his two identities of the last two years. In opposition, the figures represent two possible attitudes of the artist to reality: a standing off from the world and an attempt to accept it on its own terms. Judas Priest represents 'Dylan the public persona' – the star who betrayed both himself and his audience in pursuit of false goals. Frankie Lee represents the more private, inner man that the public never really get to see. These two aspects of character – ego and alter ego – are introduced as 'the best of friends'. As the song opens, Judas Priest attempts to seduce Frankie Lee with money, of which Frankie is in need. The money is 'on a footstool, just above the plotted plain' and causes man to stoop to the level it occupies. Frankie subconsciously or intuitively seems to recognise his peril in succumbing to the temptation of the 'roll of tens' for 'his head began to spin' as he studied the notes.

Judas hurries Frankie along and assumes the role of the Devil tempting man as he winks one of his cold eyes and promises Frankie that he'll be waiting for him in 'Eternity', adding, in a quick attempt at reassurance when Frankie's fear makes itself apparent: 'Though you might call it "Paradise"'.

Frankie feels 'low and mean' but when a message comes that Judas Priest is 'stranded in a house' down the road, Frankie rushes off in search of his friend, and of course, falls into the trap. There's no escape for Frankie now. By allowing Judas Priest to dominate him, Frankie has 'lost all control' over himself and begins to foam at the mouth, over his art – 'everything which he had made' – and his destiny. The 'house' is 'not a house, it's a home' says Judas Priest. There's no way out, and Frankie dies in Judas's arms 'of thirst' – spiritual starvation.

While Frankie appears to be a victim of Judas Priest, the real truth is yet to come. The one truly responsible for Frankie's terrible fate is 'the little neighbour boy' who has 'his guilt so well concealed'. Frankie's spectacular 'death' is, in fact, a symbolic one. They carry him out 'in jest', which is to say they don't carry him out at all, for Frankie Lee has *become* Judas Priest, having 'burst' into his arms. What the various aspects of the song symbolise is not too difficult to determine, and Dylan even adds his own moral to help clarify matters. Frankie Lee is Dylan as he was – innocent, a little gullible maybe, apprehensive at the thought of a great deal of money or status (symbolised by the 'big house as bright as any sun'), of success and its supposed rewards. The house has 'four and twenty windows' – there's little privacy – but maybe the women's faces are tempting enough to allow that to be ignored. Frankie Lee is, nevertheless, in need of money, and although he feels 'low and mean', he is a 'gambler'. He takes the chance, heads 'down the road', succumbs to Judas's temptations and loses control – loses himself. He dies after he 'raved' in a period of chaotic madness, leaping 'up the stairs' to commercial success. That success, which has caused Frankie Lee to become Judas Priest, is given to Frankie by the 'little neighbour boy'. He recalls 'every boy and girl' in 'Tiny Montgomery' or 'every girl and boy' in 'Quinn the Eskimo', whose enthusiasm, acclaim and belief make Tiny and Quinn what they appear to be. But while the kids in those songs were expected to 'get their bang' and 'jump for joy', the 'little neighbour boy' harbours only disappointment and disillusion: 'Nothing is revealed', he mutters. Frank is only a 'moderate man' after all. Dylan's tagged-on moral is appropriate enough: 'One should never be where one does not belong'.

Frankie paid his price for bounding up the stairs of the big house and allowing himself to burst into Judas Priest's arms. He won't make the same mistake again. In the album's final cut, and throughout the songs of the next few years, Dylan consistently announces that he's not going to go anywhere, except where he belongs. The significance of the second part of the moral – help your neighbour 'with his load' – is clarified in Dylan's comments in the *Rolling Stone* interview in 1969, where he says: 'If I could ease someone's mind, I'd be the first one to do it. I want to lighten every load, straighten out every burden.'

The final piece of advice – to the listener and to himself – is 'don't go mistaking Paradise for that home across the road'. This underlines the point about simply accepting and being satisfied with what you have and recognising true values and seeing through false temptations.

The album's other 'split personality' song, 'All Along the Watchtower', isn't far away either. The two characters are 'the joker' – the entertainer, the clown, the wearer of the mask (Jung's symbol of ego), the public Dylan – and 'the thief', Dylan's symbol for himself as poet, the more private persona. As 'joker', Dylan depicts himself as he did in the Basement songs and on *Blonde On Blonde* – 'stuck' and 'stranded' – he's trapped and feeling exploited, yearning for some kind of escape:

> 'There must be some way out of here,'
> said the joker to the thief
> 'There's too much confusion, I can't get no relief.'

We're back as far as 'Mixed Up Confusion', 'Stuck Inside of Mobile' or 'Please, Mrs. Henry'. The joker feels he's being exploited by people who have no understanding of the true worth of what he produces: 'Businessmen they drink my wine, plowmen dig my earth'. The 'businessmen' are like the 'managers and the advisers and the agents' from the 1969 *Rolling Stone* interview, and Dylan coupled 'farmers and the businessmen' in 'Sad-Eyed Lady of the Lowlands': 'None of them along the line knows what any of it is worth'. It's the universal complaint of the artist in a materialistic society.

The thief is much calmer. He has the wisdom of experience, having 'been through that' and learned from it. He speaks 'kindly' to the joker, with Dylan deploying another Shakespearean pun where 'kindly' means 'affectionately, compassionately' while indicating that the thief and the joker are of the same 'kind'; 'you and I' underlines this affinity. The thief's insight is that 'life is but a joke', and feelings like the joker's (who has difficulty seeing the joke) are false. The thief's lesson is the same as Lear's – as well as Hamlet's and indeed is one already learned and forgotten by Dylan, who might have announced 'It's Alright, Ma (I'm Only Bleeding) Ho Ho Ho' in 1965 but probably had more in common with the oh-so-serious 'little boy lost' a year later. The song acknowledges a lesson re-learned: the Biblical Apocalypse may be expected and watched for, even though still 'in the distance', but it's growing nearer and more imminent. 'The hour is getting late', 'the wind began to howl', 'two riders were approaching', Babylon and all her 'graven images'[103] may be about to be destroyed. All the joker and the thief can do about it is 'not talk falsely' but simply assert true values, or, as Dylan was to sing twelve years later in 'When You Gonna Wake Up?', 'strengthen the things that remain'.

This assertion of truth and rejection of the false is the concern of many of the songs on *John Wesley Harding*. Dylan's retrospective analysis of the mistakes he had made as the joker is developed in 'The Wicked Messenger', 'I Am a Lonesome Hobo' and 'Drifter's Escape' – all self-portraits in parable form.

'The Wicked Messenger' concerns the earliest part of Dylan's career. His response to the enquiries about his origins and background are not answered directly, for the messenger knows that whatever he says will be misrepresented. Instead 'he answered with his thumb' by playing his 'message' songs, which spoke the 'truth' as he then perceived it. The second verse takes us to Dylan's attempts to win fame and fortune as a 'political' singer, making his bed (or perhaps his bid – for Dylan twists the sound as he sings the word) 'behind the assembly hall'. The more success he achieves, the more ambitious he becomes. At this point the messenger becomes 'wicked' because he becomes rich – 'the leaves began to fallin'' – and what he becomes divides his public, the 'seas' to redeploy a metaphor he used in 'When the Ship Comes In'. When Dylan's public split into two factions – the 'acoustic' and the 'electric' fans – Dylan suffered a hurtful backlash from folkies and socialists who felt that he had 'sold out'[104] to commercialism, hence the final lines:

---

[103] cf. *The Book of Isaiah*: Prepare the table, watch in the watchtower … And behold here cometh a chariot of men with a couple of horsemen. And he answered and said: 'Babylon is fallen, is fallen; and all the graven images of her gods he hath broken unto the ground'.
[104] See, for example, Irwin Silher's 'Open Letter To Bob Dylan' which was printed in the November 1964 issue of *Sing Out!*.

He was told but these few words
Which opened up his heart
'If ye cannot bring good news, then don't bring any.'

'I Am a Lonesome Hobo' contains a merciless self-assessment, acknowledging former 'deceit', admitting 'shame' (and thus echoing 'Too Much of Nothing', 'Nothing Was Delivered' and 'Lo and Behold!') and attesting that material wealth merely led to spiritual poverty:

Well, once I was rather prosperous
There was nothing I did lack
I had fourteen-karat gold in my mouth
And silk upon my back.

He adds 'I did not trust my brother' and this lack of faith 'led me to my fatal doom'. The moral is clear enough, and Dylan points specifically to three lessons, or warnings:

Stay free from petty jealousies
Live by no man's code
And hold your judgment for yourself.

'Drifter's Escape' is concerned with Dylan's lack of progress in his search for self. Portraying himself as a drifter on (very public) trial, he admits to 'weakness' and bewilderment:

I still do not know
What it was that I've done wrong.

The 'judge' speaks not as a judge – he 'cast his robe aside' – but as a compassionate guide:

'You fail to understand,' he said
'Why must you even try?'

But if the judge is sympathetic, 'the crowd' who form the jury are restless. The drifter's 'escape' is both unexpected and fortuitous, leaving him to come to his own terms with what he did wrong. The allegory is of Dylan's own escape from the trials of public demand.

Another song in this vein is 'I Pity the Poor Immigrant'. What Dylan shows here is not so much pity as sympathy, for the immigrant feels guilty of his mistakes or sins – 'lies', falling 'in love with wealth itself', filling 'his mouth with laughing'. For all the 'power', 'strength', and 'wealth' the immigrant or Dylan had, he was left only with a debilitating loneliness and irredeemably shattered visions.

The album's opening song also depicts a part of the process that almost claimed Dylan as victim. John Wesley Harding is presented as a strangely unheroic hero, who is defined as much by what he didn't do as what he did. It's another thinly-veiled self-assessment. Dylan's photograph on the cover of the album depicts him as a cowboy-frontiersman who might be surrounded by Red Indians if they weren't real ones.[105] The portrait – the song is as much of a Polaroid picture as is the cover photograph – is of Dylan's first 'self', the 'friend to the poor', taking a stand 'with a gun in every hand' (a wonderful image of a multiplicity of guns being aimed at a plethora of just targets), lending helping hands, and achieving fame, or notoriety, in the process:

> All across the telegraph
> His name it did resound.

The song's tone seems to shift towards ambivalence at times, though. Michael Gray points out the 'but' in:

> He opened many a door
> But he was never known
> To hurt an honest man.

When we come to 'but no charge held against him, could they prove' we may well begin to wonder about John Wesley Harding's integrity, and though 'he was never known' to do other things, that isn't the same thing as saying he didn't do them. The ultimate

---

[105] Dylan's friends are actually the Bauls of Bengal.

irony that John Wesley Hardin was, in truth, a notorious outlaw and killer adds to the problem of our response to the song.

The Blakeian encounter of 'As I Went Out One Morning' is also enigmatic. Dylan represents himself as a would-be do-gooder and perhaps even social reformer, who goes out to imbibe some of Tom Paine's influence. He is given an immediate opportunity to put his philanthropy into practice as he's confronted by a fair and enchained damsel: 'I offered her my hand'. It's the appropriate gesture but provokes an unexpected response. Not for nothing, it seems, is she enchained. For, despite her loveliness, she is clearly dangerous. She speaks 'from the corners of her mouth' – that is, dishonestly[106] – and Dylan immediately recognises that 'she meant to do me harm' as she takes hold of his arm, a grip that is only yielded with Tom Paine's timely arrival.

The overall impact of many of the *John Wesley Harding* songs lies in what it suggests rather than what it expresses. Nevertheless, it seems to me that the damsel's chains are her own, and not kept there by Tom Paine or anyone else. His apology – 'I'm sorry for what she's done' – is not simply for her having taken Dylan's arm, but for everything she's done. She symbolises a way of living and offers a direction in her attempted 'seduction' – 'I will secretly accept you, and together we'll fly south'. But the furtiveness of that 'secretly' and her plea 'from the corners of her mouth' betrays her. What she is offering is quite clearly opposed to what either Tom Paine or his disciple-narrator of the song believe in. It involves deceit, dishonesty and self-imposed chains.

Speaking in 1964 about the Emergency Civil Liberties Committee as they appeared to him on the night of his acceptance of the Tom Paine Award, Dylan said:

> Here were these people who'd been all involved with the left in the thirties, and now they're supporting civil rights drives. That's groovy, but they also had minks and jewels and it was like they were giving the money out of guilt. I got up to leave, and they followed me and caught me. They told me I had to accept the award ... I'm not

---

[106] cf. The judge in 'Percy's Song' who speaks 'out of the side of his mouth'.

going to be part of any organisation. Those people at that dinner were the same as everybody else. They're doing their time. They're chained to what they're doing. The only thing is, they're trying to put morals and great deeds on their chains, but basically they don't want to jeopardise their positions.[107]

It's clear from 'As I Went Out One Morning' that Dylan feels himself both fortunate and thankful for having been strong enough to renounce, or escape from, such shackles.

Out of the spiritual vacuum created by the years of crisis and re-evaluation, new values and ideals had to emerge. The creation of values out of chaos was to be the work of the years to come. On *John Wesley Harding*, Dylan expresses the value of faith, truth, acceptance, understanding, self-knowledge, sympathy, and finally points towards the overriding value of compassion or love. Two songs in which 'compassion' is the key are 'I Dreamed I Saw St. Augustine' and 'Dear Landlord'. Though the first of these concludes with a frightening dream of guilt, the dream depicts St. Augustine offering love and compassion to all; indeed his appeal is to those one might feel were least in need of compassion – 'gifted kings and queens' – though whose loneliness is clearly a spiritual one. For them he has the message of faith: 'Know you're not alone'.

The first verse demonstrates that no one is beyond the redemption or salvation that love has to offer. St. Augustine is 'searching for the very souls, whom already have been sold'. He goes about his work amidst 'the utmost misery', carrying 'a blanket underneath his arm' as symbol of his compassion, but wearing 'a coat of solid gold'. And though one might expect a contradiction of values, there is none: the love St. Augustine offers makes all else irrelevant, insignificant, and the 'solid gold' coat is a reflection of spiritual worth rather than lack of it. The singer's humility and tears at the song's conclusion stem not from the terrifying dream – and the fact it is only a 'dream' is important – nor from his subsequent loneliness, but from the implicit

[107] Quoted in Nat Hentoff's 'The Crakin' Shakin' Breakin' Sounds'.

acknowledgment of his past failure to do what the dream of St. Augustine showed was possible: to combine wealth with charity, power with humility, authority with compassion, and to believe in and communicate love to all, without qualification.

'Dear Landlord' offers the lessons of St. Augustine's dream to others. 'Landlord' is a collective symbol for anyone with wealth and power over others. It is a plea for understanding, compassion and love, and the song's speaker alternates confessions with his pleas, attempting to make his demands of the 'landlord' a little less demanding. The first of these is 'please don't put a price on my soul'.

There are values that go far beyond those determined by price; the soul cannot be bartered for and cannot be the object of valuation, just as St. Augustine's compassion was not to be estimated against his 'coat of solid gold'. But this initial plea is followed by two apologies for the difficulties imposed upon the singer by his life – 'my burden is heavy' – and by his art – 'my dreams are beyond control' – and by a gesture of his own capacity for charity – 'I'm gonna give you all I got to give' – which simply expects or hopes for gracious acceptance rather than reciprocity – 'I do hope you receive it well'.

In the second verse, the singer offers the landlord understanding – 'I know you've suffered much' – but it's tempered by a warning against self-pity – 'but in this you are not so unique' – and a confession of his own weaknesses or temptations, which he indicates he feels they have in common:

> All of us, at times, we might work too hard
> To have it too fast and too much.

Throughout the song, there are gestures of conciliation, as if the singer realises that his chances of getting an appropriate response are not good before the final tempered appeal for simple understanding:

> If you don't underestimate me
> I won't underestimate you.

The album's closing songs, 'Down Along the Cove' and 'I'll Be Your Baby Tonight', are signal songs, both in lyrical content and in sound. *John Wesley Harding*'s sound is very cold, very chilling, the voice hard and sober, the harmonica piercing. With 'Down Along the Cove' comes warmth, the drumming softens, as does Dylan's voice, which mellows against the flowing pedal steel guitar. The two songs present Dylan's new self and his new commitment in life and art. They are songs that lead us directly and unerringly to *Nashville Skyline*, away from American frontiers and to the heart of the country in pursuit of values that, this time, Dylan feels may be truer than the false goals that brought his previous self to its knees. The minstrel boy decides to 'let it down easy to save his soul' and Dylan chooses love. On *John Wesley Harding*'s wintery-grey cover photograph, Bob Dylan is smiling for the first time on an album cover.

12. I'll Be Your Baby Tonight

> There are many ways to the mystic centre, as many ways
> as there are beings. But there is only one true guide,
> the self. One must follow it through horror and ecstasy,
> good and evil, life and death. It will lead the individual
> back from his mutilated, fragmented state, back from the
> ravages of the accidental and chaotic ... [the artist] must
> follow thought to the point leading him beyond itself to
> the universal self.
>
> — Edwin Casebeer, *Hermann Hesse*

Jung's three basic elements of the male personality are the conscious ego, the anima and the self, with 'anima' referring to the feminine element that remains largely unconscious. It is from the unconscious, Jung says, that man draws energy to produce creative work. But a basic male problem is the projection of one's own feminine characteristics on women. As *John Wesley Harding* moves towards *Nashville Skyline*, Dylan's wife Sara develops in importance, in his life and in his songs. She consequently becomes those women upon whom Dylan's earliest anima projections would have been fixed. She is presented as mother, sister and childhood friend. She becomes every woman Dylan ever knew, and every woman in whom he recognised aspects of himself. If ego had dominated *Blonde On Blonde*, it is the positive aspects of anima that Dylan cultivates now.

In 'Shelter from the Storm', Dylan pays tribute to Sara for being instrumental in his physical and spiritual regeneration. Coming in 'from the wilderness' like some Yeatsian beast – 'a creature void of form' – he slouches towards his rebirth, shaped anew by Sara's 'shelter'.

In his early love songs, Dylan depicted himself as wandering, 'travellin' on' restlessly, experiencing women, at times portraying them as sensual (there is the 'strength' of Ramona's skin or the 'watery and wet' mouth of the girl in 'I Don't Believe You' for example), erotic (such as the gypsy gal in 'Spanish Harlem Incident'), instinctive and intuitive (such as the woman with the sparkling ring in 'She Belongs to Me'), or as elemental ('Love Minus Zero/No Limit'). But these relationships are brief and temporary. Each woman returns to other roles and functions. Most of the later songs about women express disillusion or bitterness. The women are portrayed ironically (as in 'I Don't Believe You') or contemptuously (as in most of the *Blonde On Blonde* songs). But to gain the substance of his art, Dylan must re-enter life and explore the relationship of man and woman. Art is not only a defence against the transitory but an insight into the basic nature and problem of humanity. In the final two songs on *John Wesley Harding*, Dylan announces the emergence of his third self.

> Love is the most important thing of all. It may be important to great thinkers to comprehend the world, to explain it, to despise it. But it is my sole concern to be able to love the world, not despise it, not to hate it and myself, but to be able to contemplate the world and myself and all beings with love and admiration and veneration.[108]

The search for wholeness taking Dylan towards love is natural enough in a world of abrasive conflict and lovelessness. In 'Down Along the Cove' he celebrates for the first time his understanding of that love, an understanding that he feels is shared by 'everybody'. It's a very public presentation of feeling:

> Down along the cove
> We walked together hand in hand
> Ev'rybody watchin' us go by
> Knows we're in love, yes, and they understand.

The slightly superfluous 'together' with 'hand in hand' emphasises the bond of affection.

[108] Hermann Hesse, *Siddharta*.

The final song, 'I'll Be Your Baby Tonight', is altogether more intimate in its tone. 'Close the door' takes us within, shutting out the world, its follies and its mockeries. Dylan's anima projections are unconsciously betrayed in his terms of address. In 'Down Along the Cove' the woman is addressed as 'mama', the closest and the original female personality. Similarly, Dylan is her 'boy' or her 'baby'. It's very much a case of mutual reassurance. 'You don't have to worry anymore' and 'You don't have to be afraid' are sung just as much to himself as to his lady. They contain exactly those reassurances that would be offered to a fretting child – including the 'bottle'.

The songs on *Nashville Skyline* carry straight on. 'To Be Alone with You' and 'Tonight I'll Be Staying Here with You' are simply restatements of the sentiments expressed in 'I'll Be Your Baby Tonight'. The intimacy of the personal relationship is enhanced by the closing of the door and of the day. The night brings an intimacy which is denied in the daytime.

> 'How do you work?'
> 'Most of the time I work at night.'[109]

It's interesting here to quote an observation of Wallace Fowlie in his critical study of Rimbaud:

> In a night world … man has his deepest intuition of the void, of the limitless empire of his mind, of the eternity of time, of the innocency of the cosmos waiting for some expression of his will. Ever since Nerval and Novalis, one school of the modern poet has understood that he must be possessed by the night. Whatever union between the self and the universe can be achieved, whatever sensations can be engendered from a single sensation, night is the time when the superior ego (Je est un autre) claims its life and its expression.[110]

With these comments in mind, perhaps the lines from 'To Be Alone with You' take on just a little more significance than they might otherwise do:

[109] From Bob Dylan interview with Ephron and Edmiston.
[110] Wallace Fowlie, *Rimbaud: A Critical Study.*

200

> They say that nighttime is the right time
> To be with the one you love
> Too many thoughts get in the way in the day
> But you're always what I'm thinkin' of
> I wish the night were here.

'Tonight I'll Be Stayin' Here with You' announces the new-found permanence of the situation. As Michael Gray observes in *Song & Dance Man*: 'the habit of always moving on has been kicked and the impulse to stay has at last succeeded'. If worries and fears have been left behind, so too have 'troubles', and with them the traveller's necessities – 'ticket' and 'suitcase'. Although the singer can 'hear that whistle blowin'', he is fully prepared to renounce his seat on the train to one who is still travelling the path he was formerly on. Indeed, he even affords us a glimpse of the identity he has cast off – namely that of the 'poor boy on the street'. In a live version of the song from 1975, Dylan acknowledges the regenerative force of the love he now accepts:

> I was feelin' broke and shattered
> 'Cause your love was all that mattered
> So tonight I'll be stayin' here with you.

The next time he is to acknowledge such force is in 'Covenant Woman' from 1979.

'I Threw It All Away' is significant here not so much for its expression of regret for former folly but for its mid-song assertion:

> Love is all there is, it makes the world go 'round
> Love and only love, it can't be denied.

Dylan embraces a cliché here that he would formerly have dissected. There's a neat denial of this in the seductive 'Lay, Lady, Lay', when Dylan asserts that love enables you to 'have your cake and eat it too'; the exhortation for the lady to stay is reinforced by other statements of unwillingness to go anywhere. The new lifestyle is to be more of homely simplicity. Dylan chooses to be a husband in 'Country Pie' – 'Call me for dinner, honey, I'll be there' – renouncing his former lifestyle: 'I don't need much and that ain't no lie, ain't runnin' any race'.

These songs are the statements of a 'moderate man'; the thought, the expression, the language, the performances all reflect this. 'There's no attempt there to reach anybody but me,' said Dylan about *Nashville Skyline*;[111] but the attempt to reach oneself is something that requires lifelong dedication.

New Morning's songs present a Dylan who is more deeply committed to his new-found identity, though at least one of his contemporaries wasn't too happy with what he heard. Country Joe McDonald commented: 'I don't know where the real Bob Dylan went, but I don't believe this one.'[112] On *New Morning*, *Nashville Skyline*'s husband takes upon himself the role of father, and thus seems to find his purpose in life in an idyllic country setting:

> Build me a cabin in Utah
> Marry me a wife, catch rainbow trout
> Have a bunch of kids who call me 'Pa'
> That must be what it's all about.

Those lines are from 'Sign on the Window', and throughout the album there are celebratory exclamations of happiness, satisfaction and gratitude. 'If Not for You' is a tribute to the wife who provides not just love and sustenance but vision, significance, identity, and who represents the very turning of the world – 'If not for you, winter would have no spring' – just as Cordelia, in *King Lear*, is presented as 'a kind of beneficent Goddess of Nature whose tears … can renew and quicken the virtue of earth'.[113]

'The Man in Me' is another personal song of gratitude, whilst 'Time Passes Slowly', 'Winterlude' and 'New Morning' are celebrations of an apparently idyllic existence and marital bliss, which is valuable for its permanence and stability:

---

[111] From *Bob Dylan* by Scaduto.
[112] In *Rolling Stone*, 27th May 1971.
[113] John F. Danby, *Shakespeare's Doctrine of Nature*, Faber and Faber, 1949.

> Ain't no reason to go in a wagon to town
> Ain't no reason to go to the fair
> Ain't no reason to go up, ain't no reason to go down
> Ain't no reason to go anywhere.

But 'Time Passes Slowly' has some interesting lines. For instance, the second stanza concludes 'Time passes slowly when you're searchin' for love'. Having found love, one might expect time's speed to increase. At the end of this particular affair, Dylan is to announce: 'Time is a jet plane, it moves too fast' (in 'You're a Big Girl Now'). But the ultimate impermanence of all is acknowledged in Dylan's admission of life's transience in the song's final lines:

> Like the red rose of summer that blooms in the day
> Time passes slowly and fades away.

There's an even more interesting statement that indicates that the maintenance of such an apparently perfect lifestyle is far from being effortless: 'We stare straight ahead and try so hard to stay right'. But surely such efforts hint at weak foundations. 'Try so hard' anticipates a failure that the final lines seem to indicate as inevitable.

'Winterlude' appears straightforward enough, but it is a plea that seems to follow a disagreement with promises of better things:

> Tonight there will be no quarrelling
> Everything is gonna be alright.

'One More Weekend' takes it up:

> Things will be okay
> You wait and see.

The idea of 'one more' weekend suggests that the song is really a request for one last chance to make things work out. There's a hint of that in:

We'll go someplace unknown
Leave all the children home
Honey, why not go alone
Just you and me.

The suggestion that the relationship is not as idyllic as Dylan might like it to be is not too far-fetched. On *Nashville Skyline*, 'Tell Me That It Isn't True' was a discordant note in the midst of harmony:

I have heard rumours all over town...
To know that some other man is holdin' you tight...
All of those awful things that I have heard...

On *New Morning*, the 'Sign on the Window' publicises the quarrel:

Sign on the street says 'Y'Don't Own Me'
Sign on the porch says 'Three's A Crowd'.

The singer is left 'lonely', his feelings endorsed by sympathetic weather:

Looks like a-nothing but rain...
Sure gonna be wet tonight on Main Street...

In 'If Dogs Run Free' Dylan's belief in love may still be intact – 'true love can make a blade of grass stand up straight and tall' – but while love 'can cure the soul … can make it whole', the truth is that 'true love needs no company'. Lessons come hard in 'Sign on the Window':

My best friend said, 'Now didn' I warn ya
Brighton girls are like the moon.'

And if *New Morning* opened with a song of praise to Sara, it closes with a hymn of praise to God, the 'Father of loneliness and pain'.

For collections of songs that supposedly celebrate happiness and the joys of living contentedly in an ideal and permanent marital bliss, *Nashville Skyline* and *New Morning* contain more than a little sorrow, regret, loneliness, and pain. The persona Dylan has assumed *is* assumed. The Happy Family Man is a role he's tried to play to the best of his ability, and which he's tried to believe in as he asserts through cosy lyrics, accented clichés and embraced platitudes. But he's been unsuccessful because he can't accept it – neither the role nor its proclamation: the singer of 'If Not for You', 'New Morning' or 'To Be Alone with You' is in no way a man who has found himself.

'Tonight I'll Be Staying Here with You' may have had Dylan renouncing a former role, but 'One More Night' has him embracing it again:

> I will turn my head up high
> To that dark and rolling sky.

The reason for his leaving is telling: he found it impossible to play the part forced upon him by his relationship with a woman who was 'the only pal I had' – 'I just could not be what she wanted me to be'. On *New Morning* he tries 'so hard to stay right' and attempts to affirm the belief that a wife and 'bunch of kids' give him his identity:

> That must be what it's all about
> That must be what it's all about.

But there are plenty of indications that things aren't exactly what he'd hoped they'd be and that something has gone awry. His pictures of Elysium – whether catching rainbow trout outside a cabin in Utah or sitting beside bridges catching 'wild fishes' that swim in streams 'up in the mountains' – are conscious presentations of the unreal. 'Time Passes Slowly' is far from a celebration. It's a very sad song, a lament for the loss of someone real enough who might just have turned out to be ideal:

Once I had a sweetheart, she was fine and good-lookin'
We sat in her kitchen while her mama was cookin'
Stared out the window to the stars high above.

But they were staring towards the unattainable because it is as difficult to find true love as it is to grasp the stars; like beauty, love, youth, and 'the red rose of summer' that symbolises all three, time 'fades away'.

'I Threw It All Away' is the parallel song on *Nashville Skyline*, itself a statement of regret and profound sadness for what was 'once' and which brings only the pain of recollection. There are many other images of isolation and loneliness and sorrow on *New Morning*. The visit to the gypsy in 'Went to See the Gypsy' finds the narrator initially encouraged by a 'pretty dancing girl' who promises him that the gypsy can help:

Drive you from your fear
Bring you through the mirror.

The incident maybe owes just a little to Harry Haller's visit, with the aid of Hermine – herself a pretty dancing girl – and Pablo, the gypsy musician, to the magic theatre at the conclusion of Hermann Hesse's *Steppenwolf*. Harry finds himself looking into the great mirror of the psyche, seeing the multiplicity of his personae, images of a thousand Harrys which collectively compose the real self. But he is still 'old Harry, old weary loon' and bitterly, he shatters the mirror and turns again to the Magic Theatre, only to find it closed.

As the singer in 'Went to See the Gypsy' turns back from his contemplation of the 'river of tears' outside the hotel, he finds no one:

The gypsy's door was open wide
But the gypsy was gone
And that pretty dancing girl
She could not be found.

Having failed in his attempt to be brought 'through the mirror' to a realisation of his true self, he must begin his search again. The song's conclusion takes Dylan back to the starting point – to his birthplace and to his own birth, symbolised by the rising sun:

> So I watched that sun come rising
> From that little Minnesota town.

'Went to See the Gypsy' combines an acknowledgment of failure with a determination to begin over again and it's no coincidence that the sleeve notes to *Planet Waves* – Dylan's next album – begin 'Back to the Starting Point...' Indeed, the entire album is filled with retrospective self-analysis.

If the songs on *New Morning* admit the unreality of his former ideals and the inevitable inability to attain them, and if the songs ultimately explain Dylan's acknowledgment of his failure to become the person he tried so hard to be, at least the album concludes with indications of strength rather than weakness. 'Three Angels' takes us back from the mountains, from the country stream and the wood, to 'the street' and the 'concrete world'. The return has been harbingered in the preceding song, 'The Man in Me':

> Storm clouds are raging all around my door
> I think to myself I might not take it anymore.

The wish to get back is expressed in a just-about contemporary song 'Watching the River Flow' in which Dylan sings 'wish I was back in the city instead of this old bank of sand'.

The three angels may be ungainly symbols of a false religiosity, perched 'high on their poles' and 'with wings that stick out', but they symbolise something beyond the tatty and tawdry commercialism that put them there. They 'play on their horns all day' but the people pass by beneath unheeding, not questioning their own existences, nor acknowledging the presence of a higher one. The world may be 'a concrete world' but it is, nevertheless, 'full of souls'. And though no one hears or tries to hear the music the angels play, the music is played, continuously, 'up above the street', on a higher level of existence, perceived, it seems, only by 'dogs and pigeons' who 'fly up' whilst humanity crawls below.

'Father of Night' is sung with great determination and resolution. I've said that the record ends very strongly for a work which is, above all else perhaps, a confession of failure. But as Dylan has already said, 'there's no success like failure'. If Dylan's third 'self' has been cast off, at least he's learned a little more who he's not. With God's help, the 'Father who taketh the darkness away', he can begin over again in his search for the truth of his identity.

13. Back to the Starting Point

The river flows, it flows to the sea
Wherever that river goes
That's where I want to be
Flow, river, flow.

— 'Ballad of Easy Rider'

It's always we've rambled, that river and I.

— Woody Guthrie, 'Pastures of Plenty'

The river plays a significant role in Hermann Hesse's *Siddhartha*. From the river, Siddharta learns that there is no such thing as time. The river's beginning, middle and end are of a single piece, like the past, present and future of an individual's life. In 'Watching the River Flow', written after the *New Morning* songs, Dylan expresses the dissatisfactions that were evident enough on the previous album. The songs on *New Morning* and on *Nashville Skyline* were lyrically lightweight, and 'Watching the River Flow' opens with Dylan's acknowledgment of a period of artistic limbo:

What's the matter with me
I don't have much to say.

His artistic staleness is undoubtedly a product of his struggle for personal development and self-realisation. His exploration of his third 'self' – that of 'moderate man' – having proved unsatisfactory, Dylan seems restless and aimlessness begins to trouble him again: 'Walkin' to and fro beneath the moon'. The moon symbolises changeability and Dylan used it in the friend's advice about female fickleness in 'Sign on the Window' – 'Brighton girls are like the moon'. He also depicts himself on a 'bank of sand', a further indicator of impermanence and mutability. The song expresses wishful fancies then denies them. The wish to be 'back in the city' that opens the second stanza and the dissatisfaction with 'this old bank of sand' is immediately countered then contradicted. At the stanza's conclusion, the singer sits 'contentedly' on the bank of sand; and in the following two stanzas, he depicts the troubles of city life:

> People disagreeing on just about everything, yeah
> Makes you stop and all wonder why...
> People disagreeing everywhere you look.

There's a great deal of loneliness and pain in the city. There are people who are 'really shook' on the streets, and one man 'who just couldn't help but cry'. The remainder of the song is an extended expression of the intention to simply 'sit' and 'watch the river flow', a sentiment echoed in the lines from 'Ballad of Easy Rider' quoted above.

If Siddhartha learns from the river that there's no such thing as time, maybe Dylan can too. Time played an important part in some of the *New Morning* songs, and there seems to be a growing awareness of the transient nature of things. Of course, lines previously quoted from 'Time Passes Slowly' are significant here:

> Like the red rose of summer that blooms in the day
> Time passes slowly and fades away.

The 'rose', the 'summer' and the 'day' – all indicative of youth and beauty – inevitably pass and fade away.

In 'If Dogs Run Free', time is a 'swamp':

> The best is always yet to come
> That's what they explain to me.

To look to the future whilst the delights of the present sink to their decay and destruction in the 'swamp of time' is surely bad advice and should not be heeded. To separate past, present and future is to deny the message of the river that 'keeps on rollin'

... no matter what gets in the way and which way the wind does blow'. The river is eternal, controlled only by the 'Father of time ... who turneth the rivers and streams' ('Father of Night'); 'the whole earth' may 'in progression ... pass by' ('Three Angels'), but 'the river flows' on, timelessly. By 1975, Dylan had presumably been able to put his thoughts on the nature of time into order:

> It all exists. The past exists, the present exists, the future exists. It all exists. [The future] exists as part of the present. It's connected. It just depends how far you want to set your sights, you know. In Zen philosophy, I think it's Zen philosophy, I mean you just live in the present ... but that statement's more complicated than meets the eye really, or meets the ear. But it's all the same, the past, the present and the future.[114]

But perhaps such remarks, expressed very confidently and with no acknowledgment of Nietzsche, are the product not simply of Dylan's interest in Zen, nor of his continuing self-exploration, but also of the attempt to get back to basics, to clear away the ruins and remnants of former failures with the album *Planet Waves*.

The sleeve notes to the album are as open and personal as anything written since *Some Other Kinds of Songs* in 1964. Dylan presents a retrospective personal assessment, a thumbnail sketch of his past and some of the circumstances and influences of his formative years. In the first few words, he acknowledges his Jewishness:

> Back to the Starting Point! The Kick-off, Hebrew letters on the wall.

Brief flashes of the past enter his mind – his arrival in New York, for example:

> NYC in early autumn, leaves flying in the park.[115]

---

[114] On the *Mary Travers and Friend Radio Show*, 1975.

[115] This must be a particularly significant memory as Joan Baez also recalls a similar scene in her retrospective song about Bob Dylan, 'Diamonds and Rust', in which she sings: 'Now I see you standing with brown leaves falling all around and snow in your hair...'

He allows himself to drift into reminiscence of an earlier past, as a youth in the Midwest amid 'beer halls & pinballs, polka bands' and all the paraphernalia of the fifties:

> furious gals with garters & smeared lips … doing the Hula … Space guys off duty with big dicks & ducktails ALL wind up voting for Eisenhower … getting killed on motorcycles.

His last wry point takes us closer to his own past, to which the notes refer most specifically – beginning with an acknowledgment of the 'masks' of identity discussed in previous chapters and with which 'Dirge' concerns itself: 'We sensed each other beneath the mask'.

Dylan goes on to give an account of his career and development in the 1960s when he:

> pitched a tent in the street & joined the traveling circus, Love at first sight!

But by 1966 'the sideshow took over – what a sight'. With the accident and the subsequent spiritual search for self explored in the *John Wesley Harding* album, 'I lit out for parts unknown … searching thru the ruins for a glimpse of Buddha'. Dylan concludes this particular section with the somewhat ominous admission that he subsequently 'bought a serpent from a passing Angel'.

1974 marked the beginning of the end of Dylan's marriage to Sara. If with *New Morning* Dylan had begun to admit, artistically, the failure of reality to measure up to ideals, or his own failure to live up to an identity he had wished upon himself, the years between must have been, personally, a continuing struggle to cling to a lifestyle that the *Nashville Skyline* songs and certain *New Morning* songs attempted to celebrate, but which others were forced to deny. The traumas of separation from Sara are graphically expressed in the songs on *Blood on the Tracks*, while the dichotomy of feelings – the extremes of love and hate – are presented on *Planet Waves*. Alongside the songs of disgust and contempt are songs intended to praise, maybe even to flatter,

seduce or placate. 'Something There Is About You', 'Never Say
Goodbye', and, most notably, 'Wedding Song' and 'You Angel
You' are such songs, as is the contemporary 'Nobody 'Cept You'
– all of which collectively anticipate the last gasp 'Sara' (as do
certain *Street-Legal* songs, though in a different manner).

The remark about buying 'a serpent from a passing Angel'
refers directly to Dylan's response to his relationship with
Sara, relating it to the archetypal relationship between man
and woman represented in the Adam and Eve story: woman is
irresistible but is necessarily, and eternally, the cause of man's
fall from grace.

The sleeve notes conclude 'Yeah the ole days are gone forever
and the new ones ain't far behind'. There's a final pan across
America's landscape, with Dylan's camera-eye finally coming to
rest on the starting-point:

> Cities of the flesh – Milwaukee, Ann Arbour, Chicago,
> Bismarck, South Dakota, Duluth! Duluth – where
> Baudelaire lived & Goya cashed in his Chips, where
> Joshua brought the house down!

The adolescent identifications with poet and painter – and
the 'Joshua' recollection which makes me think of Dylan's Little
Richard act shaking high school parents in late 1955 – lead on
to the conclusion:

> From there it was straight up – a Little jolt of Mexico, and
> some good LUCK, a Little power over the Grave, some
> more brandy & the teeth of a Lion & a compass.

These are sentiments that Dylan acknowledges again years later.
The reference to Mexico is a strictly autobiographical reference to
Dylan's filming of *Pat Garrett and Billy the Kid* with Sam Peckinpah
in Durango. The crediting of his survival to 'good LUCK' is
echoed in 'Dirge's acknowledgment of 'Lady Luck who shines on
me' and 'Idiot Wind's 'I can't help it if I'm lucky'.

Street-Legal's final track, 'Where Are You Tonight? (Journey
Through Dark Heat)', concludes with the great cry 'I can't believe

it! I can't believe I'm alive!'[116] but it is in 1979 that Dylan finally identifies the source of his apparent 'power over the grave', which he defines as God's 'saving grace': 'I've escaped death so many times I know I'm only living by the saving grace that's over me'.

Planet Waves, meanwhile, offers songs in which Dylan revisits his past. 'On a Night Like This' admits 'we got much to talk about and much to reminisce', and 'Tough Mama' has brief acknowledgments of two friends from the early sixties – Ramblin' Jack Elliott and Peter La Farge:

> Jack the Cowboy went up north
> He's buried in your past
> The Lone Wolf went out drinking
> That was over pretty fast.

'Something There Is About You' questions Sara's attraction in terms of the past:

> Is it because you remind me
> Of something that used to be.

He then confronts such a past directly:

> Thought I'd shaken the wonder
> and the phantoms of my youth.
> Rainy days on the Great Lakes
> walkin' the hills of old Duluth
> There was me and Danny Lopez
> cold eyes, black night and then there was Ruth
> Something there is about you
> that brings back a long-forgotten truth.

There's also the announcement that personally he's reached a watershed. 'Going, Going, Gone' makes reference to the 'moderate man' persona that Dylan has had to abandon:

---

[116] A line which is echoed in the Craig McGregor interview of 1978 in which Dylan said, 'As you go on you begin to realise, if nothing else, at least you're alive … at least I'm alive!'

I been hangin' on threads
I been playin' it straight
Now, I've just got to cut loose
Before it gets late.

Cutting loose involved a return to the stage with a massive nationwide tour of the USA, a new record label, and renewed association with The Band, his backing group from 1965 through 1967 who accompany him on *Planet Waves* and in the 1974 concerts. Maybe the whole thing was an effort to come to terms with 'something that used to be'. Certainly Dylan's vocals are as sharp as ever. He readopts the voice of the mid-1960s, abandoning the smoothness of the vocal style used on *Nashville Skyline*, *Self Portrait* and, to a lesser extent, *New Morning*. The concerts showcase Dylan rocking and singing as hard as ever. Even his hair begins to grow again. There's no doubt that he sees it all as an important time for personal redirection. He knows where he's been and he knows who he's been, even if he doesn't know where he's going or who he is now. The point is, it would seem, that it is better to 'travel on' rather than to 'sit':

Grandma said, 'Boy, go and follow your heart
And you'll be fine at the end of the line.'

On the album's opening cut, 'On a Night Like This', as The Band rock along exuberantly, Dylan sings, 'if I'm not too far off, I think we did this once before'. If, in these songs, he seems to be cutting into a perspective from where he's been, and if he's uncertain as to where he's going other than rediscovering lost directions, he's still putting a great deal of faith in his relationship with Sara. The album contains perhaps six songs addressed to her and Dylan's working title for the record was initially *Lovesongs*.[117] If, in the 1960s Dylan refused to plead or compromise, now – to preserve maybe his conception of his own identity – he willingly does both. 'Something There Is About You' is a song of praise:

[117] And subsequently *Ceremonies of the Horsemen* – a line from the 1965 love song 'Love Minus Zero/No Limit'.

Suddenly I found you
And the spirit in me sings
Don't have to look no further
You're the soul of many things.

In 'Tough Mama', she's presented as a 'Sweet Goddess, born of
a blinding light and a changing wind' and in 'You Angel You' as
an 'angel' who is 'fine as anything's fine'. The plea in 'Never Say
Goodbye', echoed in the closing lines of 'Sara' a few years later,
is direct and unqualified:

You're beautiful beyond words
You're beautiful to me
You can make me cry
Never say goodbye.

But it is in 'Wedding Song' and in 'Nobody 'Cept You', an
album outtake, that Dylan most notably expresses his hopes in,
and his need for, his relationship with Sara. If the words of praise
above have gone some way towards deifying her, the lyrics of
these songs are conclusive. 'Nobody 'Cept You', for instance, has
Dylan declaring:

There's nothing 'round here I believe in
'Cept you, yeah, you
And there's nothing to me that's sacred
'Cept you…
Got nothing left to live or die for
'Cept you.

In 'Wedding Song', we have an equivalent statement: 'I love
you more than life itself'. The song is an expression of total love,
gratitude, admiration and need. Dylan expresses his debt to her for
her influence upon his past and the direction his life has taken as
he left former comparatively valueless lifestyles behind. He owes
her a great deal in this respect: 'you breathed on me and made
my life a richer one to live'. Not only that, but in truth 'what
is more, you saved my life'. Dylan particularly emphasises one
point, both here and in his dedication in *Writings and Drawings*,

the dedication concludes 'to Sara who made it all complete', while in 'Wedding Song' he says 'ever since you walked right in, the circle's been complete' and 'you're the other half of what I am, you're the missing piece'.

There is a desperation in 'Wedding Song' and, more significantly, in the later 'Sara' that make sense only by acknowledging that Dylan's identity – his concept of himself as it existed in 1974 – depends on his marriage to and relationship with Sara continuing. She has not just given him life, but identity; with her, he knows who he is and feels 'complete'.

Just before he acknowledges 'you saved my life' in 'Wedding Song', Dylan sings 'you ... pulled me from the hole', which is reminiscent of Lear's first words on being awoken after the exhaustion that followed his madness in the storm: 'You do me wrong to take me out o' the grave.'[118] Lear is naturally confused, knowing neither where he is nor who he is, or even *if* he is:

> I will not swear these are my hands...
> Would I were assured
> Of my condition.

But Cordelia's presence reassures him and gives him the identity he has lacked since his abdication. The storm taught him that he is a man and now he learns from her exactly who he is as a man: 'As I am a man, I think this lady to be my child Cordelia.' If she is his child, he is her father, and he knows it. Thus Lear's identity depends upon Cordelia. Dylan's identity depends upon his being defined and completed by Sara in the same way. Without her he stands to lose the only conception of self left to him, save the persona of the public performer – the mask formerly cast away having been readopted.

The passion and desperation in Dylan's pleas are thus explicable and it is clear, as it was at times in *New Morning*, that the relationship is threatened. As he sings in 'Shelter from the Storm', 'something has been lost'; in 'Wedding Song', he acknowledges 'what's lost is lost, we can't regain'. While the song has its hyperbolic

---

[118] *King Lear*, 4.7.

declarations of love – 'I'd sacrifice the world for you' or 'if there is eternity I'd love you there again' – there's also the admission of pain – 'your love cuts like a knife' – and the plea:

> Oh, can't you see that you were born to stand by my side
> And I was born to be with you
> you were born to be my bride…
> And I could never let you go, no matter what goes on.

But that last line betrays that something *is* going on, and 'can't you see' suggests an unwillingness or inability on her part to recognise just how much rests on her continued presence.

Dylan's belief in Sara's being 'the other half' of what he is and 'the missing piece' of his complete identity relates to a body of mythological material with which Jung was familiar, which describes androgyny as a residual element in the human psyche. There is a mythic theology, which is almost universally diffused, about an androgynous god as creator-creatrix. Humanity, supposedly modelled after the divine image, was itself correspondingly androgynous, but somehow mankind fell away from, or was severed from, the original wholeness and degenerated into the imperfect man and woman of this world, ever in search of completion through integration of the alienated opposite.

Plato's *Symposium* contains its own account of the origins of human nature with three original sexes: male, female and a union of the two, the androgyne. Androgynes were mighty and powerful beings who dared to scale the heavens and attack the gods until Zeus decided to humble their pride and improve their manners by slicing them in two:

> After the division, the two parts, each desiring their other half, came together when they could. Each of us now, having one side only, is always looking for their other half … and when one of them meets with their other half, the actual half of themself … the pair are lost in an amazement of love and friendship and intimacy … the intense yearning which each of them has for the other does not appear to be the desire of lovers' intercourse

but of something else which the soul of either evidently desires and cannot tell and of which she has only a dark and doubtful presentiment.

The myth of the androgyne never referred to a species existing on earth, but to the celestial world of the imagination where the immortal prototypes for creation exist. But the *Symposium* describes the sense of longing that lovers experience which transcends rational explanation. From a psychological point of view, Plato's androgyne attempts to explain why human beings' need of each other seems to transcend drives of sexuality and reproduction, or even the desire for companionship. Hence, in 'Wedding Song', Dylan sings that Sara 'satisfied the burning in my soul' and refers to her as a 'mystical wife' in 'Sara'.

Dylan's search for his other half began with his own immaturity: 'Mixed Up Confusion', one of his earliest songs, sees him 'Lookin' for a woman whose head's mixed up like mine'. In 'Love Is Just a Four Letter Word', Dylan sings of 'searching for my double, looking for complete evaporation to the core'.

The 'complete evaporation to the core' is the search for self with which this book concerns itself and is only attainable when the ego – the superficial self – is extinguished. Baudelaire wrote, in the opening sentence of his *Journaux Intimes*:

De la vaporisation et de la centralisation du Moi. Tout est là

[Everything is in the concentration and the evaporation of the ego.]

It is clear enough that Dylan had this statement in mind here. The 'evaporation of the ego' might be achieved by the attainment of a female 'double', who would be his 'other half' – the 'mystical wife' – and make him 'complete' and allow him to attain individuation and self-realisation. But psychic union can only be fulfilled outside matrimony. Although he tries hard to persuade both himself and her that she is his 'twin' in the songs to Sara, the Jungian concepts of the processes of individuation through this psychic union is extremely complicated – Jung once said that 'only a poet could begin to understand' them.[119] Briefly, in philosophic alchemy there exists the idea of the 'Soror Mystica' – the Mystical Sister – who works with the alchemist and who is with him at all times through the long process of fusion. At the end, there's a mystic wedding and the creation of the androgyne, which could not have occurred without the presence of the sister. Such a psychic union could never take place in ordinary love but only in a spirit of love, for it is a 'love without love', being a fusion of opposing factors within the psyche of each of the lovers. It is a process of magical individuation and the final union takes place, importantly, within the isolated individual.

Dylan's attempts to identify his real wife with his 'mystical wife' are doomed to fail. He faces the problem again and again in the songs on *Blood on the Tracks*, but it becomes clearer that the identities of Sara and of his searched-for 'twin' are not one and the same.

In *Renaldo and Clara*, Dylan explores the problem even further. The figure of the alchemical 'Sister', who must be present for the alchemist to realise the psychic union, can be equated with the 'Woman in White', who is played both by Sara Dylan and Joan Baez. Bob Dylan, in his persona of Renaldo the singer, confronts in turn Joan Baez (his old lover), Sara Dylan (his wife), and the Woman in White with whom he secretly attempts to communicate and whom he directly identifies as the 'mystical wife'. In a notable scene in which a bemused and somewhat drunken Renaldo is faced on one side by Sara and on the other by the Woman in White, he is asked, first by Sara, 'Do you love her?' and then by the Woman in White, 'Do you love her?' His answer is:

> Do I love her like I love you? No.
> Do I love you like I love her? No.

Thus he separates the kinds of love – human, sexual love, and psychic or 'magic' love. This echoes Christ's answer to his disciples in the Gnostic *Gospel of Philip*. When they question him as to his

[119] Quoted in *A Record Of Two Friendships* by Miguel Serrano.

relationship to Mary Magdalene, who is employed as a symbol of divine wisdom and who, as such, is Christ's most intimate companion and a parallel of the alchemical sister, Christ replies, 'Why do I not love you as I love her?'[120]

Throughout *Renaldo and Clara*, there are explorations of the cessation of the real affair between Bob and Sara Dylan – though the scenarios are acted out by various other characters – and of the nature of the psychic encounter for which Dylan is still in search. In one scene, Clara, played by Sara, approaches another writer, Rodeo, played by Sam Shepard, but enacts a scene which is symbolic of Dylan's dilemma:

> Rodeo: I'm not chasing you, I can tell you that much.
> Clara: There's no need to chase me; if I go, I go.
> Rodeo: That's what I'm afraid of.
> Clara: What do you want me to stay for? Why do you need me?
> Rodeo: I need you to perform certain magical things with me. That's all.

This is a clear parallel to the alchemist talking to the sister.

In 1974, Dylan found himself confronting a further personal crisis. The identity he assumed in 1968 and presented on *John Wesley Harding* was nurtured and maintained with increasing difficulty for more than five years until it had to be cast aside, having become restrictive and, most importantly, having proved itself to be an assumed persona and not a true identity for which Dylan was still in search. This coincides with, or perhaps becomes the cause of – or is caused by – the deterioration of the marital relationship with Sara.

Dylan's attempts to cling to his identity as husband, whilst denying the 'straight' or 'moderate man' persona that is part of the same identity, put him in an impossible dilemma. Sara's presence defines him and he feels that she is his intended and looked-for mystical twin as well as his wife. But such identities are necessarily mutually exclusive. Dylan pleads desperately, and in fact with temporary success, for Sara to stay with him. But he

[120] Quoted in *The Gnostic Gospels*, Elaine Pagels, Weidenfeld & Nicholson, 1980.

is no longer who he was. Sara leaves and, in anguish, Bob Dylan steps outside himself to achieve an objectivity to which he has previously aspired but never attained. The objectivity and pain combine to allow him to produce his most powerful lyrics in the songs that appear on *Blood on the Tracks*.

14. Tangled Up in Blue

It strikes me funny that people actually have the gall to think that I have some kind of fantastic imagination. It gets very lonesome.

— Bob Dylan, *Playboy*, May 1966

Bob Dylan can scarcely have felt more alienated from himself than he did in late 1974. Having once again adopted the persona of the public performer with the US tour, he found himself facing separation and, ultimately, divorce from Sara. In order to achieve some kind of perspective on himself and on his situation, Dylan found it necessary to go outside of himself and become completely objective – to become, in fact, completely egoless and thus achieve the goal of self-assessment which had previously eluded him.

Such self-assessment requires total honesty, and only complete objectivity can aspire towards that. The songs written for *Blood on the Tracks* include naked self-portraits. Some contain assessments of Sara and the relationship, which is accepted as being at an end. Other songs separate, for the first time, Sara and the 'other' woman figure of whom Dylan has long been in search. Just as *Renaldo and Clara* attempts to separate Dylan the artist (Renaldo) from Dylan the public figure (Bob Dylan), so *Blood on the Tracks* attempts a similar separation of identity and thus aspires finally towards self-definition in such songs as 'Tangled Up in Blue' and 'Simple Twist of Fate'.

'Tangled Up in Blue', the album's opening song, presents a retrospective account and analysis of a relationship that is both autobiographical and mythical. Through his relationship with Sara, Dylan sees himself as being in communication with all women, or with the essence of femininity. Although Sara is – or has been – his alienated opposite, such a figure exists beyond her and can be found in other women, at other times and in other places. When he sings 'I seen a lot of women but she never escaped my mind', he admits this indirectly. The 'she' he cannot forget or escape from is his other half, who exists not as a separate entity from the many women he's seen, but as a part of them. She was a part of Sara too, who is necessarily included in the song's opening:

> She was married when we first met
> Soon to be divorced.

There are other directly autobiographical glimpses of Dylan's past:

> I lived with them on Montague Street
> In a basement down the stairs
> There was music in the cafés at night
> And revolution in the air.

And of his present:

> Me, I'm still on the road
> Headin' for another joint.

The song operates on the mythic level too, though. Dylan weaves into the song a fictitious past for himself, drifting from place to place, from job to job, and from time to time encountering the 'she' to whom it is his destiny to be forever linked. The central section of the song presents one such encounter in 'a topless place'. Again Dylan perhaps owes more than a little to Hermann Hesse's *Steppenwolf* as he presents himself stopping into the bar for a beer. In *Steppenwolf*, Harry Haller, suffering 'nausea, agony and despair' finds himself wandering from bar to bar, ending up at The Black Eagle, where he too has a 'chance' encounter with a woman: 'She gave me a friendly and observant look as I came up and with a smile moved to one side to make room for me.' The first thing she does is to wipe Harry's dirty glasses before she turns her attention to his dirty shoes: 'She took me under her wing just as I needed ... she filled my glass.' All the while Harry looks at her, 'I could not tell of whom it was she reminded me', whilst she correctly identifies him as an academic whose studies have meant that he never learned to enjoy himself. Eventually, Harry can contain his curiosity no longer:

> 'But now, I really must know your name.'
>   She looked at me for a moment without speaking.
>   'Perhaps you can guess it. I should be glad if you did. Pull yourself together and take a good look at me. Hasn't it ever occurred to you that sometimes my face is just like a boy's? Now, for instance.'
>   Yes, now that I looked at her face carefully, I had to admit she was right. It was a boy's face. And after a moment I saw something in her face that reminded me of my boyhood and of my friend of those days. His name was Hermann. For a moment it seemed that she had turned into this Hermann.
>   'If you were a boy,' said I in amazement, 'I should say your name was Hermann.'
>   'Who knows, perhaps I am one and am simply in woman's clothing,' she said playfully.
>   'Is your name Hermine?'
>   She nodded, beaming, delighted at my guess.

The parallels in the encounter in 'Tangled Up in Blue' should be clear enough. Dylan sings of his fascination with her face, which he 'just kept lookin' at'. She approaches him and asks 'Don't I know your name?'[121] Her fascination with his face corresponds with his for hers, whilst his diffidence and uneasiness, and her care for him – 'she bent down to tie the laces of my shoe' – echo *Steppenwolf* exactly. Hermine plays records for Harry; the woman in Dylan's song offers a book of poems by a thirteenth-century Italian poet – maybe Dante (whom Dylan speaks of having read in the 1968 *Sing Out!* interview) maybe Petrarch (whom Dylan is to confuse with Plutarch in the 1978 Jonathon Cott interview from *Rolling Stone*). In either case:

> Everyone of them words rang true
> And glowed like burning coal
> Pourin' off of every page
> Like it was written in my soul.

---

[121] In some live versions of the song, she says 'Don't tell me, let me guess your name.'

225

It may be that Dylan had in mind Baudelaire's 'Le Balcon' here, in which the poet recalls similar evenings spent with his own 'mother of memories, mistress of mistresses ... we often said things that never will perish, on these evenings illumined by the glowing coal'.

The association with Baudelaire is confirmed when in a 1978 concert, Dylan sings:

> She opened up a book of poems
> And shouted it to me
> Written by Charles Baudelaire...

Harry Haller, in *Steppenwolf*, is an obvious persona of his creator, Hermann Hesse. The narrator of 'Tangled Up in Blue', in the officially released version of the song, speaks in the first person and thus can be confused with his creator. In the originally recorded version – one of five cuts not used on the album release – it is still 'I' who has the encounter in the topless place, but the rest of the song speaks of 'he'; in live recordings of the song, Dylan seemingly alternates 'I' and 'he' at random. As I've already pointed out, the song combines both factual and fictitious autobiography and operates on real and mythic planes concurrently. Both Dylan and Hesse separate person and persona in their art. 'Hermine' is Harry's 'twin sister', the feminine image of himself; she cares for him as a wife, sister and mother, and thus assumes symbolic proportions. As the novel progresses, Hermine's identity melts from that of 'a woman' into 'womankind' until Harry finally consummates a symbolic marriage to her, which represents the complete welding of all aspects of his nature. The extracts from their meeting quoted above indicate that Hermine is not separate from, but part of Harry and, by implication, Hesse's personas.

In 'Tangled Up in Blue', the meeting of the song's narrator with the woman in the bar is an exact parallel. She approaches him, dominates him, mothers him, loves him. Because she is the feminine part of his own nature, her communication with him through the book of poems is directly with his soul. To realise himself fully, he must embrace her and absorb her. One of Jung's symbols for the self is the hermaphrodite. In 'Tangled Up in Blue', Bob Dylan presents a mythologised version of his male role – working in the Great North Woods, or on a fishing boat, or, in the original version of the song, 'loading cargo on to a truck' at an 'airplane plant'. He projects his femininity – his emotional poetic nature – on to the mythic 'she' who offers back to him a book of poems which seems as though 'it was written in my soul from me to you'. She is, and always has been, and always will be, a part of him. She knows that any separation is temporary – 'we'll meet again someday' – for she truly is his 'other half', the 'missing piece' of the total self, of which both ego and anima are merely parts.

If 'Tangled Up in Blue' can be referred to as a 'spiritual autobiography', the distinction its author attempts to draw is between himself and his 'other self', the self reflected in the mirror of his art. The distinction is between real self and perceived self, between person and persona. Both are conscious but the 'I' who is heard singing and thus narrating his semi-mythic history exists on a different level from the author who is relating aspects of his real history. But the main difficulty comes in trying to establish reality because, through the art, the writer's objectivity and self-assessment become the persona's vision, and thus a transformation occurs. There is even a brief further confusion of identity with the lines 'he started into dealing with slaves, and something inside of him died', which calls up the figure of Arthur Rimbaud (with whom Dylan has always, if subconsciously, identified) and the dichotomy between the man and the poet that occurred with Rimbaud's ceasing to write and his journey into Abyssinia.

The original version of the song includes a verse with an internal person change, in which 'he' and 'she' are presented and then commented upon by an 'I':

> He was always in a hurry
> Too busy or too stoned
> And everything that she ever planned
> Just had to be postponed

She thought they were successful
And he thought they were blessed
With objects and material things
But I never was impressed.

Here the view of the song's author has turned into the persona's vision and coincides until it is impossible to define exactly who 'I' is. The song is an important one on an important album as Dylan is forced into objectivity by the ending of his marriage. He must confront the problematic relationship between person and persona and attempt to resolve it. *Blood on the Tracks* is a record of a crisis, both in Bob Dylan's life and in his personal development. But it is not simply a biographical account; if it were, it could not function as a work of art. The biographical roots are perfectly clear, but he turns his experiences and feelings into the product of his artistic imagination, consciously reworking them in an effort to understand them, and himself, fully. Dylan presents himself and his experiences through his own perceptions, remoulding real anguish into its artistic counterpart. Feelings of loneliness and pain recur throughout, with regret and sorrow which, at times, approach despair.

The 'she' who is left behind then reencountered only to be left behind again in 'Tangled Up in Blue', must continue to be the object of his search. Thus the song concludes with the declaration, 'So now I'm goin' back again I got to get to her somehow'. Similar statements recur throughout the set of songs. In 'Simple Twist of Fate' it's expressed as a hope – 'maybe she'll pick him out again' – lyrics that, in performance, were often changed to 'maybe he'll spot her once again'. In 'You're a Big Girl Now', he says 'I know where I can find you', but in 'You're Gonna Make Me Lonesome When You Go' it's not that easy – 'I'll look for you in old Honolulu, San Francisco, Ashtabula'.

'Simple Twist of Fate' is a good example of this mythologising of real experience. At the song's beginning, the persona presented feels alone when he is with his lover. The word 'together' emphasises their closeness, as it did in 'Down Along the Cove', yet the atmosphere seems to anticipate her departure. The darkening sky of the first stanza, the oppressive 'heat of the night' of the second, and the lonesome saxophone (or clarinet) and the blind man of the third, all take on ominous significance in retrospect. The urban scenario is tacky: 'old canal', 'strange hotel' (which becomes 'old' or 'renovated' in concert), 'beat-up shade', and the 'bare room'. This external desolation becomes internal with her leaving – 'felt an emptiness inside to which he just could not relate'. There's a brief submission to the sourest of grapes – 'he told himself he didn't care' – but in the penultimate stanza, life becomes a 'hunt', a quest for his lost love, 'how long must he wait?'

The final stanza begins:

> People tell me it's a sin
> To know and feel too much within
> I still believe she was my twin.

This is interesting not simply for the new perspective – the change of person from 'he' to 'I' indicates that Dylan is attempting to unite person and persona which have been carefully kept apart here, presumably to ensure objectivity. But the conclusion is clearly subjective. The belief that 'she was my twin' brings us back to the concept of the 'other half'. But Dylan subsequently modified the lyrics:

> People tell me it's a crime
> To know and feel [or: To remember her]
> For too long a time
> She should have caught me in my prime
> She would have stayed with me
> 'Stead of going off to sea
> And leaving me to meditate.

These lines take us back before Sara, to Suze Rotolo and her 'sailing away' to Italy; they suggest that the mythic 'she' is no individual, but part of a whole. This 'she' may be encountered in many or in all women – in Suze Rotolo, in Joan Baez, in Sara. In each lover it is the same 'she', who seems to be a projection of the anima element of the male self that remains constant and essential.

When, in 'You're a Big Girl Now', he sings 'Oh I know where I can find you, in somebody's room', he's acknowledging that she can be found anywhere and everywhere. The pain of separation is not any easier for that knowledge, though:

> I'm going out of my mind
> With a pain that stops and starts
> Like a corkscrew to my heart
> Ever since we've been apart.[122]

But at least there's the strength and belief of 'I can make it through'.

The singer's identification, in this song, with the bird – 'and I'm just like that bird ... singing just for you' – is symbolic. The bird represents his artistic soul, midway between heaven and earth, expressing truth and feeling despite the inevitable tears that accompany such truth.

A similar point recurs in the beautiful 'If You See Her, Say Hello':

> If you see her, say hello
> She might be in Tangier.

She *might* conceivably be anywhere, of course, and in live versions Dylan changes the location from 'Babylon' to 'North Saigon'! The point of the 'separation' from 'she' here is both that the pain pierces 'to the heart' and that 'she still lives inside of me, we've never been apart'. He admits further: 'I hear her name here and there as I go from town to town'. Once again there is a duality to the song's function. On the personal plane, the song is an autobiographical note to a lover's quarrel and parting:

> We had a falling-out
> Like lovers often will...
> The bitter taste still lingers on
> From the night I tried to make her stay.

[122] Here Dylan (unconsciously perhaps) echoes an image of William Cowper's in 'Sweet Meat Has Sour Sauce' where he describes a feeling of pity: 'Oh how it enters my soul like an awl!'

But on the mythic plane, the parting is one he has experienced before and knows he will experience again. Indeed, the experience also exists as part of the present: 'I replay the past, I know every scene by heart'. Again, Dylan may have had Baudelaire's 'Le Balcon' in mind – a poem in which the poet recalls similar intimate scenes and says 'Je... revis mon passé' ['I relive my past']. Dylan's 'sundown, yellow moon' also hints at Baudelaire's 'Que les soleils sont beaux dans les chaudes soirees' ['How beautiful are the suns of sultry evenings'] from the same poem. In 'replay' and 'every scene', Dylan indicates that he sees himself as playing out a pre-scripted part in a drama whose events and endings are already worked out; the play on 'by heart' is as painful as it is conscious.

A major song on *Blood on the Tracks* is 'Idiot Wind', which represents as personal a viewpoint on the ending of his relationship with Sara as anything else written at this time. In 'Fountain of Sorrow', Jackson Browne wrote:

> When you see through love's illusions, there lies the danger
> And your perfect lover just looks like a perfect fool
> So you go running off in search of a perfect stranger
> While the loneliness seems to spring from your life
> Like a fountain from a pool.

'Idiot Wind' presents exactly this sight through illusion. It is bitter and angry, but most of all it's an expression of disgust – for Sara, for himself, for the affair, for sexuality which brought them together, and maybe even for the humanity that must be borne until death.

Dylan opens the song with deliberate irrelevance – irrelevance, that is, to the song's main line of thought. The depiction of himself as the victim of misguided and deliberately misleading publicity, and of an equally misguided and frustrating public response, is clearly heartfelt. The points that prompt the opening protests are the 'stories in the press', which present fantastically exaggerated and ridiculously unreal rumour tales that Dylan has suffered since his rise to fame in the mid-sixties, and which he has borne with what must be acknowledged as remarkable tolerance. The response of the public is to deny him the basic privileges of respect or privacy: 'people see me all the time and they just can't remember how to act'. But he concedes that the public are the victims of the publicity machine. Having accepted 'big ideas, images and distorted facts' as truth, and thus having been denied knowledge of the 'person', they respond only to the 'persona'. All this must be, and has been, simply accepted and suffered by 'Bob Dylan the person', who has continued to exist behind the mask of 'Bob Dylan the performer'. But what he cannot tolerate is the adoption of such a 'public' response by a person who should know better:

> Even you yesterday
> You had to ask me where it was at
> I couldn't believe after all these years
> You didn't know me any better than that.

She has made the mistake of confusing 'person' and 'persona', which is indicative not simply of a lack of understanding or knowledge but of a lack of sympathy. When such deficiency is recognised in the woman whose greatest function is to provide 'shelter from the storm' for the 'hunted' or 'ravaged' artist, the response is understandably powerful: dismay, anger, despair and grief mingle with contempt. Dylan's juxtaposition of the ironic 'sweet lady' with 'idiot' superbly expresses this. The chorus addressed directly to her, is venomous:

> Idiot wind
> Blowing every time you move your mouth...
> You're an idiot, babe
> It's a wonder that you still know how to breathe.

Dismay transmuted into disgust is carried over to the second stanza – 'you hurt the ones that I love best and cover up the truth with lies'. While there are traces of a self-indulgent self-pity – an image of 'a lone soldier on the cross' and the lamentation about the lack of 'peace and quiet' – the viciousness of the attack culminates in the stanza's startling conclusion: 'one day you'll be in the ditch, flies buzzin' around your eyes'.[123]

Such flaming passion soon burns itself out, though there's a hit of it in the third stanza – 'your corrupt ways' – and in the next two choruses that repeat 'you're an idiot, babe'. But Dylan's aggression becomes somewhat redirected as the song progresses. As the third stanza opens, for example, he shows that he is prepared not to simply make her the scapegoat for the dissolution of the affair: 'It was gravity which pulled us down and destiny which broke us apart'. It's not that he feels himself to be her victim, but that they are both victims of forces that exist beyond either of their control. The acknowledgment of her control of his primitive or instinctual nature is expressed not in resentment but simply in acceptance – 'you tamed the lion in my cage' – and after all he's come through, it 'just wasn't enough to change my heart'.

The same point, basically, is also expressed in the second stanza: 'in the final end he won the war after losing every battle'. But in truth in such wars there are no victors: 'you'll find out when you reach the top you're on the bottom'.

Retrospection on the affair becomes filled with sorrow rather than anger. 'Springtime turned slowly into autumn', but only the beginning and the ending of the love affair seem to be memorable. The turning may be slow – in later concert versions 'slowly' actually became 'quickly' – but there's no acknowledgment, no apparent recollection of the affair's hot summer.

The final, great, stanza of 'Idiot Wind' begins:

> I can't feel you any more
> I can't even touch the books you've read
> Every time I crawl past your door
> I been wishin' I was somebody else instead.

The disgust suggested here is recorded with more than a little sorrow and regret, as seen in the fourth line. There may be one last hit, and that, of course, is a very human foible – 'I been

---

[123] cf. Shakespeare's *Antony and Cleopatra* where Cleopatra anticipates her death in: 'a ditch in Egypt. Be gentle grave unto me. Rather on Nilus' mud, lay me stark naked and let the waterflies blow me into abhorring.'

double-crossed now for the very last time' – but there is the kind
of recollection that was denied in the third stanza:

> Down the highway, down the tracks
> Down the road to ecstasy
> I followed you beneath the stars
> Hounded by your memory
> And all your ragin' glory.

These are lines that Rimbaud might have written, sung with
powerful emotion, particularly on the live version that appears
on *Hard Rain* and which is surely one of Dylan's finest moments.
Despite it all – the pain, the subsequent and uncontrollable
blame and disgust, the anger and the contempt – it is sorrow
that is transcendent. There may be triumph in the shedding of
the burden of the 'howling beast' in his soul, and in the shout
of 'now I'm finally free!', but the 'hurt' and 'pain' remain and
must be transcended. Similarly the 'memory' of the woman and
her 'ragin' glory' demands not just acknowledgment, but tribute,
which is given freely:

> You'll never know the hurt I suffered
> Nor the pain I rise above
> And I'll never know the same about you
> Your holiness or your kind of love
> And it makes me feel so sorry.

With this statement of ultimate sorrow, Dylan even allows the
previously acerbic chorus to lose most of its bitterness, and to
embrace himself:

> Idiot wind
> Blowing through the buttons of our coats
> Blowing through the letters that we wrote
> Idiot wind
> Blowing through the dust upon our shelves
> We're idiots, babe
> It's a wonder we can even feed ourselves.

It's the statement of a very mature artist. The profound sadness and profound resignation are to recur in the album's closing lines from 'Buckets of Rain':

> Life is sad, life is a bust
> All you can do is do what you must.

The sentiments here and in the final lines of 'Idiot Wind' are reminiscent of Macbeth's conclusions in his meditation on his own existence, following his receipt of the news of the death of his wife and his realisation that everything has, and will, come to nothing:

> All our yesterdays have lighted fools
> The way to dusty death. Out, out brief candle!
> Life's but a walking shadow; a poor player
> That struts and frets his hour upon the stage
> And then is heard no more. It is a tale
> Told by an idiot, full of sound and fury
> Signifying nothing.[124]

As well as the 'dust' and 'idiot' associations, and the observations on life's significance, or lack of it, the idea of sound and fury passing into nothing reflects neatly enough the emotional progression expressed in 'Idiot Wind'. But Shakespeare's lines are also appropriate in their depiction of man as 'a poor player that struts and frets his hour upon the stage and then is heard no more'.

Shakespeare is playing games with images here, for the words are spoken, not by the usurping King of Scotland, Macbeth, but by a player presenting an image of Macbeth to an audience, and who is thus, in reality, strutting and fretting on a stage. As the words are delivered, player and character played become one and the same. This unification goes further to embrace both dramatist – a 'player' himself – and audience, who, whilst they accept the performance, willingly exchange 'reality' for an image of it that may, in Macbeth's soliloquy, be closer to absolute reality than the world they left outside the theatre.

[124] *Macbeth*, 5.5.

Renaldo and Clara, as has already been observed, concerns itself with these very matters. In a revealing interview with Jonathon Cott, published in *Rolling Stone* in January 1978, Dylan speaks at length of the film's import. *Renaldo and Clara* makes use of Bob Dylan's physical image – the obvious means by which Bob Dylan is perceived by his audience – and Bob Dylan's name, which may or may not identify 'the real Bob Dylan'. The film's 'auteur' exploits this tangle and can thus move between reality and illusion and destroy the boundaries of perception that divide myth from reality. As Bob Dylan, in interview, said about the film's 'auteur': 'Bob Dylan didn't make it. I made it.' Or, as Ellen Willis wrote: 'Dylan has exploited his image as a vehicle for artistic statement.'[125] In the same essay, Willis says:

> The tenacity of the modern publicity apparatus often makes artists' personalities more familiar than their work ... If there is an audience for images, artists will inevitably use the image as a medium... Dylan's art is about celebrity.

The film opens with music. Bob Dylan appears singing 'When I Paint My Masterpiece', but he's wearing a mask. The mask, however, is transparent, but beneath it is another mask, a painted white face. Thus, for all its transparency, the mask conceals rather than reveals the man beneath. Dylan tells Cott, 'In the film, the mask is more important than the face. Renaldo [who is the performer in the mask] is oppressed. He's oppressed because he's born.'

This comment takes us back to the words spoken by the actor playing Macbeth, quoted above, and parallels words from *King Lear*, spoken by the actor playing Lear:

> We came crying hither
> Thou knowest the first time that we smell the air
> We wawl and cry...
> When we are born, we cry that we are come
> To this great stage of fools.[126]

[125] Ellen Willis, 'Dylan', *Cheetah*, 1967.
[126] *King Lear*, 4.6.

Dylan goes on, in the Cott interview: 'I'll tell you what this movie is: it's like life exactly, but not an imitation of it. It transcends life, and it's not like life.' Here, he's struggling to express the idea of art mirroring, rather than imitating life discussed earlier in this book. Reflection is an image but not an imitation, and *Renaldo and Clara* is Bob Dylan's mirror.

Late in the film, there's a scene in which Dylan is shown in front of a mirror putting on his white face, thus becoming Renaldo, whom he sees as a reflection of himself, an image but not an imitation. More from Dylan to Cott:

> I'll tell you what my film is about: it's about naked alienation of the inner self against the outer self – alienation taken to the extreme ... the film is about the fact that you have to be faithful to your subconscious, unconscious, superconscious – as well as to your conscious. Integrity is a facet of honesty. It has to do with knowing yourself.

Even though *Renaldo and Clara*, like many of Dylan's songs, is primarily concerned with this search for self-realisation, it may take the search a little further. But it offers no solutions and reaches no conclusions. Any definitions are negative ones: 'We don't really know who Renaldo is. We just know who he isn't.'

It may be that the songs on *Blood on the Tracks* function in a similarly negative way, defining aspects of self which are not, rather than which are. The songs are the record of pain, of loneliness and separation; they are a testament of experience. But if Dylan's search is to progress, it must recommence rather than continue. As with *Planet Waves*, which may be seen as a *false* start rather than a *new* one, *Blood on the Tracks* sees Dylan forced by circumstance to begin over: 'Now I'm goin' back again', he sings on 'Tangled Up in Blue'. He recalls the past – 'I was standin' on the side of the road, rain fallin' on my shoes' – but the past and the present seem to be one and the same. At the end of the song, Dylan declares 'but me I'm still on the road, headin' for another joint'. As 'You're a Big Girl Now' opens, 'I'm back in the rain' and in 'If You See Her, Say Hello', he speaks of 'making the rounds', maybe acknowledging the cyclical nature of his existence. 'I replay the past' and the previously quoted lines which conclude the album accept the concept of destiny or providence:

> All ya can do is do what you must
> You do what you must do
> And you do it well.

In a song written for *Blood on the Tracks* but not included on the album, 'Up to Me', Dylan acknowledges the fact that, despite the perils of existence, Hamlet's 'slings and arrows of outrageous fortune' bring 'money', which 'never changed a thing'; 'death', which kept 'trackin' us down'; and 'time', which 'is an enemy'. It has always been his fate to continue to live and to be an artist:

> If I'd a lived my life by what others were thinkin'
> The heart inside me would've died
> I was just too stubborn to ever be governed
> By enforced insanity
> Someone had to reach for the risin' star
> I guess it was up to me.

Reaching 'for the risin' star' is a romantic view of the poet's role as a man who seeks to go beyond the necessary limits of human existence. To be the thief of fire, to seek to reach the absolute, to become godlike and yet retain individual consciousness, however, is an old philosophical dilemma. Dylan has long been aware of the contradiction, and 'reaching for the risin' star' is very much a part of his past. The condition of human individual existence is imperfection; to have reached infinity would be to have lost one's separate personality. As Baudelaire wrote:

> Poets, artists, the entire human race would be most unhappy if the ideal, this absurdity, this impossibility, were attained.

And of course it is individuation that Dylan has long sought to realise. But the romantic role of the poet is consigned to the past, a part of 'history'. As 'Up to Me' reaches its conclusion, Dylan offers advice that he follows himself: 'So go on boys and play your hands, life is a pantomime'. This returns us to Shakespeare's 'great stage of fools', and further to Hamlet and Dylan's acceptance of apparent destiny: 'one of us has got to hit the road, I guess it must be up to me'.

In 1968 Dylan said, 'I like to play music on the stage. I expect to be playing music endlessly.'[127] In Craig McGregor's interview from January 1978, Dylan was asked, 'Tell me why you're getting back on the road again. Do you really like it?' Dylan responded: 'It's not that I like it or dislike it: it's what I'm destined to do.'

This, then, is the philosophy adopted as 1974 became 1975: to simply 'do what you must do', not necessarily because you want to, but because it's 'all you can do'. Dylan was to play almost sixty concerts between October 1975 and May 1976, one hundred and fifteen concerts in 1978 alone, a further seventy between November 1979 and May 1980. If being Renaldo, realising Renaldo fully, was the way to Bob Dylan, then Dylan most readily accepts the role that once almost killed him.

---

[127] In *Sing Out!*, November 1968.

15. Still on the Road

Whoever has not known himself has known nothing, but whoever has known himself has simultaneously achieved knowledge about the depth of all things.

— *The Book of Thomas the Contender*

Although Dylan wished to believe in the permanence of his relationship with Sara, experience forced him to recognise its transience. If, through her, he gained acquaintance with an aspect of human experience – the domestic – he discovered, painfully, the brevity and instability that was a part of that world. His love and loss of Sara completes a phase of human experience for him, though the image of springtime turning into autumn in 'Idiot Wind' is depressive, depicting the passing of happiness without real awareness of its having been experienced to the full. As the references to 'destiny' at the end of the last chapter indicate, Dylan seems to have accepted that his role as artist-author or artist-performer may well be closer to his identity than he has been able thus far to acknowledge. After the experience of disintegration and pain, all he can do to try to heal his scars is seek satisfaction in the temporal world with fulfilment 'on the road'. To accept this life again though, it is necessary to deny his 'other self'. Such denial, as Jung points out, has always been inevitable for artists:

> As a human being, he may have moods and a will and personal aims, but as an artist he is 'man' in a higher sense – he is 'collective man' – one who carries and shapes the unconscious psychic life of mankind. To perform this difficult office it is sometimes necessary for him to sacrifice happiness and everything that makes life worth living for the ordinary human being ... the artist's life cannot be otherwise than full of conflicts, for two forces are at war within him – on the one hand the common

human longing for happiness, satisfaction and security in life, and on the other a ruthless passion for creation which may go so far as to override every personal desire.[128]

Desire is the title of Dylan's next collection of songs. The back sleeve has pictures of the Empress card from the Tarot deck, symbolic of 'both the initial perfection of nature and the final perfection of art – not only of Isis but of Nephthys',[129] and of Joseph Conrad, story narrator par excellence. Dylan's brief sleeve notes quickly scan the songs contained in the album and he presents himself as poet 'on the heels of Rimbaud'. Allen Ginsberg used the phrase 'Songs of Redemption' as the album's subtitle, but the phrase 'Romance is taking over' is more interesting. One of the songs included here (and all but two are co-written with Jacques Levy) is entitled 'Romance in Durango'; others, 'Mozambique' and 'Joey' for example, present a 'romanticised' point of view. But the following literary definitions of 'romance' from the *Oxford English Dictionary* are surely closer to Dylan's intended meaning:

> 3. Medieval tale usually in verse of some hero of chivalry.
> 4. Prose or rarely verse tale with scene and incidents remote from everyday life ... set of facts, episode, love affair etc. suggesting such tales by its strangeness or moving nature.

The first of these appropriately describes 'Joey' or 'Hurricane' or the unreleased 'Catfish' – each subject being accorded, to some degree, 'heroic' status. The second definition fits 'Isis', the unreleased 'Golden Loom', and Dylan's new verse-narrative songs previewed in the earlier 'Lily, Rosemary and the Jack of Hearts', which has its own 'hero of chivalry' and is realised on *Desire* in 'Romance in Durango' and 'Black Diamond Bay'.

Of these songs, it is perhaps 'Isis' that is the most remarkable work. The narrative takes place on a surreal, mythical plane, in a timeless landscape which combines elements of nineteenth-century Western America with ancient Egypt. (The song in one

[128] C.G. Jung, *Modern Man in Search of a Soul*, Routledge & Kegan Paul.
[129] Aleister Crowley, *The Book Of Thoth*, Weiser, 1974.

sense is broadly based on 'On the Trail of the Buffalo', which Dylan recorded informally in 1961.) It functions symbolically, presenting archetypal figures and situations. The 'quest' is symbolic of the process in the psyche which is seeking its own goal. Introduced in concert in 1975 as 'a song about marriage', 'Isis' can be related to the concept of the 'sacred' or 'chemical' marriage which is the central symbol of alchemy. The concept is that man, as a result of the loss of his original 'Adamic' state, is divided within himself. He regains his integral nature only when the two powers, whose discord has rendered him impotent, are again reconciled with one another. The regaining of the integral nature of man (expressed in alchemy by the symbol of the masculine-feminine androgyne) is the prerequisite of union with God. In psychological terms, these two poles of human nature resemble the conscious and the unconscious. The 'chemical marriage' may be simply interpreted as an 'integration' of the unconscious powers of the soul into the ego-consciousness, though such interpretation is not totally justifiable and as Titus Burckhardt points out:

> It is quite vain to wish to describe psychologically the real essence of alchemy or the secret of the 'chemical marriage'. The more one strives to dispense with symbols and to replace them with scientific concepts of one sort or another, the more rapidly does that spiritual presence vanish which is the very heart of the matter and which can only be transmitted by symbols.[130]

Nevertheless, 'Isis' functions symbolically, combining the emblem of the sacred marriage with that of Isis, the Great Mother, and the song is structured around the concept of the quest. The myth of the quest is so pervasive that some scholars have argued that it determines virtually all mythic and literary patterns. According to Joseph Campbell in *The Hero with a Thousand Faces*, the 'monomyth' can be reduced to a 'formula represented by the rites of passage in separation – initiation – return'. 'Isis' begins with the 'separation':

---

[130] Titus Burckhardt, *Alchemy*, Penguin, 1971.

> I married Isis on the fifth day of May
> But I could not hold on to her very long
> So I cut off my hair and I rode straight away
> For the wild unknown country
> where I could not go wrong.

Both 'I rode straight away' and 'I could not go wrong' are neatly ambivalent. The separation seems to lead him to asceticism – the cutting off of his hair is indicative of this, as is his behaviour in the second stanza:

> I came to a high place of darkness and light
> The dividing line ran through the center of town
> I hitched up my pony to a post on the right
> Went into a laundry to wash my clothes down.

'Washing down' is also a part of the apparent cleansing process involved in the self-discipline of the would-be ascetic. The hitching of the pony to the ambivalent 'right' is also a significant response to the choice between darkness and light that confronts him, separated as they are by the central 'dividing line'. In Cirlot's *Dictionary of Symbols*, Jung is quoted on the significance of 'right' and 'left':

> The right side is masculine, representing the rational, the
> conscious, the logical and the virile, the left representing
> the converse.

Following the marriage and separation, the song's narrator rides off seeking and attempting to assert his identity as an independent being, having been defeated in his attempts to assert himself in his relationship with 'Isis' whom he 'could not hold on to'. An opportunity for such self-assertion is presented almost immediately by the approach of a man who is perceived to be 'not ordinary' and by his suggestion of the expedition for which money 'ain't necessary', which suggests that the quest does not have material treasure as its aim. But his question 'Where are we goin'?' as they set out 'for the cold in the North' is ignored, leaving the song's narrator:

Thinkin' about turquoise ... thinkin' about gold
Thinkin' about diamonds and the world's biggest necklace.

As we'll see, such thoughts are misguided.

The journey takes place in a surreal landscape. The questers set out in darkness and travel through canyons in a 'devilish' cold. The thoughts of the narrator turn back to Isis, whose identity can be expressed in terms of the Eternal Feminine discussed in the previous chapter, encountered in 'Tangled Up in Blue', and recognised as the Woman in White in *Renaldo and Clara*.

She told me that one day we would meet up again
And things would be different the next time we wed.

She directly echoes the words of the 'she' in 'Tangled Up in Blue' who reminds him 'we'll meet again some day' and anticipates not just reunion but remarriage. The thoughts about Isis neatly fill in the time it takes for the questers to reach what appears to be a goal: 'the pyramids all embedded in ice'. The mysterious man then reveals that it is neither gold nor turquoise they have been in search of, but 'a body' he's 'tryin' to find' that has its own value. He dies before the tomb is penetrated, leaving the narrator to continue alone:

I broke into the tomb but the casket was empty
There was no jewels, no nothin', I felt I'd been had.

All that's left to do is tidy up before riding back 'to find Isis' once more:

I picked up his body and I dragged him inside
Threw him down in the hole and I put back the cover.

In mythic terms, the 'quest' symbolises the urge for spiritual renewal. It has its origins in nature rituals purported to bring about and celebrate the annual regeneration of the deity whose death is synonymous with winter. One can see how this myth has been incorporated into the song. The 'body' the man wishes to 'carry out' of the tomb that is 'embedded in ice' and reached in the very depths of cold and dark winter – 'the wind it was howlin' and the snow was outrageous' – is that of the 'deity'. Its carriage out of the tomb will 'bring a good price' because it will bring about the regeneration of nature and thus of life. The concept of spiritual renewal, as opposed to natural regeneration, is also incorporated into the song.

In alchemical symbolism, the 'tomb' has its own significance. 'The grave in the great world corresponds to the womb in the less world – a place of renewal, not of destruction.'[131] The vessel in which the alchemical process takes place is the coffin of the impotent old king. It can also become the womb in which the new seed may develop and where resurrection can take place.

But the narrator doesn't take anything from the tomb and instead places a body into it. Thus he has, though perhaps neither willingly nor indeed consciously, played his part in a regenerative process of which he is himself both benefactor and beneficiary. As he journeys back to Isis, he finds her 'in the meadow' – in a spring he has played his part in regenerating. Similarly he feels renewed:

I came in from the East with the sun in my eyes.

The East is symbolic of spiritual regeneration. The idea of having 'the sun in my eyes' means not, I think, that it is shining from the West, but that he actually brings the sun from the East, signifying renewal. There are two neat examples of wordplay in the song's penultimate stanza, when he confronts Isis once again:

She said 'You look different.' I said 'Well, I guess.'
She said 'You been gone.' I said 'That's only natural.'

The reunion with the 'mystical' Isis completes the regenerative process for the narrator, who announces his intention to 'stay' at the song's conclusion.

The song's significance with regard to Dylan's search for self thus resides in the mythical operation of its symbolism. The artist

---

[131] F. Sherwood Taylor, *The Alchemists*, Paladin, 1976.

seeks the immortal self buried deep in nature and wishes to reclaim it through his art. The pyramids in ice symbolise the eternal nature of self – the timeless frozen into permanence. But the journey to the pyramids is only the beginning of a quest that ends with the second mystical wedding with Isis, in which the artist completes his own nature through the symbolic marriage with his 'other half' of whom he is always in search and yet, paradoxically, towards whom he is destined to be continually impelled.

The narrator of 'Isis' is accompanied on his journey by the mysterious stranger whom he immediately and intuitively understands and with whom he enters into a spontaneous and reciprocal agreement to embark upon the quest: 'I gave him my blanket, he gave me his word'.

What the narrator leaves behind in the casket is an aspect of himself that he has encountered and transcended. The tomb becomes the cradle of the new self – 'you look different' – who journeys back to Isis and fulfilment. The journey has thus taken him through the night to the dawn, through darkness to light, through winter to spring – symbolically through death to life.

The unreleased 'Golden Loom' draws on the same body of symbol and archetype. The Eternal Feminine here is a 'fisherman's daughter' who carries a 'golden loom'. In alchemical imagery, the masculine and feminine principles are complementary and destined to undergo a continual serial process of unification and separation. They were often spoken of in their interaction as Sol and Luna (Sun and Moon). Luna was the dark receptive one, the source of vitality. The principle she represents is a goddess identified with the moon, which the Egyptians symbolised in Isis. As 'she' approaches in 'Golden Loom', there is 'moonlight on the water'. The process of unification occurs in the second stanza, where the masculine and feminine principles merge after the familiar cleansing process:

> First we wash our feet
> Near the immortal shrine
> And then our shadows meet.

But as always, separation follows quickly:

> Then you drift away...
> You're gone and then all I seem to recall
> Is the smell of perfume
> And your golden loom.

Just before these lines in the final stanza where he lifts her veil
are two rather mysterious lines:

> I see the trembling lion
> With the lotus flower tail.

Again, Dylan is drawing on alchemical symbolism: the lotus-
flower is 'the lotus of Isis; the lotus represents the feminine or
passive power',[132] while the lion (a green lion) symbolised the
devouring corrosive acid in the alchemical process which caused
separation or dissolution.

There are two parallel examples of Dylan's drawing on this body
of symbolism, and in each case it is the alchemical symbol of the
dragon which is used. At the S.N.A.C.K. concert in March 1975,
Dylan sings an unusual version of 'Knockin' On Heaven's Door',
which is, in fact, 'Knockin' On The Dragon's Door'. In 'Señor
(Tales of Yankee Power)', he announces that he can 'smell the tail
of the dragon'. As the lion represents the devouring element, so
the dragon represents matter in its imperfect, unregenerate state;
and, of course, it must be destroyed. In his book *The Alchemists*,
Thomas Charnock writes of this dragon and its part in the great
work of alchemy in the sixteenth century:

> This is the philosopher's dragon which eateth up his own tail
> Being famished in a dongeon of glass and all for my prevail
> Many years I kept this dragon in prison strong
> Before I could mortify him.

The dragon's sister is Mercury. As the dragon is matter,
metal, body, so is his sister spirit, metallic mercury, soul. It is no

---

[132] *The Book Of Thoth.*

coincidence that Dylan sings of 'Knockin' on the dragon's door' and, in 'Oh, Sister', 'Oh, sister, when I come to knock on your door...'

The details of the alchemical processes and of the significance of alchemical symbolism are immensely complex, but Jung believed that the 'great work' of alchemy was very close to what he called 'individuation' – the shaping of an integrated personality, or what I have referred to as the search for self. The symbols are a secret language of the mind, which stand for psychological processes and stages in the 'work'. The alchemist, Jung explains in *Psychology and Alchemy,* was really exploring not the nature of matter, but his own unconscious mind:

> The real nature of matter was unknown to the alchemist; he knew it only in hints. Inasmuch as he tried to explore it he projected the unconscious into the darkness of matter in order to illuminate it. In order to explain the mystery of matter, he projected yet another mystery – namely his own psychic background – into what was to be explained.

Psychologically, the processes of dissolution or separation and combination or unification refer to the breaking down and destruction of surface psychological characteristics and attitudes that surround and obscure a man's basic self and to the creation of a new integrated personality.

The alchemist's art depended upon the presence of the Soror Mystica – the Mystical Sister – so the feminine principle is necessary for the self to be fully realised. Hence the return to Isis, and the inevitable attraction to and wedding with the 'she of the golden loom'. 'Oh, Sister' dramatises the approach of the masculine principle to the sister before the mystical encounter; just as he is compelled to seek her, she is obliged to respond:

> Oh, sister, when I come to lie in your arms
> You should not treat me like a stranger
> Our Father would not like the way that you act
> And you must realise the danger.

'The danger' of her non-response is, of course, dissolution without reunification, death without regeneration:

> We grew up together from the cradle to the grave
> We died and were reborn and then mysteriously saved.

The encounters have been and should continue to be serial. But the introduction of 'our Father' and the stressing of responsibility to Him – 'is our purpose not the same on this earth, to love and follow His direction?' – brings in a new dimension to the obligation under which both man and woman find themselves. The purpose of life is 'to love'. To 'follow His direction' is neatly ambivalent, meaning that loving is both God's will but also 'the way' to realisation of Him.

Non-response is thus equivalent to disobedience of His will and can only lead to the creation of sorrow, for time is not infinite, though it may seem to be so:

> Time is an ocean, but it ends at the shore
> You may not see me tomorrow.

'Tomorrow' takes us into eternity which could be denied by disobedience to God's will.

The alchemical processes spoken of above are reflected in the symbolism of Christianity and of the mystery-religions, in the concepts of death and resurrection. F. Sherwood Taylor writes in *The Alchemists*:

> The contemplation and practice of alchemy was rewarded by the emotional and spiritual satisfaction of one who sees living beings wonderfully fulfilling their ends appointed by God. The whole alchemical process has, as it were, a spiritual significance; it is a perfection of matter and was viewed with feelings appropriate to the sight of perfection. The alchemical process was a small illustration or example of the whole purpose of things which were impelled to seek perfection by their striving towards the perfect ideas of their kind in God; it was likewise a symbol of man whose end in life is to find bodily perfection in the

glorious body and spiritual perfection and fulfilment in
the beatific vision of God.

The imagery in 'Oh, Sister' parallels the *Song of Solomon* 5.2–3,
in which the Church is awoken by the calling of Christ:

> 2. I sleep, but my heart waketh; it is the voice of my
> beloved that knocketh, saying, Open to me, my sister, my
> love, my dove, my undefiled, for my head is filled with
> dew and my locks with the drops of the night.
> 3. I have put off my coat; how shall I put it on? I have
> washed my feet; how shall I defile them?

It may be most significant that Dylan comes to express his
personal search for self not simply through the symbolism of
alchemy or in the parallel symbolism of the Great Mystery, but in
its further parallels in Christianity. Sherwood Taylor's ideas are of
great importance here too. They go some way towards explaining
Dylan's interest in Christianity, which is emergent on *Desire* and
in the filming of *Renaldo and Clara*, and to a further extent in
the songs on *Street-Legal*, before the starker expressions of faith
in the songs of 1979 and 1980 and the announcement of Dylan's
conversion to Christianity in 1979. 'One More Cup Of Coffee'
also draws on the *Song of Solomon* to an extent.

> Your breath is sweet
> Your eyes are like two jewels in the sky
> Your back is straight, your hair is smooth
> On the pillow where you lie.

In tone, these opening lines parallel Christ's description of the
Church's graces in *Solomon* 7.1–3:

> 1. How beautiful are thy feet with shoes, O prince's
> daughter! The joints of thy thighs are like jewels, the work
> of the hands of a cunning workman.
> 2. Thy navel is like a round goblet, which wanteth not
> liquor: thy belly is like an heap of wheat set about with lilies.
> 3. Thy two breasts are like two young roes that are twins.

Like the 'sister' in 'Oh, Sister', the woman addressed here is not responding to such advances as openly as hoped for:

> But I don't sense affection
> No gratitude or love
> Your loyalty is not to me
> But to the stars above.

The song presents her outlaw father, a forbiddingly powerful figure who warns away strangers, and who is God-like in his omniscience and 'oversees his kingdom' just as God 'overlook(s) His preserve' in 'Joey'. There are also allusions to the woman's mother and sister, who have prescient powers, as she herself has, despite their lack of education. In the 1978 concerts, Dylan introduced the song with a long rap about a meeting with the 'King of the Gypsies' – a meeting also alluded to in the 1978 Jonathon Cott interview. After staying for a week at the great European gypsy festival, held, Dylan assures us, in the week of his own birthday at the end of May in the South of France, Dylan is asked by the King of the Gypsies what he would like to have to take away. 'All I could ask for,' Dylan tells the audience, 'was one more cup of coffee for the road.' The rap is pertinent both to the song's atmosphere and relevant because there is little else he *could* ask for from this woman who has no 'affection … gratitude or love … [or] loyalty' to offer, just:

> One more cup of coffee for the road
> One more cup of coffee 'fore I go
> To the valley below.

A significant development in the nature of Dylan's writing, as opposed to his poetic thought at this time, is the emergence of the narrative song that presents a 'theatre of action' in which characters are presented acting out parts in their own stories, and in which the narrator remains totally objective. 'Lily, Rosemary and the Jack of Hearts' from *Blood on the Tracks* is the first such song – a long narrative in which the narrator has no other role save that of narrator. The song has a cinematic quality to it, as the narrator, like the camera, focuses upon the figures, the actions, and the details which are significant for scene-setting or plot.

The main attraction of the song is undoubtedly its power of suggestion. As Dylan observed in 1965: 'We all think we know things, and we really know nothing'.[133] This is very true of 'Lily, Rosemary and the Jack of Hearts'. Pete Hamill, in the sleeve notes to *Blood on the Tracks*, sums it all up admirably:

> Listen to the long narrative poem called 'Lily, Rosemary and the Jack of Hearts'. It should not be reduced to notes, or taken out of context; it should be experienced in full. The compression of story is masterful, but its real wonder is in the spaces, in what the artist left out of his painting. To me, that has always been the key to Dylan's art. To state things plainly is the function of journalism; but Dylan sings a more fugitive song; allusive, symbolic, full of imagery and ellipses, and by leaving things out he allows us the grand privilege of creating along with him. His song becomes our song because we live in those spaces. If we listen, if we work at it, we fill up the mystery, we expand and inhabit the work of art. It is the most democratic form of creation.

The Jack of Hearts is a typical Dylan anti-hero character who may have his origins in Baudelaire's 'Spleen', a poem already alluded to in 'A Hard Rain's A Gonna Fall' and in 'I Want You'. Baudelaire's poem concludes:

> Cependant qu'en un jeu plein de sales parfums
> Héritage fatal d'une vieille hydropique
> Le beau valet de coeur et la dame de pique
> Causent sinistrement de leurs amours défunts.
>
> [Didst a card-pack's pestilential airs
> Dire relic of some dropsical old jade's
> The dapper Jack of Hearts and Queen of Spades
> Grimly discuss their perished love affairs.]

[133] In *Don't Look Back*.

It's probable here that 'le beau valet de coeur' is an ironic self-portrait by the dandyish Baudelaire, the 'dame de pique' being his mulatto mistress, Jeanne Duval. Dylan's 'Jack of Hearts' is an elusive shadowy figure who disturbs, in some way, the other three major characters in the song. The song's conclusion tells us – as much as it 'tells us' anything – that the Jack of Hearts belongs to the outlaw gang that robbed the bank safe. But like many Western outlaws, the Jack of Hearts is romanticised by his enigmatic presence.

The outlaw has always been an important figure in Dylan's songs. In his early concern with social misfits or outcasts, Dylan sympathises with, or expresses the points of view of transgressors of society's laws or codes and those for whom society has no place, like Hollis Brown, who lives 'on the outside of town'. Dylan's outlaws live literally 'outside the law', which, as 'Absolutely Sweet Marie' establishes, demands total honesty – above all to oneself. Alan Wall observes:

> Dylan the mythographer has always insisted that he had
> no real background – no home, no ancestry except the
> one which he chose to acknowledge which consisted of a
> mixture of musical and poetic influences.[134]

Dylan has a fondness for songs in which he can announce that he is a 'ramblin' boy' – a phrase used by Tom Paxton of Dylan. In 1961 in Minneapolis, Dylan recorded 'Ramblin' Round Your City', and a song with which he opened his 1963 New York Town Hall concert began:

> Well, I'm just one of them ramblin' boys
> Ramblin' round and makin' noise.

There are countless variations on the 'I Was Young When I Left Home' theme, and Dylan tips the wink at his own mythology in 1968 by singing Woody Guthrie's 'I Ain't Got No Home' at the Woody Guthrie Tribute concert, and by announcing 'I am a

---

[134] *The Passage of Bob Dylan.*

lonesome hobo without family or friends' on *John Wesley Harding*. Wall continues:

> He styled himself as the incomprehensible outsider, society's orphan, estranged from all its standards: 'I got nothin' ma, to live up to'. And essentially free from all its sins: 'Don't you understand it's not my problem'. He is also often deeply pitiless: 'There's no use in trying to deal with the dying though I cannot explain that in lines'. Dylan was the uncommissioned jester, living outside the court.

John Wesley Harding presents Dylan as the outlaw – both in the Polaroid cover photograph, and in the characters in the songs on the album – and in Sam Peckinpah's film *Pat Garrett and Billy the Kid*, Dylan was literally given the chance to play out the role of the outlaw. He appeared as Alias – 'Alias what?' 'Alias anything you like' he replies – who gives up his job to become a member of Billy the Kid's gang, proving himself as a deadly knife-throwing killer in an early skirmish in the film.

Pat Garrett and Billy the Kid was made in Durango, Mexico, and Dylan's 'Romance in Durango' clearly owes a great deal to the experience. The song is a presentation of the thoughts running through the mind of a nameless outlaw who is escaping with his lover to Durango after having shot a man in a cantina. The song is presented in the first person and there is little doubt that we are meant to recognise Dylan's identification with his main character. In 'Billy', a song written for *Pat Garrett and Billy the Kid*, Dylan portrayed the same wanted man – 'There's always some new stranger sneakin' glances' – which is as appropriate to himself as it is to Billy the Kid; the affinity is further emphasised in the song's request, 'Billy don't you turn your back on me'.

There's a further significance in the relationship Dylan has long felt with the figure of the outlaw; I've already pointed out Rimbaud's thief symbol, which he adopted. The artist, as much as the public performer, has more than a little in common with the outlaw: his existence is not in accordance with social acceptability or 'normality'; he does not conform and thus exists a little way beyond society. Not too far, of course, for it is his calling to look at those who make up society and present them, or reflect them, in his art.

In 'The Hunchback in the Park', Dylan Thomas presents a view of the poet in symbolic terms. He is a social misfit – his hunchback symbolises the burden of artistic responsibility which makes him 'abnormal'. He is necessarily a 'solitary mister', and though he must suffer the jeers and jibes of coarser souls, he has the last laugh, for he has the freedom they want but is denied them: 'Nobody chained him up'. This freedom comes through the role of the artist, and thus is permanent and total.

'Billy' is also 'walkin' all alone', but he too has the outlaw's freedom. The motives of his pursuers are explained: 'Billy, they don't like you to be so free'.

Louis MacNeice wrote an interesting and relevant assessment of the poet in 'To The Public':

> Why hold that poets are so sensitive?
> A thick-skinned grasping lot who filch and eavesdrop.
> Who enjoy ourselves at other men's expense;
> Who, legislators or not, ourselves are lawless.
> We do not need your indulgence, much less your pity;
> With fewer qualms, we have rather more common sense
> Than your Common Man, also, of course, more freedom,
> With our burglars' and gunmen's fingers, our green fingers.
> So, crude though we are, we get to times and places
> And, saving your presence or absence, will continue
> Throwing our dreams and guts in people's faces.

The Jack of Hearts is both actor and thief. He represents two aspects of Dylan's identity with which we have already concerned ourselves at some length. The concept of poet as 'burglar' or 'gunman' is extended in much of Dylan's writing. The 'outlaw' in 'Romance in Durango' can thus be regarded as speaking and thinking on behalf of Dylan. He is a songster and a guitar player, and though necessity required he 'sold [his] guitar to the baker's son', he asserts, 'I can get another one, and I'll play for Magdalena as we ride'.

This song operates on multiple levels: as an atmospheric

evocation of an outlaw on the run in Mexico, full of sound and colour, with its Spanish vocabulary and chorus as well as its Mexican backing music; and as a romantic self-portrait of the artist pursued for something for which he can barely acknowledge responsibility:

> Was it me that shot him down in the cantina
> Was it my hand that held the gun?

But he knows or feels that his true innocence is recognised by God and reassures his lover in the chorus:

> No llores, mi querida [Don't cry, my love]
> Dios nos vigila. [God watches over us.]

But there are even further significant suggestions about the song. The outlaw's companion is 'Magdalena' and, despite his constant reassurances to her, there is an acknowledged acceptance of his own fate throughout the song – 'what's done is done'. His affirmation that 'the end is near' is ominously prophetic. The God he feels is his protector can also be a God of Wrath, and though he can love, he can also threaten:

> The face of God will appear
> With His serpent eyes of obsidian.

There are traces of Christian allusion in the final stanza's account of the outlaw's death. As he cries, 'Oh can it be that I am slain', he hears what sounds like thunder and calls to Magdalena: 'Look, up in the hills, that flash of light!' The verse ends with a hint of loss of faith – 'we may not make it through the night' – but the hopeful chorus, with its faith in 'Dios nos vigila' and its optimism in 'soon the desert will be gone' is allowed to conclude the song.

'Hurricane' and 'Joey' both speak on behalf of outlaw characters who retain their honesty and integrity, and who thus have claims to innocence, albeit one that lies beyond the considerations of the law. Though the purposes of the songs differ, in each of them

Dylan flirts briefly with the idea that his heroes' innocence carries them close to God or gives them some affinity with Christ.

Joey Gallo is portrayed as the definitive outlaw – 'always on the outside of whatever side there was' – but though he has the reputation of a killer, 'the truth was far from that'. He is a 'child of clay', a phrase that combines suggestions of both human weakness and innocence, but he is also given the title of 'King of the streets'. In the verse in which it is asserted that later in life he wouldn't carry a gun, Joey gives his own explanation: 'I'm around too many children'. Dylan presents him as a victim of persecution by the forces of society – 'the police department hounded him' – on an obviously trumped-up charge – 'they got him on conspiracy, they were never sure who with'. He finally dies trying to save others – 'he pushed the table over to protect his family' – and is mourned by 'mother Mary' and his 'old man' who 'had to say one last goodbye to the son that he could not save'. With Joey's death, 'the sun turned cold' and the song's narrator concludes with an expression of belief that 'if God's in heaven', Joey's killers will eventually 'get what they deserve'.

Hurricane Carter is also portrayed as the victim of a trumped-up charge and an apparently farcical trial – a 'pig-circus'. He is 'the man the authorities came to blame for somethin' that he never done' – just like Joey, just like Jesus. Hurricane likes to spend his time in 'some paradise', and like Joey he is called 'crazy'. Just as Joey is 'King' in his world, Rubin 'coulda been the champion of the world' and is described in prison as 'just like Buddha'.

These observations are simply suggestive, though it must be accepted that Dylan's sympathies lie with Hurricane and Joey, just as they did with Donald White, Percy, George Jackson (who, incidentally, is described as the possessor of awesome 'power' and 'love') and with the countless other outlaw-victims of society; as a singer and an artist, he is an outlaw himself. Thus, society's villains become the artist's heroes, for it is only the artist who can see through falsity to the truth, through the identity perceived by the public eye to the true self behind it. Only the artist or the poet can make sense of the assertion that 'to live outside the law you must be honest', for only they can respect true honesty, true integrity of spirit, and true innocence of the kind society will always fail to recognise.

Such identification – the product of artistic sympathy – has always played a significant part in Bob Dylan's search for self. The affinity he recognises between himself and the outlaw – whether the man on the run to Durango, Hurricane, Joey, or Jesus Christ – emerges startlingly in the lyrics of 'Shelter from the Storm', in which Dylan presents himself unequivocally as Jesus Christ, and is understandable. It points forward to the realisation of such affinity in *Renaldo and Clara* and in the songs on *Street-Legal*. The figure of Christ becomes more significant as Dylan's search for self progresses, for it is to be in Christ that Dylan finally comes to realise and fulfil himself. Jung can provide a further illumination of this point:

> The self is a circle whose centre is everywhere and whose circumference is nowhere. And do you know what the self is for Western man? It is Christ. For Christ is the archetype of the hero, representing man's highest aspiration. All this is very mysterious and at times frightening.[135]

[135] Miguel Serrano, *A Story of Two Friendships*.

16. Changing of the Guards

The mantle of 'hero' that Dylan's role of public performer forced him to assume led to the identification – initially by his audience but later by himself – with the archetypal hero, the figure of Jesus Christ. There are early traces of this, particularly in Dylan's youthful work, when he tended to take both himself and his role somewhat too seriously. The self-righteousness of his accusations, his protests and his striking out at injustice, hypocrisy and the evils of the world often included the invocation of Christ's name and indeed the threat of divine retribution. Dylan's identification with, rather than invocation of, Christ, may be glimpsed in the conclusion of what I have argued to be his first major song, 'A Hard Rain's A-Gonna Fall', when he expresses his intention to 'reflect' the truth of mortality 'from the mountain so all souls can see it' or to 'stand on the ocean until I start sinkin''.

The burden of such an identification was borne lightly for a number of years. Whilst some of the public were hailing him as a 'messiah' bearing messages of enlightenment for benighted modern man, Dylan parodied the persona light-heartedly. His arrival in London in May 1965, for instance, bearing an enormous industrial light bulb, was much more of a joke than people were, at the time, prepared to understand or perhaps willing or able to admit. There's a similar joke in 'Bob Dylan's 115th Dream', when the hobo-sailor is refused help by the surly patriot:

> I said 'You know they refused Jesus, too.'
> He said 'You're not Him.'

The patriot seems more clear-sighted than many of Dylan's followers. As acclamation and flattery worked on Dylan's ego, however, the myth began to take over. If Dylan had already become a saviour for some of his audience, he began to see himself as one, just as David Bowie's Ziggy Stardust became a 'leper messiah'. Scaduto quotes an 'Australian actress' expressing her thoughts on Dylan in April 1966:

> I came to believe that Dylan was Christ revisited. I felt that everything fitted, without being Christian-religious or anything, I felt that what he had to say about living and communication with people was the truest, most honest and most Christ-like thing I've ever heard. I began to feel that Dylan was sacrificing himself in his whole philosophy, his thinking. That he would eventually die or that something horrible would happen to him. I felt it psychically. I felt it strongly. I must have been going slightly unhinged. But I know that other people felt Dylan was a Christ, sacrificing himself ... Dylan knew it and he was so afraid of it. So very afraid. In that context, of being afraid of it, he said to me, 'I'm only a musician.' He said it with that kind of child-like thing when people say they are something they know they're not, when they know they're more. I know he didn't want to think himself as any sort of prophet or that important, but he knew other people thought it of him and he was afraid of it. So was Christ, he was afraid of it too.[136]

Scaduto's comment is a pertinent one:

> If you are not Jesus Christ, but many people believe you could be and are asking you to cure their blindness and perform other miracles, then even crucifixion in the twentieth century could seem a very real possibility.

I've already pointed out that Dylan's retrospective self-portraits often present images of Bob Dylan, the star persona, as messiah. In 'Dirge' for example as:

> Man forever stripped
> Acting out his folly
> While his back is being whipped.

In 'Romance in Durango', the cowboy-angel guitar player rides

[136] Scaduto, *Bob Dylan*.

towards his destruction with Magdalena by his side and God's watchful eye above; and in 'Shelter from the Storm' he remembers his 'crown of thorns' and his passion:

> They gambled for my clothes
> I bargained for salvation an' they gave me a lethal dose
> I offered up my innocence and got repaid with scorn.

Dylan's life has been a 'bargain for salvation'. The 'dose' of the mid-sixties may have been lethal, but what died and what was left behind was a self that was a burden, a load that needed to be discarded. The journey through night to the morning, the ever-continuing search for self, led Dylan many times to confront God and to attempt to define the nature of God and the significance of Jesus Christ. Dylan's Jewishness was a major consideration in the early 1970s, but in 1967 he had spoken of his 'worries' about 'the sign on the cross'. In Dylan's self-penned 1966 *Playboy* interview, the following exchange occurred:

> Playboy: What do you have to look forward to?
> Dylan: Salvation. Just plain salvation.
> Playboy: Anything else?
> Dylan: Praying.

Salvation or redemption for Dylan undoubtedly lay in the process of individuation – the realisation of the self that lies beyond the individual and which is at one with the concept of God.

'Seek and you will find' said Jesus in the Sermon on the Mount (Matthew 7.7/8), 'knock, and the door will be opened'. Dylan was still a seeker in the early 1970s 'knock, knock, knockin' on heaven's door' without apparent response, though he had relinquished the 'badge' – a 'star' of course – which had been pinned upon him.

In the 1974 song 'Up to Me', Dylan wrote, 'we heard the Sermon on the Mount and I knew it was too complex'. But his investigation of the complexities continued, notably in the making of *Renaldo and Clara* in the latter part of 1975. The Rolling

Thunder tours of 1975 and 1976 included Roger McGuinn, Steven Soles, David Mansfield and T Bone Burnett – all of whom later became born-again Christians. Soles and Mansfield were also part of the 1978 tours and, although they don't consider themselves very influential in the effect their conversations about religion had on Dylan, Soles does remember Dylan responding to his profession that faith in God was so much more rewarding than faith in man.

With regard to new thoughts and attitudes in Dylan's songs, *Renaldo and Clara* granted a snippet of the unreleased song, 'What Will You Do When Jesus Comes?':

> Tell me what will you do when Jesus comes?
> Tell me what will you do when Jesus comes?
> Will you tear out your hair?
> Will you sit down in your chair?
> Tell me what will you do when Jesus comes?
>
> Tell me what will you do when Jesus comes?
> Tell me what will you do when Jesus comes?
> Oh will you kick him out in the street?
> Will you drive him out in the heat?
> Tell me what will you do when Jesus comes?

The rehearsal take of Curtis Mayfield's 'People Get Ready' included in the film anticipates, in its content and imagery, Dylan's later 'Slow Train' and Regina Havis's lengthy spoken introduction to the gospel concerts in November and December 1979 – a story of a penniless old woman being allowed to ride the train to visit her dying son because, as she is told by the stationmaster, 'Jesus got your ticket.' In 'People Get Ready', it is a 'train to Jordan' and 'all you need is faith … don't need no ticket'. Then again, 'there ain't no room for the hopeless sinner'.

There is a good deal of Christian imagery in *Renaldo and Clara*, a film cut and edited shortly before the writing of the songs for the *Street-Legal* album, and thus there are many parallels in imagery and concepts between film and album. I don't wish to present a full analysis of *Renaldo and Clara* here, in a book which is primarily concerned with tracing the development of Dylan's poetic thought in his writing, but during 'Isis', as it is performed in the film, Dylan makes the sign of the cross with his hands; in their encounter with the truck driver, Helena and Clara actually come face to face with the smiling 'Devil' who has 'an honest face'; and the girlfriend presents herself to Renaldo in a crowded cafe with the words 'just stand and bear yourself like the cross and I'll receive you'.

'Bob Dylan' is shown trying to get by a security guard played by Mick Ronson and identified by Dylan in the Cott interview as 'the Guardian of the Gates'; then follows a shoddy cabaret scene before the film cuts to scuffling preachers, one of whom says of a heckler, 'the boy's not fit to go to hell'.

The train image recurs throughout *Renaldo and Clara*, heading, Dylan says again in the Cott interview, to the 'holy crossroads'. In the film, the Masked Tortilla complains that he 'doesn't seem to be able to get off this train', a remark pertinent to 'Señor'. Later on the train, Dylan and the Masked Tortilla talk about a mysterious man with a black beard who seems to be following them, and who 'seems ready to make his move' but 'he'll wait until dark'; the film cuts to Renaldo singing 'It Takes a Lot to Laugh, It Takes a Train to Cry'. There are countless more images and allusions – even specific scenes such as Dylan and Ginsberg looking at the cross on Kerouac's grave, or walking around the stations of the cross towards the film's conclusion, before Dylan is shown buying tickets at a railway station. Renaldo's last song is 'Knockin' On Heaven's Door'.

Two quotations from the Cott interview should serve to take us neatly towards *Street-Legal*: 'Jesus is the most identifiable figure in Western culture' and:

> I believe in life, but not this life ... real life ... I experience it all the time, it's beyond this life ... You know, I'll tell you lately I've been catching myself. I've been in some scenes, and I say, 'Holy shit, I'm not here alone.' I've never had that experience before the past few months. I've felt this strange, eerie feeling that I wasn't all alone, and I'd better know it.

Dylan admits later, 'My experience with film helped me in writing the [new] songs.' Some of the songs were written in Autumn of 1977 including 'Is Your Love in Vain?', 'Changing of the Guards', and 'Her Version of Jealousy'. Others were completed during the tour of the Far East, Australia and New Zealand during the first months of 1978. Although Dylan denies in the Craig McGregor interview of February 1978 that he's got into any 'dedicated religion', there seems little doubt that Dylan's religious and specifically Christian awareness was growing throughout the time of the composition of *Street-Legal*'s songs.

Paul Williams describes *Street-Legal* as 'a portrait of a man suffering from a profound and unconscious alienation'.[137] In the Cott interview Dylan describes *Renaldo and Clara* as being about naked alienation of the inner self against the outer self. There's a bitten-off understatement of this soul-dissatisfaction in the bridge of 'Is Your Love in Vain?':

> Well, I've been to the mountain
> And I've been in the wind
> I've been in and out of happiness
> I have dined with kings
> I've been offered wings
> And I've never been too impressed.

It's a superb compression of life-history – the image of fame and fortune at their height in the symbol of the mountain Dylan scaled and conquered, the 'wind of changes' ('Forever Young') which shifts the sands of time turning spring into autumn, time moving like a 'jet plane ... too fast' so that happiness becomes an illusion that is sacrificed to transience.

Dylan's marriage to Sara was formally terminated in 1977 just before the release of *Street-Legal*, and, as Paul Williams observes, some of the album's songs are 'Dylan's final words on marriage and lovers before *Slow Train Coming*'. As Dylan sings, 'I've been in and out of happiness', he continues to equate happiness with marriage, just as he did in 1974's 'Wedding Song', when he

---

[137] Paul Williams, *Dylan – What Happened?*, Entwhistle, 1979.

sang to his wife 'happiness to me is you'. Following the loss of such happiness, all other worldly comforts, indulgences and consolations count for nothing.

The litotes of 'I've never been too impressed' conceals a loneliness that is presented for what it is. This time the song is addressed to the second person 'You', but once again we should recognise Dylan the artist confronting Dylan the man, looking into the mirror, staring into the eyes of one whose mind retains images of a past that cannot be regained. The song is a product of the divorce.

In 'No Time to Think', the vision of 'a wife who sleepwalks through your dreams' is a reflection of a scene in *Renaldo and Clara*, when 'Mrs Dylan' looks at herself in a mirror only to be haunted by the ghost of her dead lover, Ramon (the character shares the name, more than coincidentally perhaps, with the victim of the fugitive's gun in 'Romance in Durango'). Such haunting visions are too painful to be borne by the conscious mind and are thus relegated to the unconscious but merely lie dormant until they are summoned into consciousness in dreams. They must be exorcised if he whose mind is haunted is to survive. Thus the artist looks into his own eyes and paints himself as he perceives himself – as a victim of loneliness: 'you travel alone, unknown as you slowly sink'. The moaning assonances convey the emptiness within.

The artist has a vested interest in the man's spiritual well-being for without the man's strength, the artist cannot function. No matter if 'the empress attracts you', if there is mental or spiritual 'oppression', which is the product of the memory of betrayal 'for pieces of change' in the 'Federal City', the resultant feelings of strangeness and violence towards the 'tyranny' and 'hypocrisy' that succeeded former 'ecstasy' preclude the creation of beauty or truth which are the artist's 'ideal[s]'.

As the third stanza opens with the acknowledgment that the Federal City 'judges will haunt' the man in the mirror for some time to come, the singer confesses his own depression, which is just as debilitating:

I've seen all these decoys through a set of deep turquoise eyes
And I feel so depressed.

There is an interesting example of 'selves' suddenly converging in mid-song. The 'deep turquoise eyes' are those that Joan Baez described as being 'bluer than robin's eggs' in her song about Dylan, 'Diamonds and Rust'. They are the eyes through which the poet perceives the world he mirrors in his art, yet they are the eyes of the man who now is condemned to 'travel alone' and 'slowly sink'. Depression leads to 'alcohol', to further polarisation of 'duality', and inevitably to the long-time obsession with mortality that Dylan shares with Hamlet on his return to Denmark. Here the song's reiterated title attains its significance: there's 'no time to think' for the Gemini whose destiny is ruled by the quicksilver, androgynous Mercury – 'the messenger of the Gods [who] accompanied the soul after its death – bodily or mystical – through all the realms of the world of shadows, to its final place of rest'.[138]

But Mercury is also 'the creative Mercury ... who is the messenger of the gods [who] transmits their will by hieroglyphs intelligible to the initiate and records their acts ... he is duality, he represents both truth and falsehood, wisdom and folly'.[139] Psychologically, he represents the agency of consciousness, which increases our awareness of our own powers of discrimination and evaluation as it comes into being. Small wonder, then, that 'destiny fools you like the plague with a dangerous wink' for Mercury is tricky and is related to the Juggler of the Tarot deck who bears 'the hollow wand of Prometheus that brings down fire from heaven'.[140] Thus we come full circle to Dylan as Rimbaud would have dubbed him: the 'thief of fire'.

The stanzas begin to interweave. In the fourth, the 'tyranny' from the second stanza reappears, once again accompanied by betrayal, and 'mortality' recurs. 'The lion lies down with the lamb' in 'Paradise', but the attainment of Paradise demands

[138] Titus Burckhardt, *Alchemy*.
[139] *The Book Of Thoth*.
[140] Idem.

'sacrifice'. 'Mortality' is 'reality' which holds fear only for those who are faithless.

The 'anger and jealousy' that accompany the feelings of violence and strangeness are the symptoms of a distressed soul. The self-analysis continues as the artist looks into the mirror at his own reflection, which in turn looks back to the artist, though Dylan seems to allude to Magritte's *La reproduction interdite* as:

> You glance through the mirror and there's eyes staring clear
> At the back of your head.

But:

> You can't find no salvation, you have no expectations
> Anytime, anyplace, anywhere.

From these lines it appears that the object of the quest remains 'just plain salvation'. The essential duality of the Gemini nature precludes the attainment of individuation. The aspects of personality that exist on each side of the looking glass are the joker and the thief, the madman and the magician. When the magician holds sway, 'anger and jealousy' predominate. 'Madmen oppose him' by showing 'kindness, humility, simplicity' – qualities found most readily and most abundantly in God's true innocents, his 'natural' fools. But folly is not far removed from madness. The haunting dreams of the wife are recurrent and distracting: 'You know you can't keep her' one part of him says to another. But such rationality cannot be maintained: 'the water gets deeper' as 'the brink' of distraction is approached and sanity is 'buried' and lost as stanza six moves into stanza seven.

The man becomes ghost-like. As he is forced to 'resist' pleasure, new lovers begin to doubt his very existence. Indulgence of the flesh and neglect of the spirit can lead only to despair. Following 'the bridge that you travel on' to 'the Babylon girl with the rose in her hair' can lead only to faithlessness. She is *Revelation*'s 'mother of whores' (17.5) who is 'a haunt for every unclean spirit' (18.2).

She symbolises 'every obscenity on earth' (17.5) and to pursue her is to guarantee damnation. He sings:

> Stripped of all virtue as you crawl through the dirt
> You can give but you cannot receive.

'Mortality' is contemplated once again with all the obsessive horror of former years. On his desk, Baudelaire had a clock which had no hands, but bore the words 'It's later than it seems'. The final stanza has Dylan acknowledging himself desperately as 'the victim' who has:

> No time to choose when the truth must die
> No time to lose or say goodbye.

Without anything to believe in and without the hope of 'salvation' there remains only the inconsolable recognition of humanity's imperfection.

Dylan has always seen 'fear in a handful of dust': 'bullets can harm you and death can disarm you' and quickly too if fate so chooses – 'no time to suffer or blink, and no time to think'. The song becomes an expression of despair when supposedly therapeutic self-analysis leads only to recognition and confession of emptiness and negativity, frailty and vulnerability, and loneliness, which is initially identified as social but subsequently recognised to be spiritual, and which is absolute.

Such despair is present in other songs on *Street-Legal*. What Dylan calls tersely 'my pain' in 'Is Your Love in Vain?', is expressed, for example, in the following phrases – admittedly out of context – from 'We Better Talk This Over', itself an analysis of the state of a relationship that is no longer a relationship, formally or legally at least:

> I feel displaced, I got a lowdown feeling...
> I'm exiled...
> I'm lost...

Or from 'True Love Tends to Forget':

> Every day of the year's like playin' Russian roulette...
> This weekend in hell is making me sweat.

He describes his aimlessness, the futility of an existence that can be summarised as simply 'knockin' about from Mexico to Tibet'. In 'Where Are You Tonight? (Journey Through Dark Heat)', 'horseplay and disease is killing me by degrees'. In 'Señor (Tales of Yankee Power)', he sings 'I just gotta pick myself up off the floor' and 'this place don't make sense to me no more'. In 'Baby, Stop Crying', 'I can't tell right from wrong'. Such sentences collectively convey not simply a world-weariness but a sickness of soul which is the product of final separation from his wife, which has torn certain aspects of his psyche asunder. In certain ways, the love that was once between them exists within him still. 'Where Are You Tonight?' begins:

> There's a long-distance train rolling through the rain
> Tears on the letter I write
> There's a woman I long to touch and I miss her so much.

In 'True Love Tends to Forget', he sings 'You're a tearjerker baby, but I'm under your spell' and in 'We Better Talk This Over' it's 'I'm lost in the haze of your delicate ways'. But there needs to be resolution and acceptance of finality.

'We Better Talk This Over' is, of all the songs that are the product of his divorce, the one that most specifically refers to it. The annulled marriage was 'the bond that we've both gone beyond'. The speaker seems at first to be speaking very coolly and there seems little indication of pain or sadness, regret or blame. There's no trace of bitterness or recrimination no accusation, at least in the song's opening stanza. Talking things over seems an eminently sensible thing to do and the speaker admits that neither he, nor the she who is addressed, is quite 'sober' and thus perhaps not able to see things as clearly as they might or indeed as they ought. There are traces of apprehension – 'this situation can only get rougher' – and 'rougher' the situation gets. For although he sings 'you don't have to be afraid of looking into my face', by the second stanza the control and the level-headedness is slipping away with his sobriety and the accusations fly: 'you been two-faced, you been double-dealing'. As the song progresses, the love and the pain the singer's brave face conceals are inevitably betrayed. Although he is prepared to face up to the finality of the situation – 'the vows that we kept are now broken and swept 'neath the bed where we slept' – the statement betrays his bitterness in consigning the vows to the metaphor of the dirt which, though it is readily concealed, does not cease to exist.

His continuing love makes itself felt in a confession that may be reluctant but forces itself: 'I'm lost in the haze of your delicate ways with both eyes glazed'. Again it is the drunkenness that allows self-control to slip. Wishful thinking – 'It'd be great to cross paths in a day and a half, look at each other and laugh' – must give way to the acknowledgment of reality – 'I don't think it's liable to happen'. And although the song ends with apparently strong and confident advice or instruction – 'be grateful for what we've shared together and be glad' – it is clear enough that being 'glad' in retrospection is most unlikely for the singer.

'New Pony' is the album's only statement of apparent recovery from such depressions. But it is a kind of death-like state, which Dylan describes himself as barely living out on *Street-Legal*, just as alcohol induces a state in which truth drifts towards illusion and ultimately merges with it. At the end of the Jonathon Cott *Rolling Stone* interview, Dylan said, 'I live in my dreams, I don't really live in the actual world.' The withdrawal, conscious or not, to the world of illusion may be a retreat from reality, but if it is, it is not one that brings reassurance or consolation.

In concert in the latter part of 1978, Dylan prefaced his performance of 'Señor' with a short story that followed the lines of this speech from Savannah on the 8th December:

> I was riding on a train one time through Mexico, from Durango to San Diego. I fell asleep on this train and when I woke up the train had stopped in a yard. And people were

getting on the train. An old man stepped on the train. I was kind of in a daze and I was sitting watching it all through the window of the train like through a mirror. And I was watching through the mirror as this old man stepped up on the train and walked up the aisle to the seat across the aisle. He was carrying nothing but a blanket. He must have been about a hundred and fifty years old. Anyway I just kept on looking out through this mirror and I felt this strange vibration, so I turned to look at him. And as I turned to look at him, I saw that both his eyes were burning and there was smoke coming out of his nostrils. Well I immediately turned away, but after thinking awhile, I thought that this was a man I wanted to talk to. So I waited a little while longer and the train pulled out of the station and I turned to talk to him and he'd disappeared. I searched for him in the next town but he was gone.

There is an obvious dream-like quality here and, of course, in the song itself, beautifully set in dramatically evocative music. Dylan's use of the 'mirror' image brings us back to the artist's view of the world and of himself as a perceived image, rather than a reality. The speaker asks the mysterious señor a series of questions, though no answers are forthcoming, if indeed they are even expected. The first of the singer's queries is concerned with his destination – 'Lincoln County Road or Armageddon?' – and presents conflicting alternatives. They are apparently en route for the 'holy crossroads'. The road travelled seems to be familiar and the singer allows his mind to wander and to drift back to former times, producing flashing images of dream-like episodes from the past, one of which evokes a recollection of 'the last thing I remember before I stripped and kneeled'. The last words he remembers hearing are those of 'a gypsy' who points out to him, 'Son, this ain't a dream no more, it's the real thing'.

As the journey continues, the singer is concerned to learn more about his fate: 'will there be any comfort there?'. Towards the song's conclusion he asserts 'I'm ready when you are, señor'. But the final lines convey an impatience and impetuousness born out of frustration and confusion, the products of waiting for the indefinite.

The song's effect lies much more in what it suggests than what it expresses. To offer interpretation, as so often happens with Dylan's lyrics, would be to deny many of the song's possibilities. Nonetheless, in the context of the album, when one bears in mind the expressions of the feelings of aimlessness and spiritual desolation, and of the awareness of mortality, which are so prevalent in other songs – particularly of the expression of despair, which has no apparent remedial salvation to counter it – one can respond more meaningfully to the suggestions inherent in 'Señor'.

The encounter described in the dream-like prologue to the song helps too. The 'old man' carries a blanket and is thus presented to us as was St. Augustine in the earlier 'I Dreamed I Saw St. Augustine', where the blanket is symbolic of spiritual 'comfort' or reassurance of possible salvation and even redemption. Yet St. Augustine has 'fiery breath' and thus resembles the old man with his 'burning' eyes and 'smoke coming out of his nostrils'. 'Señor' takes us closer to Dylan's ultimate fundamentalism, yet here he is still uncertain of exactly whom he is addressing. As the journey progresses, curiosity gives way to anxiety, anxiety begets fear, and fear begets despair. The singer initially assumes that the journey has an end, that there is a destination. Initially he keeps his 'eyes glued to the door' hoping it will be opened or will disclose the 'she' he left behind. Either way, his hope is for 'comfort'. But hopes, too, are left behind and replaced by fears: 'I can smell the tail of the dragon'.

But the true 'hell' the singer will apparently have to endure is an eternity of non-contact and of waiting. He will never be told 'where she's hiding' nor 'who to contact' nor 'what we're waiting for' because they are not waiting for anything to happen at all – they're simply waiting. Such a realisation remains beyond the comprehension of the singer – 'this place don't make sense to me' – and he can only respond to the 'suspense' by striking out wildly and blindly – 'let's disconnect these cables, overturn these tables'. But as the gypsy reminded him, this is no dream but 'the real thing'. The true horror of his situation will only be appreciated when he acknowledges that his 'riding' (like that of the Masked Tortilla stuck on the train in *Renaldo and Clara*) will never end; his questions will never be answered by a señor, who will be eternally tight-lipped, being himself perfectly accustomed to such a fate.

The American psychoanalyst Rollo May contended that modern man is plagued by feelings of emptiness and loneliness which are a part of the greater experience of anxiety. Loneliness is the product of the emptiness that is the product of man's sense of powerlessness. In *The Encyclopaedia of Reality*, Katinka Matson follows this through:

> Anxiety becomes 'a confusion and bewilderment about where we are going', both in an individual and social context. May defines anxiety as 'a human being's basic reaction to a danger to his existence, or to some value which he identifies with his existence'. May interprets our response to these changes as a loss of sense of self, of relationship to nature, of a language that effectively conveys personal feelings, and of the tragic significance of human life. What is needed, therefore, are individuals who are rediscovering their sources of inner strength and integrity. This implies that we should work to re-establish self-awareness through rediscovering our feelings about what we want ... and confirm our aliveness in creative activity.[141]

'Señor' is very much, therefore, a product of what Rollo May terms 'anxiety' – a 'reaction to a danger ... to some value which he identifies with his existence'.

'Where Are You Tonight?' is *Street-Legal*'s powerful and moving concluding song. It opens with the narrator making a profoundly sad personal confession of his loneliness, his aimlessness and his despair. The long-distance train might as well have no direction or destination, for all such considerations are irrelevant when the singer acknowledges the emptiness within his heart. Memories of 'light' and 'laughter' are consigned to the past, and the sounds become a knell – 'a lonesome bell tone' – for a dead affair.

The parting of the singer and his lover was, it seems, fated. Just as in 'Idiot Wind', it had been 'destiny which pulled us apart', so

---

[141] Katinka Matson, *The Encyclopaedia of Reality*, Paladin, 1979.

here their parting is 'predicted' by a prescient Cherokee as being not just inevitable but pre-determined. 'In the last hour of need' he sings, 'we entirely agreed, sacrifice was the code of the road'. The affair is sacrificed along with the singer's self-belief and happiness. He is given over to 'despair', which is sensed by his partner, who is now seen objectively for the first time. No longer looking through the eyes of involvement, he feels that separation has enabled him to perceive 'her invisible self' for the first time. His visions of her begin with the image of 'a babe in the arms of a woman in a rage' and as objectivity offers clarity, it is as if she is a 'stripper on stage' and he can see more of what has long been concealed, or what he was unable or unwilling to recognise in her. In 'Idiot Wind', he had told her that she had 'tamed the lion in my cage'. Here, as he recalls his leaving, he announces the liberation of the instinctual nature that was repressed by the relationship. He has attained a new freedom – 'there's a lion in the road, there's a demon escaped' – and though there is profound sadness in that 'there's a million dreams gone', time, distance and objectivity work to undo the love that was once so powerful: 'her beauty fades and I watch her undrape'.

Though the song progresses to a statement of apparent achievement of an ideal freedom – 'a new day at dawn', a feeling of having 'finally arrived' of having 'survived' – the great shout of triumph – 'I can't believe it, I can't believe I'm alive' – surrenders to the despair with which each stanza ends: 'Oh, where are you tonight?'

The attainment of what may seem comparatively to be a 'sweet paradise' of liberty has cost him dear: 'just remind me to show you the scars' he shouts. These are the scars incurred in the terrible and futile struggle within himself, the financial scars of the divorce settlement – 'your partners in crime hit me up for nickels and dimes' – but mostly the scars on his soul. There seems little possibility of the rediscovery of self-awareness within the near future without great strength and great effort from beyond and within. The song's concluding lines hardly 'confirm aliveness', in May's words, for the singer 'can't believe' that he's alive, after all. In any case, 'without you it just doesn't seem right' and the song ends with a piercing cry of pain and terror – the cry of a soul in despair, totally alienated from itself.

Dylan's previous experience of this state of 'nigredo' was expressed in the songs of spleen that constituted the *Blonde On Blonde* album – an album only lightened by the presence of 'Sad-Eyed Lady of the Lowlands', its final track. It was Sara who gave him shelter from the storm portrayed on *The Basement Tapes* and who gave him definition, locus and identity. But that identity was perceived to be assumed, and the search for true self had to be resumed at the cost of the marriage. In the songs on *Blood on the Tracks* and, to a lesser extent, on *Desire*, the pain of separation and solitude is expressed side by side with the relief of freedom and the opportunities it afforded for the continuation of the process towards the realisation of self. 'Now I'm finally free', he triumphantly exclaimed in 'Idiot Wind', and he portrayed himself as the dapper Jack of Hearts – the handsome, unattached, enigmatic, outlaw-hero who, like John Wesley Harding, 'was never known to make a foolish move', intrigued women and stole their hearts, and disturbed men and stole their money.

Such freedom was attained only at a price: 'I'm going out of my mind with a pain that stops and starts', he sang on 'You're a Big Girl Now'. The desire, expressed on the album *Desire*, to 'spend some time in Mozambique', where there are 'lots of pretty girls and plenty time for good romance', is set against the reality of 'sittin' home alone … in L.A. watchin' old Cronkite on the seven o'clock news' (from 'Black Diamond Bay'); or of the failure to seduce the 'mysterious and dark' hearted girl in 'One More Cup Of Coffee', who has no 'affection, no gratitude or love' for him; or the 'sister', who treats him 'like a stranger' by turning away and refusing to acknowledge his knock at her door. The romantic ride to Durango ended uncertainly for the outlaw-hero – 'we may not make it through the night' – despite God's supposed vigilance, and the album concludes with the abject surrender of 'Sara', of which Dylan was later to say 'Some songs you figure you're better off not to have written.'[142]

Street-Legal is a further expression of a new state of nigredo — an analysis of feeling, or lack of it, about a relationship that has

[142] Craig McGregor interview, 1978, featured in *Bob Dylan: A Retrospective*, Angus & Robertson, 1980 edition.

been finally terminated and legally concluded. Dylan reaches a point from which he cannot turn back, even if he may look back. The songs are, for the most part, written by a man who feels as though he is as far from himself as he has ever been; they are songs of anxiety, loneliness, confusion, bewilderment and despair, but there is a reaching out.

The album's opening song, 'Changing of the Guards', puts Dylan's state of mind in late 1977 into kaleidoscopic perspective. The song's imagery is obscure and full of enigmatic symbolism, but its impact is clear enough. As the song opens, the singer finds himself just one more of the 'desperate men, desperate women' of the world, and after 'sixteen years' of searching for himself, he has failed to find salvation or faith and has lost all that he had. For such lost souls, 'the good shepherd grieves'.

Dylan presents a brief life-history. He remembers stepping 'forth from the shadows to the market place', though by 1974 he had become disillusioned enough to declare 'I ain't a-haulin' any of my lambs to the market-place any more' (in 'Tough Mama'). He'd found only 'merchants and thieves, hungry for power' or 'businessmen' or 'ploughmen', who could not 'know what any of it is worth'. His 'shelter from the storm' marriage was a temporary refuge from a world devoid of values. The 'beloved maid' who was 'sweet like the meadows where she was born', like Isis, offers her mysterious self: 'I couldn't help but follow, follow her down past the fountain where they lifted her veil'. The removal of the mystery, however, coincides with the dissolution of their love-affair. But a fall can, paradoxically, put a man back on his feet: 'I stumbled to my feet'. Survival is the name of the game now: 'I rode past destruction in the ditches with the stitches still mending'. The wounds will heal, though there may be 'heart-shaped' scars. Such an experience puts a man on his guard. 'Don't trust anyone', he sang to himself in 1967 in 'I'm Not There', certainly not 'renegade priests and treacherous young witches'. Freedom has its own price: loneliness, purposelessness, the pain of memory:

> The endless road and the wailing of chimes
> The empty rooms where her memory is protected.

But after the fall comes the resurrection. With imagery from the 'good shepherd's' own rebirth:

> Forty-eight hours later, the sun is breaking
> Near broken chains, mountain laurel and rolling rocks.

Purpose supplants purposelessness. 'Eden is burning' and there are two choices; it's either 'elimination' or 'the changing of the guards'. This latter change is of such magnitude that it requires great courage if it is to be contemplated at all.

Dylan has faced 'elimination' before, and he's survived, only to face further threats some eleven years on. The great 'changing of the guards' which is the alternative, and the contemplation of which demands a courageous heart, offers considerable rewards for the lost soul. 'False idols fall' before the might of God. Acceptance of faith in God will ensure salvation of a kind that has previously been beyond conception: 'Peace will come with tranquility and splendour on the wheels of fire'. Heaven guarantees eternal life, and ensures the complete victory over 'cruel death', who surrenders like a snivelling wretch 'with its pale ghost retreating' to God and the Church of Jesus.

The journey has been long and hard, but the 'cold-blooded moon' of change has given way to the rising 'sun'. 'Changing of the Guards' announces Dylan's conversion to Christianity.

18. Lost or Found?

Throughout this book, I've been concerned with Dylan's many separate identities. Public and private personae are, in effect, separate selves whom Dylan recognised, confronted, explored and discarded as he has searched, through his art, for his true self. His greatest works are the products of this search.

In *Dylan: What Happened?*, Paul Williams writes of two Bob Dylans, which he terms the 'inner man' and the 'outer man'. The 'inner man', he argues, 'has a deep personal relationship with God … and his whole life is focussed in on the daily struggle to submit to and serve the will of the Lord'. The 'outer man':

> Sees that the inner man has turned to Christ and so he takes on the intellectual and moral and political attitudes of the 'born-again' Christian community, [and] tries them on for size.

Dylan's power resides in his art and, to an extent, in the charisma that continues to be projected onto him by his audience, for whom he still serves as a mirror, through which – individually and collectively – they may continue to perceive their own selves. As the greatest poet of his generation, who has communicated directly with more people at any one time than any poet in history, Dylan continues to affect individual and collective consciousness to a considerable degree.

Conclusions are always much more difficult than introductions. To come to conclusions about anyone still living is almost impossible; they are simply drawn 'on the wall' to be erased and replaced by new ones as time passes and fades away, like any graffiti or, indeed, like any wall – which, in 1965 at least, was a suitable canvas for Dylan's 'latest works of art'.

In an essay in *The Sacred Wood*, T. S. Eliot wrote:

> The more perfect the artist, the more completely separate in him will be the man who suffers and the mind which creates.

The most important thing Dylan has given us is the experience of himself. His art has always embodied the man who made it, and Dylan's depth of feeling at every stage of his development has always been clear and expressed with total honesty. Care, passion and intensity came and went; disgust, disillusion, spleen, understanding and acceptance led to faith, trust, hope and belief. Failure gave rise to depression. And depression always returned to self-analysis, which gave way to insight, which, in turn, fed personal and artistic maturity.

Dylan has attempted to realise himself by living the many and various phases he's experienced through to their conclusions. He always began with an idea of who he thought he would like to be, or who he thought he was. In the 1950s, it might have been Little Richard. Later Hank Williams, Jimmie Rodgers or Leadbelly. Subsequently it might have been Woody Guthrie, Jack Kerouac, Arthur Rimbaud, William Blake, T. S. Eliot or Lord Byron, where before it was Bertolt Brecht, which it might be again. It might have been the frontier-cowboy, Napoleon in rags, the civil rights champion, James Dean, the visionary, the mystic, the detached observer, the social commentator, the Zen master, the moderate man, or the Fool. It could also have been the Hasidic, the planter of gardens and catcher of trout, the rock'n'roll star who 'made it too far', the messiah, or Renaldo the masked man, the actor, the entertainer, the trapeze artist, the song and dance man, the evangelist or St. John, the prophet of the blackest of all apocalypses. But he has always been Bob Dylan.

Acknowledgements

It has taken forty years to bring *The Chameleon Poet* to publication. A great many people, all of whom knew John Bauldie, have helped along the way.

Bill Allison would like to thank:

Ian Woodward
Richard Lewis
Nigel Hinton
Dave Heath
John Lindley
Barry 'Swifty' Swift
Pete Long
Peter Doggett
Mike Wyvill
John Wraith

Special thanks to:
Clinton Heylin – still *il miglior fabbro*.
Ian Daley and Isabel Galán of Route who saw the need to publish *The Chameleon Poet* and who possess editorial skills and patience that most writers can only dream of when working with a publishing house.
Ben Summers-McKay for his editorial eye.
Margaret Garner for trust from the very beginning.
Jeff Rosen and David Beal for their help and support.

Finally to Julia, my other half, who knows too much to argue or to judge, and our wonderful daughters, Lucy and Helen – may God bless and keep you always.

John Bauldie Appendix
Telegraph *Articles & Wanted Man Study Series Titles*

List of articles John Bauldie wrote for *The Telegraph*, with issue number and year.

1982
No.9   Visions of Johanna

1983
No.11   Jacques Levy
No.11   Dirge
No.14   Tangled Up in Blue

1984
No.16   Give Me a TV Dinner
         – The Plugz
No.18   Blind Wille McTell and
         Lenny Bruce

1985
No.19   The Old Dylan Place
No.19   Tonal Breath Control
No.20   Ceilings and Basements:
         Woodstock July 66–October 67
No.20   Returning What Was Owed
No.21   I Dreamed I Saw Bob Dylan –
         Live Aid

1986
No.24   'Hard Times in NY Town'–
         Bob Dylan in NYC 1961 Pt 1
No.24   On the Heels of Rimbaud
No.24   The Beat Goes On –
         The Death of Richard Manuel
No.25   'Hard Times in NY Town'–
         Bob Dylan in NYC 1961 Pt 2
No.25   *Hearts of Fire* Press Conference

1987
No.26   D.A. Pennebaker Interview
No.27   Conversation with
         Robert Shelton
No.28   Richard Marquand
         Hearts of Fire Interview
No.28   Iain Smith
         Hearts of Fire Interview

1988
No.30   Miles Interview
No.31   Bob Spitz Interview
No.31   Hurricane

1989
No.32   It's Not a House, It's a Home
No.33   The Ron Wood Interview
No.34   Daniel Lanois and *Oh Mercy*

1990
No.35   Great Shows:
         Paris and London 1990
No.35   The Joel Bernstein Interview
No.35   Pounding Away on his
         Old Typewriter
No.35   'A Day at Warhol's Factory
         Remembering Gerard Malang':
         Interview
No.36   Bob and The Blues Breakers
No.36   A Scene-by-Scene Guide to
         Pennebaker's *You Know That*
         Something is Happening
         Early Cut of *Eat the Document*:
         Interview with Pennebaker
No.37   A Conversation with
         Charlie Quintana

1991
No.38   A Conversation with
         John Jackson
No.41   House of JB
No.41   *Tarantula*

1992
No.43   America's Greatest Living Poet
No.43   Tony Write Interview

1993
No.45   Madhouse on Castle Street
No.46   Ken Pitt Interview
No.47   Harvey Brooks Interview

1994
No.48   The Great White Wonder
No.48   Dink's Song

1995
No.53   The Odd But True Story of
         Hearts of Fire

1997
No.56   Tom Petty Interview
No.56   Mickey Jones Interview

Wanted Man Study Series: List of Titles

1. *Bob Dylan's Slow Train* John Hinchey
2. *Bob Dylan & Desire* John Bauldie
3. *Bob Dylan: Escaping On The Run* Aidan Day
4. *The Bible In The Lyrics Of Bob Dylan* Bert Cartwright
5. *Jokermen & Thieves: Bob Dylan And The Ballad Tradition* Nick de Somogyi

Copyright Information
Songs used by permission

'Masters of War' written by Bob Dylan. Copyright © 1963 by Warner Bros. Inc.; renewed 1991 by Special Rider Music

'Million Dollar Bash' written by Bob Dylan. Copyright © 1967 by Dwarf Music; renewed 1995 by Dwarf Music

'Minstrel Boy' written by Bob Dylan. Copyright © 1970 by Big Sky Music; renewed 1998 by Big Sky Music

'Mixed-Up Confusion' written by Bob Dylan. Copyright © 1962, 1968 by Warner Bros. Inc.; renewed 1990, 1996 by Special Rider Music

'Most Likely You Go Your Way (and I'll Go Mine)' written by Bob Dylan. Copyright © 1966 by Dwarf Music; renewed 1994 by Dwarf Music

'Mozambique' written by Bob Dylan and Jacques Levy. Copyright © 1975 by Ram's Horn Music; renewed 2003 by Ram's Horn Music

'Mr. Tambourine Man' written by Bob Dylan. Copyright © 1964, 1965 by Warner Bros. Inc.; renewed 1992, 1993 by Special Rider Music

'My Back Pages' written by Bob Dylan. Copyright © 1964 by Warner Bros. Inc.; renewed 1992 by Special Rider Music

'Never Say Goodbye' written by Bob Dylan. Copyright © 1973 by Ram's Horn Music; renewed 2001 by Ram's Horn Music

'No Time to Think' written by Bob Dylan. Copyright © 1978 by Special Rider Music

'Nobody 'Cept You' written by Bob Dylan. Copyright © 1973 by Ram's Horn Music; renewed 2001 by Ram's Horn Music

'Nothing Was Delivered' written by Bob Dylan. Copyright © 1968, 1975 by Dwarf Music; renewed 1996 by Dwarf Music

'Obviously Five Believers' written by Bob Dylan. Copyright © 1966 by Dwarf Music; renewed 1994 by Dwarf Music

'Oh, Sister' written by Bob Dylan and Jacques Levy. Copyright © 1975 by Ram's Horn Music; renewed 2003 by Ram's Horn Music

'On a Night Like This' written by Bob Dylan. Copyright © 1973 by Ram's Horn Music; renewed 2001 by Ram's Horn Music

'One More Cup of Coffee (Valley Below)' written by Bob Dylan. Copyright © 1975, 1976 by Ram's Horn Music; renewed 2003, 2004 by Ram's Horn Music

'One More Night' written by Bob Dylan. Copyright © 1969 by Big Sky Music; renewed 1997 by Big Sky Music

'One More Weekend' written by Bob Dylan. Copyright © 1970 by Big Sky Music; renewed 1998 by Big Sky Music

'One Too Many Mornings' written by Bob Dylan. Copyright © 1964, 1966 by Warner Bros. Inc.; renewed 1992, 1994 by Special Rider Music

'Open the Door, Homer' written by Bob Dylan. Copyright © 1968, 1975 by Dwarf Music; renewed 1996 by Dwarf Music

'Outlaw Blues' written by Bob Dylan. Copyright © 1965 by Warner Bros. Inc.; renewed 1993 by Special Rider Music

'Percy's Song' written by Bob Dylan. Copyright © 1964, 1966 by Warner Bros. Inc.; renewed 1992, 1994 by Special Rider Music

'Please, Mrs. Henry' written by Bob Dylan. Copyright © 1967 by Dwarf Music; renewed 1995 by Dwarf Music

'Pledging My Time' written by Bob Dylan. Copyright © 1966 by Dwarf Music; renewed 1994 by Dwarf Music

'Poor Boy Blues' written by Bob Dylan. Copyright © 1962, 1965 by Duchess Music Corporation; renewed 1990, 1993 by MCA

'Positively 4th Street' written by Bob Dylan. Copyright © 1965 by Warner Bros. Inc.; renewed 1993 by Special Rider Music

'Queen Jane Approximately' written by Bob Dylan. Copyright © 1965 by Warner Bros. Inc.; renewed 1993 by Special Rider Music

'Quinn the Eskimo (The Mighty Quinn)' written by Bob Dylan. Copyright © 1968 by Dwarf Music; renewed 1996 by Dwarf Music

'Rainy Day Women #12 & 35' written by Bob Dylan. Copyright © 1966 by Dwarf Music; renewed 1994 by Dwarf Music

'Romance in Durango' written by Bob Dylan and Jacques Levy. Copyright © 1975 by Ram's Horn Music; renewed 2003 by Ram's Horn Music

'Sad-Eyed Lady of the Lowlands' written by Bob Dylan. Copyright © 1966 by Dwarf Music; renewed 1994 by Dwarf Music

'Sara' written by Bob Dylan. Copyright © 1975, 1976 by Ram's Horn Music; renewed 2003, 2004 by Ram's Horn Music

'Saving Grace' written by Bob Dylan. Copyright © 1980 by Special Rider Music

'Señor (Tales of Yankee Power)' written by Bob Dylan. Copyright © 1978 by Special Rider Music

'Seven Curses' written by Bob Dylan. Copyright © 1963, 1964 by Warner Bros. Inc.; renewed 1991, 1992 by Special Rider Music

'She Belongs to Me' written by Bob Dylan. Copyright © 1965 by Warner Bros. Inc.; renewed 1993 by Special Rider Music

'She's Your Lover Now' written by Bob Dylan. Copyright © 1971 by Dwarf Music; renewed 1999 by Dwarf Music

'Shelter from the Storm' written by Bob Dylan. Copyright © 1974 by Ram's Horn Music; renewed 2002 by Ram's Horn Music

'Sign on the Cross' written by Bob Dylan. Copyright © 1971 by Dwarf Music; renewed 1999 by Dwarf Music

'Simple Twist of Fate' written by Bob Dylan. Copyright © 1974 by Ram's Horn Music; renewed 2002 by Ram's Horn Music

'Something There Is About You' written by Bob Dylan. Copyright © 1973 by Ram's Horn Music; renewed 2001 by Ram's Horn Music

'Spanish Harlem Incident' written by Bob Dylan. Copyright © 1964 by Warner Bros. Inc.; renewed 1992 by Special Rider Music

'Standing on the Highway' written by Bob Dylan. Copyright © 1962, 1965 by Duchess Music Corporation; renewed 1990, 1993 by MCA

'Stuck Inside of Mobile with the Memphis Blues Again' written by Bob Dylan. Copyright © 1966 by Dwarf Music; renewed 1994 by Dwarf Music

'Subterranean Homesick Blues' written by Bob Dylan. Copyright © 1965 by Warner Bros. Inc.; renewed 1993 by Special Rider Music

'Talkin' New York' written by Bob Dylan. Copyright © 1962, 1965 by Duchess Music Corporation; renewed 1990, 1993 by MCA

'Talkin' World War III Blues' written by Bob Dylan. Copyright © 1963, 1966 by Warner Bros. Inc.; renewed 1991, 1994 by Special Rider Music

'Tangled Up in Blue' written by Bob Dylan. Copyright © 1974 by Ram's Horn Music; renewed 2002 by Ram's Horn Music

'Tears of Rage' written by Bob Dylan and Richard Manuel. Copyright © 1968 by Dwarf Music; renewed 1996 by Dwarf Music

'Tell Me That It Isn't True' written by Bob Dylan. Copyright © 1969 by Big Sky Music; renewed 1997 by Big Sky Music

'Temporary Like Achilles' written by Bob Dylan. Copyright © 1966 by Dwarf Music; renewed 1994 by Dwarf Music

'The Ballad of Frankie Lee and Judas Priest' written by Bob Dylan. Copyright © 1968 by Dwarf Music; renewed 1996 by Dwarf Music

'The Death of Emmett Till' written by Bob Dylan. Copyright © 1963, 1968 by Warner Bros. Inc.; renewed 1991, 1996 by Special Rider Music

'The Lonesome Death of Hattie Carroll' written by Bob Dylan. Copyright © 1964, 1966 by Warner Bros. Inc.; renewed 1992, 1994 by Special Rider Music

'The Man in Me' written by Bob Dylan. Copyright ©1970 by Big Sky Music; renewed 1998 by Big Sky Music

'The Times They Are A-Changin'' written by Bob Dylan. Copyright © 1963, 1964 by Warner Bros. Inc.; renewed 1991, 1992 by Special Rider Music

'The Wicked Messenger' written by Bob Dylan. Copyright © 1968 by Dwarf Music; renewed 1996 by Dwarf Music

'This Wheel's On Fire' written by Bob Dylan and Rick Danko. Copyright © 1967 by Dwarf Music; renewed 1995 by Dwarf Music

'Three Angels' written by Bob Dylan. Copyright © 1970 by Big Sky Music; renewed 1998 by Big Sky Music

'Time Passes Slowly' written by Bob Dylan. Copyright © 1970 by Big Sky Music; renewed 1998 by Big Sky Music

'Tiny Montgomery' written by Bob Dylan. Copyright © 1967 by Dwarf Music; renewed 1995 by Dwarf Music

'To Be Alone with You' written by Bob Dylan. Copyright © 1969 by Big Sky Music; renewed 1997 by Big Sky Music

'To Ramona' written by Bob Dylan. Copyright © 1964 by Warner Bros. Inc.; renewed 1992 by Special Rider Music

'Tombstone Blues' written by Bob Dylan. Copyright © 1965 by Warner Bros. Inc.; renewed 1993 by Special Rider Music

'Tomorrow Is a Long Time' written by Bob Dylan. Copyright © 1963 by Warner Bros. Inc.; renewed 1991 by Special Rider Music

'Too Much of Nothing' written by Bob Dylan. Copyright © 1967, 1970 by Dwarf Music; renewed 1995, 1998 by Dwarf Music

'Tough Mama' written by Bob Dylan. Copyright © 1973 by Ram's Horn Music; renewed 2001 by Ram's Horn Music

'Train A-Travelin'' written by Bob Dylan. Copyright © 1968 by Warner Bros. Inc.; renewed 1996 by Special Rider Music

'True Love Tends to Forget' written by Bob Dylan. Copyright © 1978 by Special Rider Music

'Up to Me' written by Bob Dylan. Copyright © 1974 by Ram's Horn Music; renewed 2002 by Ram's Horn Music

'Visions of Johanna' written by Bob Dylan. Copyright © 1966 by Dwarf Music; renewed 1994 by Dwarf Music

'Wanted Man' written by Bob Dylan. Copyright © 1969 by Big Sky Music; renewed 1997 by Big Sky Music

'Watching the River Flow' written by Bob Dylan. Copyright © 1971 by Big Sky Music; renewed 1999 by Big Sky Music

'We Better Talk This Over' written by Bob Dylan. Copyright © 1978 by Special Rider Music

'Wedding Song' written by Bob Dylan. Copyright © 1973 by Ram's Horn Music; renewed 2001 by Ram's Horn Music

'Went to See the Gypsy' written by Bob Dylan. Copyright © 1970 by Big Sky Music; renewed 1998 by Big Sky Music

'What Will You Do When Jesus Comes?' written by Bob Dylan. Copyright © 1977 by Special Rider Music; renewed 2005 by Special Rider Music

'Whatcha Gonna Do?' written by Bob Dylan. Copyright © 1963, 1966 by Warner Bros. Inc.; renewed 1991, 1994 by Special Rider Music

'When I Paint My Masterpiece' written by Bob Dylan. Copyright © 1971 by Big Sky Music; renewed 1999 by Big Sky Music

'When the Ship Comes in' written by Bob Dylan. Copyright © 1963, 1964 by Warner Bros. Inc.; renewed 1991, 1992 by Special Rider Music

'When You Gonna Wake Up?' written by Bob Dylan. Copyright © 1979 by Special Rider Music

'Where Are You Tonight? (Journey Through Dark Heat)' written by Bob Dylan. Copyright © 1978 by Special Rider Music

'Winterlude' written by Bob Dylan. Copyright © 1970 by Big Sky Music; renewed 1998 by Big Sky Music

'Yea! Heavy and a Bottle of Bread' written by Bob Dylan. Copyright © 1967 by Dwarf Music; renewed 1995 by Dwarf Music

'You Angel You' written by Bob Dylan. Copyright © 1973 by Ram's Horn Music; renewed 2001 by Ram's Horn Music

'You're a Big Girl Now' written by Bob Dylan. Copyright © 1974 by Ram's Horn Music; renewed 2002 by Ram's Horn Music

'You're Gonna Make Me Lonesome When You Go' written by Bob Dylan. Copyright © 1974 by Ram's Horn Music; renewed 2002 by Ram's Horn Music

For more information on this book, other Bob Dylan titles in our list, and for our full catalogue, please visit:

www.route-online.com